D0828812

Henry Martyn

Constance Padwick

MOODY PRESS
CHICAGO

Moody Press Edition, 1980

ISBN: 0-8024-3513-0

Printed in the United States of America

CONTENTS

Author's Preface 5

Table of Dates 9

1. Calcutta of the Nabobs 13

2. Cornwall 30

3. Undergraduate 39

4. Fellow of St. John's 59

5. A Curacy among the Evangelicals 78

6. The Lover 96

7. The Nine Months at Sea 108

8. Calcutta, 1806 131

9. Dinapore 149

10. The Linguist 165

11. Cawnpore 183

12. To Shiraz 202

13. A Year among the Doctors 221

14. The Traveler 235

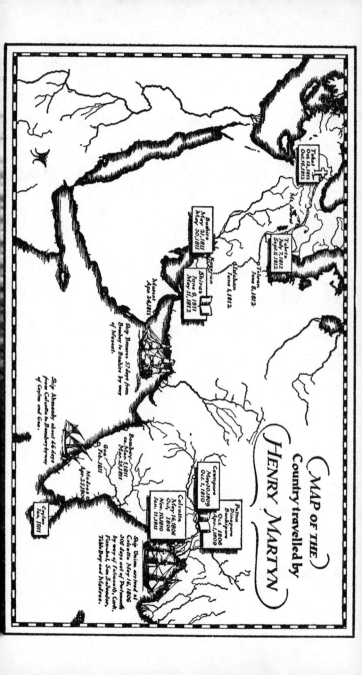

MAP OF THE Country travelled by HENRY MARTYN

Tabas
Oct. 1812
Oct. 16, 1812

Bushire
May 24, 1811
May 30, 1811

Shiraz
June 9, 1811
May 11, 1812

Kazerun

Ouzhaun
June 1, 1812

Tebriz
July 7, 1812
Sep. 2, 1812

Mt. Ararat

Muscat
Apr. 24, 1811

Ship Benares 51 days from Bombay to Bushire by way of Muscat.

Ship Almondy about 46 days from Calcutta to Bombay by way of Ceylon and Goa.

Bombay 1811
can. Nov. 25, 1811

Goa
Feb. 1811

Madras
Apr. 25, 1806

Ceylon
Jan. 1811

Dinapore
Oct. 1806
Bankipore

Patna
Oct. 1806
Apr. 1, 1809

Cawnpore
May 30, 1809
Oct. 7, 1810

Calcutta
May 16, 1806
Oct. 10, 1810
Jan. 11, 1811

Ship Union arrived at Calcutta May 16, 1806 308 days out of Portsmouth by way of Falmouth, Cork, Funchal, San Salvador, Funchal, Table Bay and Madras.

AUTHOR'S PREFACE

WHEN Henry Martyn's journals reached England after his death, Charles Siméon, Mrs. Thomason and John Sargent sat closeted together for three mornings of six or seven hours each, reading those travelled pages. In that reading they discovered their friend as sometimes, a monk being dead, his brothers find a hair shirt and a scourge of which they had not guessed. For Martyn's friends knew a man who played with children and with little dogs; and a friend who bubbled over with welcoming joy; and a scholar of luminous, beauty-loving mind; and an adventurer who flung himself unquailing into paynim camps; and a saint whose face sometimes abashed them by its shining. But now they were admitted into the confessional, and they saw laid bare before the heavenly Surgeon all the wounds and festering sores of a turbulent soul. They saw the Surgeon's knife and the quivering wince of the penitent spirit; and they caught the ineffable glance of confidence that passed from time to time between the two. "In every disease of the soul," said their friend, "let me charge myself with the blame and Christ with the cure of it, so shall I be humbled and Christ glorified."

His journal of self-examination before God is the first and greatest source of our knowledge of Martyn, and this book about him, like the rest, is built chiefly on the study of it.

But there is danger from the use of such a source, that we know our Martyn chiefly as the great penitent. The first friends, to whom the journal came as a surprise, had in mind the good hours when someone showed Martyn a copy of verses or a new Arabic grammar, when he caught the twinkle in Corrie's eye at Sabat's bombast or the tricks of the Cawnpore school-children, or when the jasmine smelt sweet in the sunset and he drove

Mrs. Sherwood a devious course in his gig, absorbed in urging upon her the joys of the study of Hebrew.

But we who never saw him romp with a child may be misled by meeting him most intimately in hours of penitence. Sargent, his first biographer,[1] "perhaps his dearest friend" and like himself a saint, knew the man so well and all his friends, and their manner of life, that he could not suppose description necessary. Simeon and Wilberforce might yet be met in the street, letters from Corrie and Thomason might come by any mail. It was not for Sargent, with his supreme delicacy, to draw the portraits of the men who might ride to visit him in his rectory under the Downs. Therefore he painted the spiritual story of his friend with the barest earthly background, as in that brief biography which says that "Enoch walked with God."

Yet as the generations pass and the scenes grow dim, we could wish that Sargent had gone down to Cornwall to seek out some old serving-maid of good John Martyn, who could tell us about Laura and Henry and Sally and call to mind the ways of the plain little boy with warts on his fingers. And had he but once described to us how Henry looked up when a friend broke in upon him in his college rooms! For when the second great biography of Henry Martyn was published in 1892[2] all who had known the man were gone, and the modest family life in Cornwall had left very little trace on the memory of the neighbourhood. Yet under such disadvantages Dr. George Smith, who brought to his book a knowledge of India which Sargent could not claim, put into his task a wealth of research which must make it the standard reference book on Martyn.

There is nothing new in the present little book. The Church has held most of the records for the greater part of a century: Sargent's *Life*; the great *Journal;*[3] then, as Martyn's

---

[1] *Henry Martyn*, by John Sargent, 1816, and numerous later editions.

[2] *Henry Martyn, Saint and Scholar*, by George Smith, LL.D.

[3] Edited by Bishop Samuel Wilberforce when Rector of Brighstone, Isle of Wight, 1839.

generation died, the sidelights from a host of biographies and memoirs of the day; the Diary of Lydia Grenfell;[4] stray letters and magazine articles published from time to time; and at last Dr. Smith's great biography in 1892. It is a mass of material, yet with it all there is danger of forgetting a life which is one of the treasures of our spiritual heritage.

For Sargent's book in the religious language of 1816 is almost strange to the children of another century; and Dr. Smith's generous copiousness makes his too costly for those of us who count our pence. We shall always turn gratefully to him in the library; he cannot be superseded: but for those who are poor and busy he may, nay probably he *must,* be supplemented, as the Church in each generation looks with fresh eyes on the stores of her spiritual heritage, and catches the glint of fresh colours in the "variegated" grace of God.

This is not a new book then, but a re-reading of old records, and that not unaided but with the good help of kind people in Cornwall, Cambridge and London too numerous to mention by name, but who have given generous and ready help in regard to anything and everything in which ignorance or carelessness stood in need. They know that they have my gratitude.

Martyn has never been and never will be the hero of the multitude, but each generation holds some who are his spiritual kindred. Across the lapse of years and blurred by the clumsy transmission of biographers, these will still catch with understanding ears the response of his spirit to the call of Christ.

C. E. P.

July, 1922

---

[4] Deposited in the Royal Cornish Institute, Truro. Extracts from it were published by a grand-nephew in 1890.

TABLE OF DATES

1774 Warren Hastings governor general of India
1781 Henry Martyn born at Truro, February 18
      In this year Herschel discovered Uranus; Lord George Gordon was tried in Westminster Hall; Cowper was 50; Sheridan 30; Fanny Burney 27; Crabbe 27; William Godwin 25; Burns 22; Cobbett 19; Samuel Rogers 18; Wordsworth 11; Scott 10; S. T. Coleridge 9; Jane Austen 7; and Charles Lamb 6.
1782 Charles Simeon began work at Trinity Church, Cambridge
1783 American Independence gained
1784 Samuel Johnson died
1786 Earl Cornwallis governor general of India
     David Brown landed in Calcutta
1787 Charles Grant and David Brown sent home their "Memorandum" asking for missionary schoolmasters
1788 Henry Martyn entered Truro Grammar School
1789 Fall of the Bastille
1790 Burke's *Reflections on the French Revolution*
     Charles Grant elected to one of the Chairs of the East India Company
1791 Thomas Paine's *Rights of Man*
     John Wesley died
1793 Execution of Louis XVI
     Sir John Shore governor general of India
     William Carey reached India in a Danish ship
1797 Death of Burke
     Henry Martyn entered St. John's College, Cambridge, October
1798 Battle of the Nile
     Earl of Mornington (afterwards Marquis Wellesley) governor general of India
     William Carey set up his printing press

1800 David Brown provost of Fort William College
1801 Martyn senior wrangler and first Smith's Prizeman
1802 Martyn fellow of St. John's
1803 War declared against Napoleon, May
Martyn ordained at Ely, October
1805 Wellesley recalled and Cornwallis appointed to India
Death of Cornwallis
Sir George Barlow temporary governor general
Martyn sailed for India as chaplain to the East India
Company, July 16th
Battle of Trafalgar, October
1806 Martyn at the capture of the Cape of Good Hope,
January
Death of Pitt, January
Martyn landed in Calcutta, May
Martyn proceeded to Dinapore, October
1807 Lord Minto governor general of India
Martyn began the Hindustani New Testament
1809 Martyn transferred to Cawnpore, April
1810 The Prince of Wales appointed regent for George III
Complete Hindustani New Testament finished for press
Martyn left Cawnpore with Persian and Arabic versions
of the New Testament, October
1811 Martyn reached Shiraz in Persia, June
1812 Martyn set out from Shiraz, May, and died at Tokat,
Asia Minor, October 16th
1815 Martyn's Persian New Testament published in St.
Petersburg
1816 Martyn's Persian New Testament, and the Arabic New
Testament made by Sabat under his supervision, published in Calcutta

Chapter 1

CALCUTTA OF THE NABOBS

NABOB, *noun substantive*. [Nobobb, a nobleman, "in the language of the Mogul's Kingdom which hath mixt with it much of the Persian," Sir T. Herbert. *Travels*, p. 99.] The title of an Indian prince; sometimes applied to Europeans who have acquired great riches in the East Indies.—*Johnson's English Dictionary* (Ed. 1827).

The style we prefer is the humdrum.—*Traditional answer of Directors of East India Company to an official who asked for guidance in writing despatches.*

WORDS HAVE their day, and the word "nabob" has all but passed out of currency with the passing from English life of the rather pitiable person for whom it stood. But in the last decades of the eighteenth century no better villain could be desired for stage or story than "a rich nabob" returned from Bengal. Macaulay, who with his sisters burrowed much among the three-volume novels of the eighteenth century, writing in 1840 said,[1] "If any of our readers will take the trouble to search in the dusty recesses of circulating libraries for some novel published sixty years ago, the chance is that the villain or sub-villain of the story will prove to be a savage old Nabob, with an immense for-

---

[1] In the *Essay on Clive*.

13

tune, a tawny complexion, a bad liver and a worse heart." All
but an alien on his native soil, this villain added to his other
crimes, real or imagined, the crime of differing from his caste.
"For your nabobs, they are but a kind of outlandish creatures
that won't pass current with us."[2] What more could comedy or
melodrama want?

Yet the nabob-to-be began life much like other small boys
of the day, perhaps as one of Squire Roger's younger sons, for
whom were neither family acres nor a family living, or maybe
as a son of the rectory, where Parson Brown had word one day
from an uncle in Leadenhall Street that he had bespoken a
writership in the East India Company for "poor Charlotte's
boy." At sixteen such a boy spent his last morning rabbiting
with his brother and the dogs in the churchyard spinney
(thicket), while his mother sobbed her heart out over piles
of lavender-scented linen. The coach bore away a ruddy English lad with a smattering of the classics and a capacity for
honest affection.

Forty years later the countryside would know him again as
"the rich nabob" who called for curricles (carriages) with the
airs of a prince, and showed a pitiable disregard for the cost
of living and the laws of fox-hunting. "Why, wherever any of
them settles, it raises the price of provisions for thirty miles
round," cries the mayor in Foote's comedy quoted above; while
Lady Oldham explains to the audience the family embarrass-
ment when "preceded by all the pomp of Asia, Sir Matthew
Mite, from the Indies, came thundering amongst us; and, pro-
fusely scattering the spoils of ruined provinces, corrupted the
virtue and alienated the feelings of all the old friends of the
family."

The process to which the nabob-to-be was submitted from
the moment when the East Indiaman left Tilbury on her voy-

---

[2] Foote, *The Nabob*, acted at Theatre Royal, Haymarket, 1778.

age of seven or more months is little enough pictured by us now.

"Such things as I should not want till my arrival in India were made very large, the Captain saying I should grow very much during the passage," one of those young "writers" tells us.[3]

We are forgetful of the completeness of exile in those days of long, slow travel, when often enough it took eighteen months to receive the reply to a letter sent home. We hardly realize the gradual wearing down of standards as home memories grew faint and the physical and moral climate did their enervating work. We are apt to see the India of the Company through the stories of men like Clive, Warren Hastings, or Wellesley the imperious. Such as these could not but be chief actors on any stage. They were men of vivid, restless genius, and of political imagination, in whose actions, good or bad, we find something of "the grand style." For men of such gifts life is not dull, and through their eyes we see romance.

But for the boy of ordinary gifts life in "the East Indies" was often a tedious affair. "The waste of spirits in this cursed country is a disease unconquerable, a misery unutterable," wrote Francis, the arch-foe of Warren Hastings. At the age when his brother entered the university our boy was cast upon a Calcutta that had only one carriage road, the dusty "Course," and one small theater, built by subscription and managed by amateur actors, who in their zeal for the drama were apt to undertake parts beyond their power, with the result that "many went to see a tragedy for the express purpose of enjoying a laugh."[4] He found indeed a little coterie of English hostesses who received every evening, and beyond a doubt were kind to striplings fresh from home. But the balls of Calcutta provided no blushing English maidens for the boy to adore or play with.

---

[3] *Travels in India a Hundred Years Ago*, Thomas Twining, 1893.
[4] Mrs. Eliza Fay, *Original Letters from India*, p. 279.

Ladies he found there of strange descent and stranger history, and Hicky's *Bengal Gazette*, the first English newspaper in India (published Calcutta, 1780), shows plainly enough how the little, bored society looked for the enlivenment of their hard, hot lives to the relish of betting and unsavory scandal.

"I don't think the greatest sap at Eton can lead a duller life than this," Lord Cornwallis wrote to his schoolboy son, during his first governor generalship (1786-1795). And our nabob-to-be soon learned to echo the sentiments of that industrious and high-minded chief, and to seek distraction in arrack punch and heavy dinners or in stables for which his salary during his first five years as an "apprentice" was inadequate. But "a Company's servant," as a contemporary letter tells us, "will always find numbers ready to support his extravagance; and it is not uncommon to see writers within a few months after their arrival dashing away on the Course four-in-hand."[5]

The boy's intercourse with the people of that eastern world, in which his station was a tiny island of European life, would seem to have been of the slightest. Unless he aimed ambitiously at diplomatic tasks—when he studied Persian, the language of eastern court etiquette—he did not take seriously the learning of any oriental language. And when he did take lessons, his teacher was regarded by this young lord of creation as only another servant of a rather superior grade, "permitted by many of the more liberal students to enter the apartments without taking off his shoes; an omission for which the other servants would be severely punished."[6]

Throughout his long years of exile, the Company's English servant may never have experienced the intellectual and spiritual adventure of friendship with an eastern gentleman. When even Sir William Jones, who reached European fame as an orientalist, was yet "quite unintelligible in Calcutta to

⁵ *Ibid*. Letter written on August 29, 1780.
⁶ D'Oyley, *The European in India*, 1813.

any native in any eastern tongue," it is not surprising that our more ordinary boy never reached converse with the more thoughtful minds of India. "Portuguese was the ordinary medium of communication between the Europeans and their domestics.... Even in Calcutta Portuguese was more commonly used by the servants of the Company and the settlers than the language of the country.... Down to so late a period as 1828, the governor of Serampore,[7] a Norwegian, received the daily report of his little garrison of thirty sepoys from the native commandant, a native of Oude, in Portuguese."[8]

The ordinary boy's intercourse with the people of India was limited to business relationships in which he depended much on the clumsy aid of the interpreter, and to his dealings, some of them, alas, deplorable, with what seemed to him at first a vast and wondrous docile army of servants round his new home —a cringing and salaaming population whose servility tempted him to think them made for his good pleasure. The charge sheet of the Calcutta superintendent of police in 1778 contains the following among similar items:

"129. A slave girl of Mr. Anderson, Piggy, having run away from her master and being apprehended by the Chowkedar—ordered her five rattans and to be sent to her master."

So late as 1800 Lord Wellesley, his imagination aflame with the vision of his ideal administrator, was pulled up short by what he knew of the downward, sensuous pull of a servile population. Of English boys sent to up-country stations he wrote in unvarnished words that "sloth, indolence, low debauchery, and vulgarity are too apt to grow on those young men who have been sent at an early age into the interior part of the country and have laid the foundations of their life and manners among the coarse vices and indulgences of those countries."

---

[7] Serampore was a Danish settlement on the Hooghly sixteen miles above Calcutta.

[8] Marshman, *History of the Serampore Mission*, pp. 21, 22.

John Clark Marshman, who knew his Calcutta as few men knew it, tells the same tale:

> The number of English ladies in the country was lamentably small.... In the days of Warren Hastings (Governor 1772-85) the arrival of a spinster from England was an event, and it was inaugurated by a succession of balls. The great bulk of the Europeans both in and out of the service, lived unmarried with native females, and their leisure was spent in the most debasing associations. The young civilian was told that one of his first duties was to "stock a zenana."

William Macintosh, a political journalist, who sheltered his possibly libelous attacks on the friends of Warren Hastings under the transparent veil of initials and dashes, published in 1782 an account[9] of "The Manner in which the Day is commonly spent by an Englishman in Bengal." Political opponents criticizing his book said that he made an unfair use, in writing the sketch, of the hospitality of a plump, good-natured soul who gave him the freedom of his Calcutta house. They do not call in question the truthfulness of the picture, though they would have us remember that there were other more energetic households, and that as a general rule "the young gentlemen, as soon after their arrival as they can, muster money to buy a horse, ride a little before daybreak until eight o'clock, then breakfast and go directly to the public offices."[10] Macintosh's description must be read with his own spelling:

> About the hour of seven in the morning, his durvan [porter or door-keeper] opens the gate, and the viranda [gallery] is free to his circars, peons [footmen], harcarrahs [messengers or spies], chubdars [a kind of constable], houccabadars and consumas [or steward and butler], writers and solicitors. The head-bearer and jemmadar enter the hall and his bedroom at eight o'clock.... The moment the master throws his legs out of bed, the whole possé in waiting

---

[9] In his *Travels in Europe, Asia, and Africa.*

[10] Captain J. Price, *Some Observations on a late Publication entitled "Travels in Asia,"* 1783.

rush into his room, each making three salams, by bending the body and head very low, and touching the forehead with the inside of the fingers, and the floor with the back part. He condescends, perhaps, to nod or cast an eye towards the solicitors of his favour and protection. In about half-an-hour, after undoing and taking off his long drawers, a clean shirt, breeches, stockings and slippers are put upon his body, thighs, legs and feet, without any greater exertion on his part than if he were a statue. The barber enters, shaves him, cuts his nails, and cleans his ears. The chillumjee and ewer are brought by a servant, whose duty it is, who pours water upon his hands to wash his hands and face, and presents a towel.

The superior then walks in state to his breakfasting parlour in his waistcoat; is seated; the consumah makes and pours out his tea, and presents him with a plate of bread or toast. The hair-dresser comes behind, and begins his occupation while the houccabadar softly slips the upper end of the snake or tube of the houcca into his hand. While the hair-dresser is doing his duty, the gentleman is eating, sipping, and smoking by turns. By and by his banian presents himself with humble salams, and advances somewhat more forward than the other attendants. If any of the solicitors are of eminence they are honoured with chairs.

These ceremonies are continued perhaps till ten o'clock; when, attended by his cavalcade, he is conducted to his palanquin, and preceded by eight to twelve chubdars, harcarrahs and peons with the insignia of their professions, and their livery distinguished by the colour of their turbans and cumberbands (a long muslin belt wrapt round the waist) they move off at a quick amble; the set of bearers, consisting of eight generally relieve each other, with alertness, and without incommoding the master. If he has visits to make, his peons lead and direct the bearers; and if business renders his presence only necessary, he shows himself, and pursues his other engagements until two o'clock, when he and his company sit down, perfectly at ease in

point of dress and address, to a good dinner,[11] each attended
by his own servant. And the moment the glasses are introduced, regardless of the company of ladies, the houccaba-
dars enter, each with a houcca, and presents the tube to his
master, watching behind and blowing the fire the whole
time.[12] As it is expected that they shall return to supper,
at four o'clock they begin to withdraw without ceremony,
and step into their palanquins; so that in a few minutes, the
master is left to go into his bedroom, when he is instantly
undressed to his shirt, and his long drawers put on; and he
lies down on his bed, where he sleeps till about seven or
eight o'clock: then the former ceremony is repeated, and
clean linen of every kind, as in the morning, is administered;
his houccabadar presents the tube to his hand, he is placed
at the tea table, and his hair-dresser performs his duty as
before. After tea, he puts on a handsome coat, and pays
visits of ceremony to the ladies:[13] returns a little before ten
o'clock, supper being served at ten. The company keep
together till between twelve and one in the morning, preserv-
ing great sobriety and decency. . . .

The record gives rise to many reflections, among them one
as to the comparative modernness of the habit of the daily tub.[14]
It must be remembered that the Englishmen who suffered
themselves to be dressed and carried like luxurious dolls were

---

[11] Mrs. Eliza Fay gives an account to her sister at home of the daily dinner
in her Calcutta home, a household of only moderate means, in the summer
of 1780. She and her husband dined on "a soup, a roast fowl, curry and rice,
a mutton pie, a forequarter of lamb, a rice pudding, tarts, very good cheese,
fresh churned butter, fine bread, excellent Madeira." This tiffin was eaten
without ice. There were giants in those days!

[12] If ladies were present it was considered a delicate compliment for a
beau to whip from his pocket a silver mouthpiece, fix it to his hookah and
offer it to the lady at his side.

[13] Mrs. Eliza Fay again enlightens us as to the ways of that almost forgotten little world. "Formal visits are paid in the evening," she tells her
sister. "Gentlemen call to pay their respects and if asked to put down their
hats, it is considered as an invitation to supper."

[14] D'Oyley's *European in India*, published thirty years later, tells us that
three or four pots of cold water were sometimes thrown over the master's
head to brace him before dressing for dinner.

living in a Bengal where the swing punkah (fan) was yet unknown[15] and from which there was no escape to a hill station. Yet even so, one whose daily life is here described has traveled far in spirit, and his mother's seven-or-eight-months-old letters must strike a wistful note when she writes in her Italian hand to tell of little Fanny's first ball and the moss rosebuds in her hair.

No one can read the despatches to the India House without realizing that in the great affairs of the Company many men must have lived more laborious lives than this. Yet it is significant that the lively author of the description quoted above felt impelled to no further comment than the remark that "with no greater exertions than these do the Company's servants amass the most splendid fortunes."

One is forced to the conclusion that, with the great exceptions of high-minded men like Cornwallis, Shore, Wellesley, or Grant, the latter eighteenth century had settled down quite complacently to regard "the East Indies" as a gold mine.

There is more of the spirit of the counter than one likes to confess among "The Honourable the Court of Directors for the affairs of the United Company of Merchants of England trading to the East Indies" *Auspicio Regis et Senatus Angliae.* They were decorously anxious for dividends. Warren Hastings was appointed to Bengal for his good management of warehouses in Madras, and his first business was to make Bengal pay. The Directors suffered many a financial tremor in the days of the patrician Wellesley "who endeavoured in redundantly eloquent despatches to reconcile his deeds with the pacific tone of his instructions."[16] They felt that creator of great schemes and enterprises to be an ornament to their administration, but how expensive an ornament! Small wonder if their servants caught their spirit. Sir Harry Verelst described the

---

[15] It was still a novelty in 1801.
[16] A. F. Pollard, *History of England.*

English in Bengal as "a colony of merchants, governed by laws and influenced by principles merely commercial."[17]

> We looked no further than the provision of the Company's investment. We sought advantages to our trade, with the ingenuity, I may add the selfishness of merchants. ... All our servants and dependents were trained and educiated in the same notions; the credit of a good bargain was the utmost scope of their ambition.

Little guessed that old, bourgeois Calcutta of the merchants that she was the stage set for a drama of spiritual adventure. Yet so it was. The saints were coming to town. As when a Christian man first trod the forum of some lustful Roman city, and his spirit, fain of the eternal beauty, felt the unclean life around him to be "earthly, sensual, devilish"; or as when two brothers of St. Francis, their hearts singing with the beauty of poverty for Christ, first visited the greedy court of an Italian merchant prince, so when men who had caught the spirit of Christ first touched the sordid life of old Calcutta, there followed struggle and the hardness of moral choice in many lives.

They came in the rather prosaic garb of chaplains of the East India Company: in matters of taste, men of their day, with a power of enjoying if not of producing "poetical effusions" that leave us cold, and a habit in penitent moments of describing themselves as "contemptible and wretched worms." But behind the high neck-cloths and the language of eighteenth-century religious diaries we find the infallible marks of the friends of Jesus.

The precursor and father of the little group arrived when Calcutta was sweltering in the hot weather of 1786, with his wife and a baby born at sea. The Company had sent for "a clergyman and a married man" to take charge of their new Military Orphan Asylum. The Reverend David Brown who responded to their call was the son of a Yorkshire farmhouse, who

---

[17] Letter to Council of Fort William, December 1769.

brought to his Calcutta home, along with a solid classical education, a certain wholesome shrewdness, and the tradition of hearty and generous hospitality. Through twenty-five years of service with only one fortnight of furlough, he kept the countryman's fresh coloring. He was no pallid saint. But Calcutta found in that Yorkshireman a spirit that was strange to her.

When he discovered that he was to have the charge of five hundred orphans instead of the forty-five of whom he had been told, and that the salary was considerably less than had been represented, he accepted the situation with the remark in his diary that "since a larger field of usefulness was thus opened to my view, I regretted not the diminution of salary."[18] This Yorkshireman must be reckoned with. He had a disconcerting habit of continual reference to a standard that Calcutta had forgotten. "I now sit down in a house of my own," he wrote, "but my good Master had not where to lay His head. . . . He emptied Himself of all and was literally the poorest of men."

His habit of reference to another standard led David Brown to do strange things. He found in the city an ugly, and at that time glaring, building known as "The Red Church" (now "The Old Mission Church," Mission Row), built sixteen years before his coming at the private expense of a Danish missionary, and still the only church in Bengal.[19] Calcutta society affirmed that the place is only fit for stable-boys and low Portuguese." Church-going was not modish, and Sunday was the day for races. Moreover it was impossible to go to church without considerable ceremony. "If you were a person of fashion yet did not choose to go to church in your yellow chariot, you would arrive in a neat sedan chair, gleaming with black lacquer. You brought at least seven servants with you—four chair-bearers, two running footmen with spears and one parasol

---

[18] *Memorial of the Rev. David Brown*, 1816, p. 298.

[19] But another was then abuilding and was consecrated in June 1787 as St. John's Church, now generally known as "The Old Cathedral."

bearer."[20] A lady told David Brown that "she had been more than twelve years a resident of Calcutta, and twice married; but it had been out of her power in all that time to go to church, because she had never had an offer from any beau to escort her there and hand her to a pew."

The very small group of very mixed parentage that looked to "the Red Church" for help, was now without a shepherd, and David Brown "thought of those with whom his Divine Master associated" and offered himself as unsalaried chaplain. Calcutta sniffed, but in spite of herself was drawn to the big-hearted man who never took a baptism or a marriage service without a deep human emotion that could not be altogether hidden from the men and women he had come to serve.

Like draws to like, and David Brown had not been many days in Calcutta before he was asked to dine with the "Senior Merchant" of the Company and found a friend.

Charles Grant, later to be celebrated in the Councils of the East India Company "for an understanding large enough to embrace, without confusion, the entire range and the intricate combinations of their whole civil and military policy, and for nerves which set fatigue at defiance,"[21] was a Highland Scot whose father had been fighting for the Stuarts at Culloden at the very hour of his birth. He was known in Calcutta as a man long of limb and long of face, his sagacious countenance under massive brows singularly steadfast and immovable, but softening when he glanced at the adorable wife whom he had brought to India as a bride of seventeen, an apt musician and a charming dancer. She made his house a home of rare delight and gave him two baby girls, loved by both parents with the almost desperate affection that surrounds the delicate babes of a household in the tropics. The head of the house, for all his home affections, followed the ordinary standards of Calcutta society,

[20] Hyde, The Parish of Bengal, p. 190.
[21] Sir James Stephen, Essays in Ecclesiastical Biography.

and the one shadow in the household was cast by the master's gambling debts which piled up far higher than his means of payment.

Then, with dreadful suddenness, the light went out from their home as, within a few days, first one little daughter and then the other was carried off by smallpox, and the twenty-year-old mother was left distraught with grief, springing up now and then in the belief that she was waking from a nightmare and would find her babies in their nursery, only to suffer her first agony over again when she reached the empty room.

To the father's conscience it seemed "a judgment from heaven" on his selfish and worldly courses. Atonement must be made. In agony of soul he broke through his lifelong reserve and went to Dr. Kiernander the old Danish missionary who had built the Red Church. "I found him lying on the couch. My anxious enquiries as to what I could do to be saved appeared to embarrass and confuse him exceedingly; and when I left him the perspiration was running from his face in consequence, as it appeared to me, of his mental distress."[22] Charles Grant came away from the only religious specialist within his ken, as miserable as he went. It was his young wife who brought him peace. She noticed, even in her sorrow, his heavy spiritual anxiety and turned to search such good books as she had, for help for both of them. In the New Testament she found the way of peace and wrote her Charles a letter to tell of her discovery:

> Now is not this the sinner whom our blessed Saviour invites to come unto Him with promises of lightening his burden and giving him rest? I think it is.[23]

He thought so too when her faith led the way, and together they remodeled the life of their household, as those who openly confessed that One was their Master, even Christ. Charles Grant set himself grimly to the task of paying off his gaming

---

[22] George Smith, *Twelve Indian Statesmen*, p. 12.
[23] Morris, *Life of Charles Grant*, p. 64.

debts and cleared them in four years. His work for the Company, in which his calmly sane intellect shone out, became the work of one who cared for India and her peoples with a disinterested love that rose above party politics or dividends. "The views which are entertained by statesmen and others for the welfare of India," he wrote in a letter of 1784, "are so disturbed by party as to be sometimes indistinct. Ambition and party, in a word, have marred all that has been intended for the benefit of this country for ten years past.... How few... rise above the mists of present passions to objects having respect to 'Him who is invisible.'"

To one trying to guide his personal and public life by standards so different from those current in Calcutta, the coming of David Brown was a great event. In nothing were these two more unique than in their relationships with the people of India. David Brown at once "dedicated some attention to the languages of the country" and though he made it plain to Calcutta that he was not the man for nautch (dancing) displays, he proceeded to go "among the Hindoos in a way not usual with the English. He attended, in their domestic circles, their literary and religious entertainments" and behaved there "with urbanity and respect."[24] David Brown, Charles Grant, and two like-minded friends,[25] persisted in seeing in the people of India men and women with spiritual struggles as interesting to God as their own. With all appearances in church and state against them, they dared to see a vision of spiritual kinship with India, and to believe that her people might come to share in what was for them the supreme experience of life, the touch of the living Christ on the spirit of a man.

They did not stop at dreaming, but wrote out a proposal which they sent home to clergy and members of Parliament,

---

[24] *Memorial of the Rev. David Brown*, p. 71.
[25] Mr. William Chambers, the East India Company's chief linguist, and Mr. George Udny, indigo planter.

calling for volunteer missionary schoolmasters to come to Bengal where the Company had not yet raised a finger for the intellectual or moral enlightenment of its eastern subjects. They asked for "fit men, of free minds, disinterested, zealous, and patient of labour, who would accept of an invitation, and aspire to the arduous office of a missionary.... His work must be his business, his delight, and reward.... Men who are ready to endure hardships and to suffer the loss of all things."

Knowing their England they sent this appeal to ardent souls, clergy whose zeal had earned them the name of "Methodist," and philanthropists like William Wilberforce and Robert Raikes. Raikes in his reply suggested that they had made a false step in asking the "methodist" clergy to forward their adventure, for, said he, the bishops "never like to give the reins into the hands of men of warm imaginations."

Charles Grant and David Brown, for all their spiritual daring, were government officials used to working through official channels; and while they were under no delusions as to the difficulties ahead, it yet never occurred to either of them that their new scheme should be independent of the official sanction of the leaders of church and state. They were before the day when great private and voluntary societies within the church undertook her missionary enterprises. The immense growth of these in the nineteenth century was at once a forward and a backward step; forward in that the societies revealed a number of the church's sons and daughters awakening to a forgotten fundamental of that church's life, but backward in so far as the primary task of the whole church was thereby relegated to smaller groups within her.

But that day had not yet come, and to Charles Grant and David Brown it seemed a natural course to approach the Archbishop of Canterbury and good King George the Third. They were not over-sanguine as to official countenance for they knew the age-long character of Christian teachers as those who "turn the world upside down," and measured the probable opposition. "The truth, as we presume to think," they wrote, "is, that all objections to the extension of Christianity arise rather from Indisposition to the thing itself than any persuasion of its Impracticability.... Some may oppose political Considerations, the danger of disturbing the present Order of things, and of introducing a spirit destructive of that subjection and Subordination, which have made the Natives of Bengal so easy to govern."

It was a true forecast. When Charles Grant went home in 1790 to one of the "Chairs" of the East India Company's Directors, he found an England increasingly panic-stricken by the news of revolution in France, and regarding the church as an institution for the moral policing of the nation and the support of the existing powers. In such an atmosphere he made his main purpose in life the enlisting of that church in spiritual service for India. He knocked unbidden at the door of Lambeth until he had persuaded the bland and very bourgeois prelate, Dr. Moore,[26] to step into his purple-liveried coach and lay before King George himself a copy of the scheme drawn up with such eager hope by the group of friends in Calcutta.

Dr. Moore did not like the task; but Charles Grant's pertinacity and his own sense of duty at last drove him to St. James's. We are told what the King said, and can picture the interview; the light from the high windows falling on the amiable and full-bodied prelate as he knelt on the carpet (for George III was a stickler for this posture) in his purple coat, full wig and abbreviated cassock; the elderly, stooping king with his good, obstinate face, a born lover of mediocrities, "testy at the idea of all innovations and suspicious of all innovators," [27] grunting a little at first, then, with the usual oscillations of his body and precipitate, tumbling speech find-

[26] The only gentleman to appear on the walls of the National Portrait Gallery in a pair of immaculate grey gloves.
[27] Thackeray, *Four Georges.*

ing words to say that he "hesitated to countenance such ideas" owing to "the alarming progress of the French Revolution and the proneness of the period to movements subversive of the established order of things"; the kneeling Archbishop hastily assuring his "royal patron" that an exactly similar hesitation arose in his own mind, then rising ponderously from the floor, only too thankful to be quit of an ungrateful task.

Charles Grant had to report to David Brown that the whole of officialdom, whether in Parliament, in Leadenhall Street or in episcopal palaces, proved prosaic and timid. The Bishop of Llandaff did send his copy of the scheme to Pitt, but with an apologetic covering letter doubting "whether the present is the fittest time for making the attempt."[28] Leadenhall Street in a panic decided to give no license to any captain of an East Indiaman for any passenger calling himself a missionary, and the friends now found their hopes of spiritual service for India limited to the possibility of sending out as official chaplains of the Company men with hearts as high as their own and with an equal sense of the spiritual rights of every human soul.

To this end Charles Grant now used his ever increasing influence in the Councils of Leadenhall Street, with the result that David Brown was joined in the course of years by a group of younger men who dared to share his vision. Among them came Henry Martyn, that youth in years who yet knew the abasement and the rapture of the saint, and who flung at the feet of Christ a scholar's dreams and the heart of a lover.

---

[28] Bishop Watson's *Anecdotes of his Life*, p. 197.

Chapter 2

CORNWALL

Not lolling at ease or in the indecent posture of sitting, drawling out one word after another; but all standing before God, and praising Him lustily, and with good courage.—JOHN WESLEY.

There is a fair prospect in Cornwall from Launceston to the Land's End.—WESLEY's *Journal* August 27, 1789.

THE CURATE of Truro in the year 1747 received a surprising letter from the master of the grammar school. That good man explained that his physician had ordered him French wines, but having failed to obtain any in Cornwall that had not been smuggled into the country he now desired to pay the duty himself on the quantity he had bought. He enclosed a sum of money and requested the clergyman, as a well-known and respectable character above suspicion by the excise men, to hand it in to the authorities as conscience money from an anonymous source. The obliged writer would in that way gain the satisfaction of having tried to keep the precept of Jesus about the things that should be rendered to Caesar.

The Reverend Samuel Walker was a genial clergyman whose company was often sought by neighboring squires "to supper on a roasted pig." He was interested in character, and never having met on that smuggling coast with such sensibility on a point of conscience, he forthwith sought the friendship of the ingenious and respectable writer. Their friendship was momentous in the life of Truro; for Samuel Walker, level-headed, and well-known in his Oxford days for devotion to logic, now saw in the grammar school master an aspect of religion which had hitherto escaped him, and which transcended logic. He witnessed in his friend a personal relationship with Christ which became central for the man who experienced it and altered all his thinking. He went further and sought that vital experience for himself, and in the power of it he transformed Truro. There was a new force about the man which drew all the city to him, so that they had to shut up the cockpit for want of patrons. Of a Sunday the people flocked now to their lovely perpendicular parish Church of St. Mary in such numbers that "you might fire a cannon down every street in Truro in church time without a chance of killing a single human being."

Samuel Walker, a careful organizer, drew the "serious people" of his flock into what would nowadays be called a guild or fellowship for mutual stimulus and prayer. He was untiring in the preparation of courses of sermons and lectures, and his people must have been among the most instructed Christians.

Among the regular members of his "Society" was one John Martyn, cashier in a Truro mercantile office and himself in a modest way a citizen of substance, with shares of his own in the Wheal Unity mine.

"Whether at Church or at Prayer-meetings, John Martyn always attended Mr. Sam Walker, the Curate of St. Mary's, but at Mr. Walker's decease seemed to prefer the Prayer-meeting to the Church."[1] Be that as it may, John Martyn together with most of Samuel Walker's flock remained in connection with the mother church throughout those days of stir. Samuel Walker before his death in 1761 had considerable cor-

---

[1] So writes Polwhele in his *Biographical Sketches of Cornwall*, i. 91,

respondence with John Wesley, that most arresting leader who came more than any other man of dominant spirit into immediate contact with the masses of the people.

In Cornwall, as in all England, John Wesley was facing and taming ill-conditioned mobs, and he could not but appreciate the changes in Truro that he found through Samuel Walker's lifework. He wrote in his journal for August 30, 1755, of his first contact with Walker's flock: "As I was riding through Truro one stopped my horse and insisted on my alighting. Presently two or three more of Mr. Walker's society came in, and we seemed to have been acquainted with one another many years."

The two men, both priests of the English Church, akin in spiritual experience and both preachers now of "the new birth," yet differed in policy. Walker dreaded the masses. "It has been a great fault all along," he wrote to Wesley, "to have made the low people of your council." So he tilled his own plot, working no stupendous upheaval but a gradual transformation in the life of the little city.

When Walker died, leaving a sober and a godly Truro, John Wesley was only at the beginning of his series of marvelous meteoric visits to a half-pagan Cornwall, whose miners and fisher folk (not without the spur of some local persecution) flocked to hear him in the open fields and made his hymns their folksongs.

Meanwhile "serious" John Martyn attended his prayer meetings, took to himself a wife, begat a son named John after himself, and amused his leisure with the study of mathematics. The mail coach for London would carry up to the office of

---

adding: "It is much to be lamented that Mr. Walker should have instituted prayer meetings." Mr. Polwhele sees so red if the word methodism be but breathed never so softly that his account of Henry Martyn is malicious and unreliable. His scorching *Anecdotes of Methodism* are a breath from the heated atmosphere in which the spiritual upheaval of the evangelical revival took place in Cornwall.

The Gentleman's Diary or Mathematical Repository John Martyn's solutions to problems which beginning airily "Suppose a fire engine" required the discovery of "the diameters of the cylinder and pumps, the height of the stroke, the depth of the engine pit shaft, and the quantity of gallons of water this engine will draw in one hour, friction excepted."

Young John's mother died early, and John Martyn the elder brought home a new bride from Ilfracombe to his house in Truro near the Coinage Hall. Her name was Fleming; she gave him a daughter Laura, then on February 18, 1781, when young John was fifteen, a second little son whom they named Henry. Two years later another baby, Sally, had been born and the mother had died, leaving to her children a constitution of singularly weak resistance.

The baby Henry opened his eyes upon a discreet and dignified little city which lived its life without much reference to the rest of England. One of the aldermen had never traveled farther than Bodmin, and news trickled in slowly when the journey by stage to Exeter took two days. The gentry of the Cornish countryside instead of careering up to London had their town houses of sober grey stone in Truro, where they might meet one another for routs and dances and the high affairs of matrimony between families of standing.

It was a trim city, but even while the stage rattled over the cobbled street you could hear if you listened the call of the gulls among the shipping, and catch a tang of the salt sea from the estuary below the bridge. Henry Martyn's childhood was spent in a house of two aspects. Its fairer face looked down a garden to the little river just before it emptied itself into the estuary where the curlews whistle; but the back of the house looked out on the very heart of the city's life. Coinage Hall Street was narrow[2] but just opposite the Martyn's house the buildings gave way to leave a little open square before the pil-

---

[2] Coinage Hall Street and Powder Street with the houses between them

lared cloister of the Coinage Hall. Years afterwards in dreams in India, Henry would find himself walking down that street, with the discreet dwellings of the citizens (for it was not yet the shopping quarter of the town) and brother John's house on the other side a few doors lower than his own, and the cloisters of the ancient Coinage Hall where his father, tall and erect, would take a daily constitutional.

Under those early English arches Wesley preached on more than one of his fifteen visits to Truro, with the people in the square before him, "enabled to speak exceeding plain on 'Ye are saved through faith.' "[3] The little boy in John Martyn's house might still sometimes see the erect figure of that "human gamecock," though he no longer rode up the street on horseback but stepped out of a chaise. "His face was remarkably fine; his complexion fresh to the last week of his life, his eye quick and keen and active. When you met him in the street of a crowded city he attracted notice, not only by his band and cassock and his long hair, white and bright as silver, but by his pace and manner, both indicating that all his minutes were numbered and that not one was to be lost."[4]

One day when Henry was eight years old, the street east of his door was blocked with soldiers, and westward with "numberless tinners, a huge multitude, nearly starved" assembled to demand a living wage. Into the heart of the throng stepped John Wesley, and standing in front of the Coinage Hall, between the two opposing hosts, he preached his gospel to them all alike. Whether or no the child Henry listened to those sermons of the veteran, he was growing up in a world half-molded by the Wesleys. Their hymns were the songs of his home to which he turned again and again for solace in the remote places of the earth.

known as Middle Row were thrown into the present spacious Boscawen Street.
[3] John Wesley's *Journal*, August 27, 1776.
[4] Southey's *Life of Wesley*.

There is no record of a beloved nurse or any woman who took the place of the lost mother in the lives of John Martyn's little children. Physically Henry sounds a neglected and untempting child with hands covered with warts, and red eyelids devoid of eyelashes set in a plain little face; but the father who gave his own leisure to those problems in the *Gentleman's Diary* saw with delight uncommon promise in his small son.

At the age of seven he entered little Henry at the Truro Grammar School and never ceased to hold before him a career of scholarship. The seven-year-old child trotted across the square and dived down an opposite lane to find himself in a large low room that held the wonderful new world of school.

Opposite the door was a molded painting where the civic ship rode yellow on very blue waves; and below the ship stood a throne whereon sat one of Truro's great ones. The Reverend Doctor Cornelius Cardew, a magistrate, a member of the corporation, twice mayor of the city, and its schoolmaster for more than a generation, looked out over a formidable beak with the searching quizzical glance of one who knew what was in boys. He thrashed soundly, he believed his boys to be "good material," and assisted by only one usher he turned out able men, so that in the distant universities they began to speak with respect of the little western grammar school.

Down either side of the room as in the choir of a church were yellow benches carved with the names of the more daring scholars; and here sat the sixty boys, more terrible to the new seven-year-old than the master himself, who thought him a babe of promise. There they sat, while bland plaster angels looked down from the green and white vaulted ceiling with perfect unconcern on despairing faces turned up in search of an answer. It soon became noticeable that little Henry, though no one called him studious, showed a happy faculty for hitting on the right answer without consulting the angels.

The "great boys" were wonderful. There was Clement

Carlyon who was going to be a doctor; there was John Kempthorne from Helston whose father was a real live admiral and
fought on the high seas; and most wonderful of all was Hum-
phry Davy from Penzance, the son of a wood-carver, round-
shouldered and clumsy, a youth who dipped his finger in the
inkpot when he wanted to blot out a mistake in his exercise,
but the inventor of wonderful things to do. He could make
lamps of scooped-out turnips, and tales of chivalry and gory
ballads and Latin verses that pleased Dr. Cardew, and he in-
vented fireworks that really went off, and "thunder-powder"
which exploded on a stone. You paid in pins to see it.

Only while these great ones were occupied with their work
and their plans for fishing, Henry finding his level among the
"lesser boys" had his temper sorely tried. He was "a good-
humoured plain little fellow," Carlyon said, and no coward;
"he quailed before no man." But he was considerably under
the average in size and in staying power, and in the hurly-burly
of the small-boy world he was always pushed to the wall, when
he broke into the bitter rages of one who is helpless before his
tormentors yet uncowed. His puny but intensely violent rages
made him a tempting subject for the bullies of that boy community and Henry's schooldays would have been dark for him
but for the searching critical eye of the pedagogue in white
bands at the end of the room.

Dr. Cardew saw that Henry's knowledge of the classics
would be small unless he had protection. He turned the
whippersnapper over to the great, beneficent Kempthorne, a
diligent senior boy who was later a clergyman and lord of a
manor in the Lizard district. Kempthorne "had often the happiness of rescuing him from the grasp of oppressors" and never
forgot "the thankful expression of his affectionate countenance
when he happened to be helped out of some difficulty."

Seated near the big, safe presence, little Martyn blossomed
out, into no very great diligence at his book it is true—he

seemed in those days rather to absorb the classics than to learn them—but into marked sociability, forgetting his helpless rages and becoming one of the friendliest souls in the school.

So the years passed and Henry Martyn, still small for his years, was no longer one of the babes but played the big boy to his own younger cousin Fortescue Hitchins, learned to shoot, and began to look to the future. Oxford was the university of most of his acquaintance, for the Cornishmen went in numbers to Exeter College, and when Henry was fifteen, they sent him up to compete for a scholarship at Corpus. The fact that in spite of his extreme youth he all but won the prize is a testimony to the classical training of Dr. Cardew's boys. Henry now sat among the "great boys" at the annual school sermon in St. Mary's and on holidays scoured the country with a gun.

He belonged to a family of mine agents that never intermarried with the great gentry of the land, but had a sprinkling of cousins and relatives by marriage up and down the Cornish countryside in the ranks of solicitors, clergy or mining accountants. It was a hospitable world and what with schoolfellows and cousins Henry could ride all over the county and be sure of a welcome at some townplace sheltering among sycamores or in the one street of some country town. There grew in him a great love of the Cornish land so that later even Cambridge seemed "a dreary scene" when he thought of misty headlands crowned with scilla or sea pink above the slow wash of an opal sea.

The holiday rides that meant the most to him were those to St. Hilary Vicarage where a little church among its trees stood as a landmark to the sailors in Mount's Bay. Here lived his father's cousin, Malachy Hitchins. He was a man of varied interests, who in youth had helped to make a survey of Devonshire, and now divided his energies between his work as the parson of the villages of Gwinear and St. Hilary (a preacher of formal old-fashioned sermons) and his other task as assistant

to Greenwich Observatory in compiling the *Nautical Almanac*.
He wrote to the *Gentleman's Magazine* under the signature
"ultimus vatum" ("You know that Malachi was the last of the
prophets") and he loved his garden. In that house of many
interests Henry Martyn always found a welcome, and with
his cousins Tom and Josepha and Fortescue in the old vicarage
garden his happiest hours were spent.

So the Cornish land bred him and made him forever her
own—small, passionate, affectionate, a boy of parts and of imagination, wholly incapable of passing easily and light-heartedly
through sunny shallows, a born plunger into the depths
whether of good or of evil.

In the winter of 1796-97, when the west country was set
buzzing by the daring of three French frigates that sailed into
Ilfracombe harbor, and when eyes were beginning to turn
to an officer named Nelson who first hoisted his flag that spring
as Admiral of the Blue, John Martyn told his boy that he should
leave school at midsummer and prepare for the larger world
of the university.

Chapter 3

UNDERGRADUATE

The gentleman's Muse wears Methodist shoes; you may know by her pace, and talk about grace, that she and her bard have little regard for the taste and fashions, and ruling passions, and hoidening play of the modern day.—W. COWPER *to the* REV. JOHN NEWTON, *June*, 1781.

Unless God has raised you up for this very thing, you will be worn out by the opposition of men and devils.—JOHN WESLEY *to* CHARLES SIMEON, *February*, 1791.

HENRY MARTYN left the grammar school in the summer of 1797, and after a September spent in "his favourite employment of shooting and . . . reading for the most part travels and Lord Chesterfield's *Letters*" he went up to St. John's College, Cambridge, following in the steps of his beloved Kempthorne.

In that summer when Henry left the grammar school, Jane Austen, all unknown in a Hampshire village, was putting the final touches to *Pride and Prejudice*; Charles Lamb spent his brief, idyllic holiday with Coleridge and Sara at Nether Stowey; and Coleridge, "the rapt one of the godlike forehead," writing a few weeks later to the excellent Mr. Cottle, announced that "Wordsworth and his exquisite sister" were staying with him.

But none of these voices had stirred the Cambridge to which Martyn went. Rather was she still listening to the rolling echoes of the most sonorous of English voices, hushed only that summer with the death of Burke.

Fanny Burney said of Burke that when he spoke of the French Revolution his face immediately assumed "the expression of a man who is going to defend himself against murderers." Just such a look stole into the faces of the authorities at Cambridge when, turning for a moment from the worship of Newton, they heard the strange clash of revolutionary forces in politics or literature. Every year saw its goodly crop of orthodox pamphlets against the writings of Thomas Paine—pamphlets in which the forces seen to be fighting in confusion on the wrong side of the battle. For Tom Paine with his harsh earnestness, his daring if unlettered mind, his championship of common folk, and his life of self-forgetful adventure seems far nearer in spirit to the Christ whom he denied, than the comfortable gentlemen who, with more dignity and learning but with less of love and sacrifice, wrote tracts under such stimulating titles as *A Layman's Protest against the Profane Blasphemy, false Charges, and illiberal Invective of Thomas Paine.*

But Henry Martyn, with four months yet to run before he was seventeen, was still outside the warring world of pamphlets. There was Cambridge, with all her beauty calling to his Cornish soul; his own college, St. John's, of whose "blushing bricks" old Fuller writes, not the least fair, its three courts containing some of the loveliest Tudor brickwork in that city of rare brick. The music at King's College chapel became one of Martyn's dear delights, and another he was to find in St. John's walks and Fellows' Gardens, where yet

> . . . *The elm clumps greatly stand*
> *Still guardians of that holy land,*

and whence in Martyn's day, when patches of heath crept

almost to the gates of the colleges one looked out over open champaign country that grew "the best saffron in Europe."

In the then much smaller city of Cambridge the eighteenth century was dying hard. Pitt was a familiar figure there, coming twice a year to visit his constituency, and walking the college courts with a cocked hat and almost military step. Men who might have stepped out of the pages of Fielding yet walked the Cambridge streets. A certain well-known Dr. Glynn, Fellow of King's and champion of the old school of physicians, took his walks abroad in a scarlet cloak, powdered wig and three-cornered hat, wielding an enormous gold-headed cane, while he ordered blisters for his patients with the unvarying and depressing formula "emplasma vesicatorium amplum et acre."

Cambridge still thought umbrellas effeminate, and there was said to be but one in all the city, kept at a shop in Benet Street and let out by the hour. But even in Cambridge old ways were passing, and fathers who brought boys to the university were shocked to see M.A.s in round hats rather than cocked ones. Powder too was going out of fashion, though the graver seniors still wore powdered wigs which went to a shop on Saturday to be curled and dressed for Sunday, and Trinity cherished a joyful story of the bribing of the shopman, and of certain statues seen at dawn with curled wigs on their heads, while college dignitaries fumed into Sunday morning chapel in their second-best headgear. But very few junior members of the university wore powered hair. Pitt had done much to change the fashion by his hair-powder tax to pay for the French war, and young poetic democrats like Coleridge, and Southey and Savage Landor at Oxford, had done their part by railing against powder "as inconsistent with republican simplicity." It was necessary, however, to wear your hair curled at Cambridge, unless you would be classed among the "very rustic and unfashionable."

Undergraduates were bound to wear white stockings, garterless and reaching to short knee-breeches, and men who cared for appearances donned white waistcoats and silk stockings for dinner in hall at about two o'clock. Dinner was followed by disputations in the mathematical school at three o'clock, but these were much deserted for the sake of exercise, and from three till half-past five, men rode or walked. The richer and the gayer sort drove curricles, and kept racehorses and hunters, but as yet the rowing man was not, and the river was left to lonely dreamers.

After five-thirty chapel, for missing which at St. John's one was ordered an imposition, men made tea in their rooms, or, in the fireless days of summer, repaired to coffeehouses in the town. Reading men then settled in for a long unbroken evening, and social spirits sat down to hazard (an old dice game) and burgundy. Few cared to disturb the evening for the supper served in hall at eight forty-five.

Tutors did not in those days give individual lessons, but lectures on the set books for the degree examinations, chiefly "treatises by Wood and Vince on optics, mechanics, hydrostatics and astronomy." Rapid bookwork was in great demand, and King's College used to quote an answer to a question in a tutor's lecture: "Sir, I do not know what the center of percussion is, but I can work the problem upon it."

Martyn's tutor, Mr. Catton, was an astronomer who had been fourth wrangler, but in Cambridge opinion should have been senior. He lived for a little observatory on one of the towers at St. John's. When he came down from his observations of occultations and contemplated his new pupil, he found a spare boy under the usual height, who had been taught no mathematics, and whose idea of learning it seemed to be the committing of Euclid to memory. The astronomer called in the help of T. H. Shepherd a second-year man, who thus tells the tale:

"Mr. Catton sent for me to his rooms, telling me of Martyn, as a quiet youth, with some knowledge of classics, but utterly unable as it seemed to make anything of even the First Proposition of Euclid, and desiring me to have him into my rooms, and see what I could do for him in this matter. Accordingly, we spent some time together, but all my efforts appeared to be in vain; and Martyn, in sheer despair, was about to make his way to the coach office, and take his place the following day back to Truro, his native town. I urged him not to be so precipitate, but to come to me the next day, and have another trial with Euclid. After some time light seemed suddenly to flash upon his mind, with clear comprehension of the hitherto dark problem, and he threw up his cap for joy at his Eureka. The Second Proposition was soon taken, and with perfect success; but in truth his progress was such and so rapid, that he distanced everyone in his year."[1]

"A quiet youth" Mr. Catton had called the slight demure boy, whose faintly ceremonious manners bore to the end of his life a trace of his studies in Lord Chesterfield before coming up to Cambridge. The undergraduate who stopped that despairing rush to the Blue Boar Inn for the next western coach saw that the "quiet youth" was an impetuous one. With friends he was known also as a sociable one, showing a bright delicacy of spirit and a liveliness all too apt to pass into quivering irritation. But few guessed what a storm center was the inner life of this freshman not yet seventeen. The Henry Martyn of those early Cambridge days had his being in a spiritual whirlwind. He was swept by great devastating emotions, longings, exaltations, rages, ambitions; raised to an ecstasy by music; cast to despair by a slip in mechanics. "A life of woe" he called it, looking back on those early storms from the comparative security of twenty-three.[2] In general the outward visible sign of the inward stress was only an "exquisite irritability," but now and again passion would master him. In such a moment he flung a knife at his

---

[1] Smith's *Henry Martyn*, p. 19, note.
[2] *Journal*, June 27, 1804.

friend Cotterill, and those who saw it quivering in the wall knew that the inner Martyn was no "quiet youth."

The safeguards of his storm-swept soul lay in his always warm affections. It is true that there was no mother to be impressed with each new Cambridge phase, to be teased, and to be trusted for unfailing love. But at Cambridge there was Kempthorne, and at home there was his father. The big, safe Kempthorne of the Truro Grammar School was still one of the great ones in Martyn's world, having become the senior wrangler of 1797. From these heights he was a good friend to "little Henry Martyn" from his old school. He found the boy swept away by the new delights and freedoms of a first term, and told him he must work. Kempthorne believed in work. He had won his own honors by unflagging diligence, covering more reams of paper, it was said, than any man in the university, as he worked out every problem in a fair hand, perhaps a hundred times, till he had first stripped the argument of each unnecessary step, and then reduced the necessary steps to the most lucid economy of word, line and letter. Such diligence he recommended to Martyn.

The beloved Kempthorne had spoken; and work Martyn did, with a greedy ambition only stimulated by his quick success in the college examinations, then conducted twice a year by the fellows in hall on the lecture subjects for the term. Martyn was never for half-measures. The boy who knew no mathematics when he came up was soon "nettled to the quick" when he took second instead of first place in his college examinations. He now set his heart on following Kempthorne's footsteps as the senior wrangler of his year, no small ambition in a student whose natural bent was for literature and above all for language.

The good Kempthorne dreaded so engrossing a concern with examination results and tried "to persuade me that I ought to attend to reading, not for the praise of men, but for the glory of God. This seemed *strange* to me, but *reasonable.*" Reasonable, no doubt, but also quite uninteresting to the Martyn of those days.

His love for his father fostered his ambition. The gentle and sympathetic old man, himself a self-trained mathematician, who all along had set before Henry a career of scholarship, was now waiting as eagerly as the boy himself for tidings of each examination. When at Christmas 1799 Henry was first in the college examination it "pleased my father prodigiously."

Only sister Sally, aged sixteen, and a devout Christian girl after the type of piety left in Cornwall by the Wesleys, was full of heavy concern for Henry's passionate soul. Her overtures, nay her exhortations on religion when he went home were "grating" to the ears of a brother two years older than herself, and he was apt to reply to her "in the harshest language." (Oh Henry!) The maiden did extract a promise, one day, that he would read the Bible for himself. "But on being settled at college, Newton engaged all my thoughts."[3] It was in the autumn term of 1799 that Newton so held the ascendancy, and it was at the Christmas examinations of the same term that Henry obtained that first place which so "prodigiously" pleased his father.

It seems that Henry did not that Christmas make the tedious journey to Cornwall. The vacation listed four weeks exactly, and the journey would cut out the best part of two of them. Although there was daily communication with London there was but one coach weekly from Cambridge to Birmingham. This left Cambridge early on Thursday morning and carried western passengers, at a fare at £1. 11s. 6d., to Birmingham by Friday evening, in time for a Cornishman to catch the night coach to the west. On the western coach there were

---

[3] Twelve years afterwards on a ship in the Indian Ocean Martyn wrote: "I bless God for Sir. I. Newton, who, beginning with the things next to him, and humbly and quietly moving to the things next to them, enlarged the boundaries of human knowledge more than the rest of the sons of men."

two days between Birmingham and Exeter, and Henry had
further yet to go; but even such speed was too much to hope for
through the miry lanes of winter. Henry did not go home, but
letters from Truro told him that his father was "in great health
and spirits."

What then was my consternation, when in January I
received from my [half] brother an account of my father's
death.

The affectionate boy, too young to remember his mother's
death, found his first great sorrow staring at him, and he quite
alone, in what seemed only a greater isolation because, with
the chimes of Trinity and St. Clement's, there floated in the
sound of eager talk on the staircase, and shouting and sudden
spurts of laughter from the court below.

Alone, Martyn found himself shivering before realities he
would gladly have forgotten.

I began to consider seriously that invisible world to
which he had gone and to which I must one day go. As I
had no taste at this time for my usual studies, I took up my
Bible [how often had the pious little Sally in Cornwall
prayed for that moment!] thinking that the consideration
of religion was rather suitable to this solemn time.

But tormented as he was by memories of his own "consum-
mate selfishness" at home, as set against his father's unfailing
"patience and mildness," Martyn found no peace of forget-
fulness through his effort at Bible reading. He was turning
for escape to other books when Kempthorne came in. That
steady, comfortable friend, the link between Cambridge and
the world of home, now advised Martyn "to make this time an
occasion for serious reflection."

Once more Kempthorne had spoken, and Martyn obedi-
ently turned again to his Bible. "I began with the Acts . . . but
I found myself insensibly led to enquire more attentively into
the doctrines of the apostles." His interest once awakened, he
remarked with approval how the notions he had gathered as a

little child from the Cornish Christians of the evangelical revival "corresponded nearly enough" with what he now read in the epistles.

It was not Martyn's habit at that time to pray, but prayer seemed a suitable exercise for one urged by Kempthorne to "serious reflection." He knelt and "began to pray from a pre-composed form, in which I thanked God in general for having sent Christ into the world." It was his first stumbling footstep in the way of prayer, wherein his spirit was to know such hard-won and such exquisite delight.

Kempthorne not only advised "reflection" but lent Martyn one of the religious classics of the day to guide him in it. He chose Doddridge's *Rise and Progress of Religion in the Soul,* a book to which young William Wilberforce owed the awakening of his spirit, and a book in which the wonderful confidence of the eighteenth century in the power of reason may be seen extending even to her evangelists, who sought to save men by a logical order of convictions, starting in this case with the proposition of the guilt of all created beings before an offended Creator. "I will labour to fix a deep and awful *Conviction of Guilt* upon his conscience, and to strip him of his vain *Excuses* and his flattering hopes" says Doddridge in the "general plan of the work." And he does labour. Good and sincere man as he is, we feel with Leslie Stephen that he is "lashing a jaded imagination rather than overpowered by an awful vision." "I am sensible I can do it no otherwise," Doddridge tells us, "than by way of deep Humiliation." Henry Martyn, dejected though he was, read and rebelled. "It appeared to make religion consist too much in humiliation" he said. "I was not under great terror of future punishment" he tells his sister; and moderns feel a sneaking gladness the he would not be terrified into the kingdom of heaven.

But in despite of too logical "plans of salvation" the vision of a living Person was slowly stealing into Martyn's heart. "I am brought to a sense of things gradually" he wrote. He still "read the Bible unenlightened" but having worked through the Acts and the epistles he now turned to the Gospels. "Soon I began to attend more diligently to the words of our Saviour in the New Testament, and to devour them with delight." Then when the same voice made "offers of mercy and forgiveness" Martyn's heart responded and he found himself, he knew not how, praying "with eagerness and hope." His spirit had discovered not a doctrine but a Person. None was to know more than he of the humiliation that marks the saint, but he learned it, not under Doddridge's guidance by the contemplation of his guilty state, but under Other guidance when he came to see "the light of the knowledge of the glory of God, in the face of Jesus Christ."

This was a conversion. Four years later he could. write, "The work is real. I can no more doubt it than I can my own existence. The whole current of my desires is altered, I am walking quite another way, though I am incessantly stumbling in that way."

Henceforth we know the same Martyn, but with a liberating change: a Martyn with emotions still intense, perhaps even intensified; all his life more quickly moved than most men whether to delight or tears; his heart raised to rapture by music or by quiet scenery; while, as the price of ecstasies too intense for his physical frame, he must know a fastidiousness and quivering irritation almost inconceivable to men of firmer build.

But no longer was this Martyn to be the slave of his own storms. In finding a Master he was set free. No more pent up in himself, his whole spiritual being found a great escape through contact with the infinite life of his Lord. That vital contact now begun was maintained, as it seemed to himself, precariously enough and with difficulty at first, through what he felt to be a surprising "reluctance to prayer, unwillingness to come to God the fountain of all good." But for all that, the

contact was maintained and cultivated, growing daily more
sure, until he became at home in the new realm that he now
entered, "tasting the powers of the age to come," and growing
into gradual harmony with that "undisturbed song of pure
concent" whose notes were for the first time stealing into his
ears as he read "the words of our Saviour in the New Testament" in January 1800.

Martyn was far too rapturous a being ever to reach a stoic
composure, but he came at last very near to the quite different
composure of the charity that "beareth all things, hopeth all
all things, endureth all things," and those who read his story see
that most sensitive and irritable of beings grow to such indomit-
able patience that a friend, in writing of a maddening character,
could say, "There is little hope that any person but Martyn
could bear with him."[4]

But the life of inner discipleship, then as ever, had to find
expression in outward relationships, and Henry Martyn made
new friendships both at Cambridge and at home. The little
religious sister in Cornwall, now recognized as a comrade in
experience, received, as she also delightedly wrote, long letters
on their common experience in Christ. The brother and sister
used, naturally enough, the vocabulary of the evangelical revival under the Wesleys, which had created the religious
atmosphere that Sally breathed. For them, any "means of
grace" from the holy communion to personal study of the
Scriptures was "a sacred ordinance," a group meeting for Bible
study was "a Society"[5] and united prayer was "engaging in a

---

[4] D. Corrie to D. Brown, October 4, 1810.

[5] John Wesley's *Journal* for May 1, 1738, after his visit to the Moravians,
tells of the first meeting of such a "society" in Fetter Lane. It was to meet
weekly in groups of not more than ten for confession, spiritual conference
and mutual prayer. This was the forerunner of the Wesleyan Class Meeting.
Charles Simeon, in order to know his flock more individually, started something between a cottage meeting and a Bible class which he also called "a
society." He had six "societies" meeting regularly, each with about 20
members.

social exercise," while private devotions were "secret duties" as against church services or "public duties." The evil which distressed them in their inner life they commonly referred to as their "corruption," over which indeed they were in deep concern as they strove by "a realizing faith" to reach a "happy frame" of "breathings after God" and a "lively view of eternal things." The vocabulary may be studied in the hymns and religious diaries of that day. Its historical lineage is interesting, many of the phrases leading one back to sixteenth century divines and worthies, or to the Moravian brethren and the German pietists. Today when it is almost obsolete as an expression of life it sounds stilted enough, but for Martyn it was pulsing with the unconquerable vitality of

> The children of the Second Birth
> Whom the world cannot tame.

Almost the same phraseology was in use among the small group of religious men at Cambridge, with whom Henry Martyn was now to ally himself. The usual nickname for those in the University who took Christian discipleship with any seriousness was still "Methodist," a tribute to the amazing influence of John Wesley's work. In Martyn's time a few such "Methodist" undergraduates were found at Queens' under the mastership of Isaac Milner, genial and full-bodied, "a man of boundless good will to his fellow creatures at every period of life, provided that they were not Jacobins or sceptics,"[6] and the most brilliant talker in the university. "He was equally at home on a steeplechase and on final perseverance; and explained with the same confidence the economy of an ant-hill and the policy of the Nizam."[7] His lectures on optics, illustrated both by his humor and by "experiments" of the nature of "exhibitions of the magic lanthorn," were among the joys of undergraduate life.

---

[6] Trevelyan, *Life and Letters of Lord Macaulay*, p. 40.
[7] Stephen, *Essays in Ecclesiastical Biography*.

Another group of religious men belonged to Magdalene where the master wailed that there must be "something in the air of Magdalene that makes men Methodists. We have elected fellows . . . whom we considered to be most anti-Methodistical but they all become Methodists." The central personality here was Professor Farish, a chemist of distinction and a man of charm, later to become well known to Martyn.

But the strongest religious influence in the university, and as some said in all England, was wielded by a fellow of King's, whose erect soldierly figure might any day be seen riding to the Gogmagog Hills on one of the best-bred horses in the neighborhood. Undergraduates who a few decades later would be designated by the first syllable of the word "pious" then had the first syllable of the word "Simeon" shouted under their windows at night, in compliment to the Reverend Charles Simeon of King's College, one of the most typically English saints that ever lived, and perhaps the most intrepid and arresting personality of Martyn's Cambridge.

Twenty years before Martyn, Charles Simeon had come up to King's College from Eton, a most active, vehement and vivid black-eyed boy, given to dominating the circle in which he found himself. He combined an intense interest in clothes, then largely expressed in shoe-buckles and silk waistcoats, with a yet intenser interest in horseflesh, that abode with him to the day of his death. Under the noise of his vehement talk, Charles Simeon had in him an unguessed depth of reverence, and when he found, three days after his arrival, that undergraduates were, by a now vanished college rule, compelled to take the sacrament at half-term and again on Easter Day, his soul revolted from a formal and official entrance to the holy of holies. He set himself to preparation, reading *The Whole Duty of Man*, "the only religious book I had ever heard of."

For three months his discomfort only grew, until in Passion Week when he was in "distress of soul," light came like a flash to his always vivid mind. "Has God provided an Offering for me, that I may lay my sins on His head? Then God willing, I will not bear them on my own soul one moment longer." To Simeon as later to Martyn came the revelation of a Person. On Easter Sunday he awoke with the words "Jesus Christ is risen to-day, Hallelujah!" upon his lips and in his heart, and went to church in a passion of glad conviction. After the service some morsels of the consecrated bread remained, and the clergyman handed them to Simeon and some others. Simeon, his heart still at worship, covered his face in prayer while he ate, then looked up to find that, inconceivable as it may now seem, the clergyman was smiling at so rare and so unnecessary a display of "enthusiasm."

From that day the taint of "enthusiasm," so much dreaded in the eighteenth century, made Simeon a marked man in the university and a considerable anxiety to his family, his brother writing plaintively enough "I trust that in the common course of things your zeal will slacken a little." Simeon suffered under his isolation, for he was warm-hearted; but there was also that in him which leaped to the call of battle.

Henceforth there were two sides to Charles Simeon. On one side he lived, almost unhelped by men, a life of very simple discipleship, of which we learn by stray phrases that reveal the man; as when he breaks out wistfully, "Oh that Jesus were to be at the wedding, with what joy I should go then"; or as when a friend, failing to make him hear, burst into his room to find that active, dominating person lost in contemplation and murmuring again and again "Glory, glory, glory to the Son of God." This little-known side of his life he maintained by rising at four, and spending the hours till breakfast in meditation with his "little old quarto Bible."

He had another and a very different side "to face the world with" as he proceeded magnificently to defy the scorn of Cambridge. Shortly after his ordination to a fellowship of King's

in 1782 he accepted, against a fury of local opposition, a living
of the value of £40 a year, in order that Trinity Church might
give him a pulpit from which to speak his message to the city.
It is doubtful whether Simeon in all his long life ever knew
what it was to speak in an uncertain tone; and in his pulpit,
preaching, as he would have said, to perishing souls of the
truths of eternity and the deepest convictions of his own heart,
his vehement earnestness of voice and gesture struck Cambridge as "lively" but "grotesque." "Oh, Mamma, what is the
gentleman in a passion about?" cried a little girl who heard
such preaching for the first time. Mamma might very properly
have replied that Simeon was in a passion, and never out of it,
for the neglected honor of his Lord.

It went the round that this fellow of King's (like the
members of the Holy Club at Oxford half a century before)
was in the habit of visiting poor felons in the jail and of poking
into cottages in insalubrious lanes. But the limit was reached
when the respectability of Trinity Church was invaded by the
great unwashed. The same treatment was meted out to Simeon
as had been given to Romaine when his preaching drew "the
unsavoury multitude" into the sacred precincts of St. George's,
Hanover Square. The respectable pew-holders locked up their
square family pews and sat in satisfied propriety at home, leaving Simeon to preach to such of the peasantry of the neighboring villages (for these tramped miles to hear him) and Cambridge lanes as could stand in the aisles. He placed benches
in the aisles, but the churchwardens, with all the joy of battle,
threw them out into the churchyard. He started an evening
service, a shocking innovation in days when evensong was
generally droned through in the sleepiest part of Sunday afternoon, and the cost of candles saved.

Such a "Methodist" with such outrageous practices was
fair game for undergraduate wit, and it became a regular Sunday "rag" to bait Simeon. You could stand outside and throw

pebbles at the windows while you waited to harry the congregation on their way out; or you could go inside and stand upon
the seats or stroll about the aisles, with suitable cat-calls to a
friend in another part of the church, and witty comments on
all that Simeon did. "Why, how long the old hypocrite goes
on apraying!" you felt bound to say, as he bowed his head
before the sermon which was to be for you an opportunity of
aping his grotesque and passionate gesture.

The sermon was the great encounter, and Simeon knew
it, and knew too that he could expect no support from university authorities. He had only his own dominating personality
and his terrible eye with which to oppose the rowdies. And
Sunday after Sunday the miracle happened, and the man with
his overwhelming earnestness imposed silence so long as he
chose to preach, the hurly-burly breaking out again when he
left the pulpit and they were no longer under the domination
of that flashing eye. As an old man he used to say that he had
never met but two gownsmen who "ever were daring enough
to meet my eye."

But Simeon did more than quell men to silence; week after
week he drove the plowshare of conviction deep into some soul
to whom he became ever afterwards a father in God, a robust
and fearless leader.

In Martyn's days he was midway in his career, still doubtful
whether another fellow would be seen to walk across the grass
of the college court with him; his disciples still running the
gauntlet of university scorn, but forming now a perceptible
group, in which "Father Simeon" held his half-tender and half-
autocratic sway. When Henry Martyn became a regular attend-
ant at Trinity in 1799, Simeon had already started tea-drink-
ings, later to become his famous "conversation parties" for
gownsmen, at which, after welcoming his guests with the polish and the dignity of a courtier, he sat erect in a high chair,
by a scientifically mended fire (a special crotchet) and dealt

out the counsel of a tried and courageous Christian, while two servants handed tea to the slightly embarrassed undergraduates.

This was Martyn's leader in the new path; a man always vivid, often quaintly humorous, generally domineering, but with touching gentlenesses; a man of whom the landlady of the "Eagle and Child" was heard to remark confidentially in the London coach, "He looks proud, he walks proud, he talks proud, and he *is* proud," but a man in whom his relationship to Christ worked wonderful flashes of humility: as when he wrote in apology to a groom whom he had rated for putting the wrong bridle on his horse, "I earnestly beg his pardon, and am sorry for what I said to him": or as when, after snapping at an undergraduate for trampling the yellow gravel of King's College court into the carpet of his bachelor domain, he would return after a few moments to say, "My brother, I was annoyed and spoke too strongly, but [and how human is that but!] I do love a clean carpet."

The literary sense was not strong in Simeon, who was rather a born organizer. He had none of Martyn's love for pure scholarship, but in him common sense was carried almost to the point of genius, and his counsel to the delicately sensitive Martyn "without one torpid nerve about him," was nearly always robust. A specimen of the guidance Martyn had is found in Simeon's treatment of what was still the favorite subject for theological worry—the Arminian and Calvinistic controversy. A letter written long after Martyn had left Cambridge may yet serve to show us Simeon's habitual and most independent treatment of such questions:

> The truth is not in the middle, and not in one extreme but in both extremes. . . . Here are two extremes, Calvinism and Arminianism (for you need not to be told how long Calvin and Arminius lived before St. Paul). "How do you move in reference to these, Paul? In a golden mean?" "No" —"To one extreme?" "No." "How then?" "To both extremes;

today I am a strong Calvinist, tomorrow a strong Arminian"
—"Well, well, Paul, I see thou art beside thyself; go to
Aristotle and learn the golden mean."

But I am unfortunate; I formerly read Aristotle, and
liked him very much; I have since read Paul and caught
some of his strange notions, oscillating (not vacillating)
from pole to pole. Sometimes I am a high Calvinist, at other
times a low Arminian, so that if extremes will please you,
I am your man; only remember, it is not one extreme that
we are to go to, but *both* extremes.

. . . We shall be ready (in the estimation of the world,
and of *moderate* Christians) to go to Bedlam together.[8]

In lesser questions his "young friends" found his advice
both fatherly and robust. He would have them work; but "remember," said he, "your success in the Senate House depends
much on the care you take of the three-mile stone out of Cambridge." Most sound counsel for one of Martyn's build who in
1799 and 1800 was all but a recluse, working with the eagerness that gained for him the title of "the man who never lost
an hour"; yet working without the old frenzy, since he knew
now a deeper interest than his work, and was almost jealous
of the necessary absorption in reading. "The labourer as he
drives on his plough," he wrote Sally, "and the weaver as he
works at his loom, may have his thoughts entirely disengaged
from his work, and may think with advantage upon any religious subject. But the nature of *our* studies requires such a
deep abstraction of the mind from all other things, as to render
it completely incapable of anything else, and that during many
hours of the day."

The examination for degrees took place in January 1801.
Henry knew that, having no advantage of family or wealth, his
social prospects, and in part those of his sisters also, depended
upon the honors that he took. It was true that he was now

---

[8] H. C. G. Moule, *Charles Simeon*, p. 97.

easily first in his college examinations; but the year was said to be an unusually brilliant one in the university. Among leading names from other colleges were those of Charles and Robert Grant of Trinity, the two sons of Charles Grant of Calcutta, who had learned their first Latin from the Reverend David Brown.

The examination of those days began before breakfast on a January morning, a moment at which spirits are apt to be at a low ebb. As Martyn passed under the fluted columns of the Senate House portico, there flashed into his agitated mind the text of a sermon heard not long ago—"Seekest thou great things for thyself? Seek them not, saith the Lord." Steadied, as an over-excited child by his father's voice, he went in and wrote with a mind "composed and tranquillized," and retained his calm through the three long mornings of the *viva voce*, when the honors men sat around a table in the ice-cold Senate House with an examiner at their head, who propounded a problem which all worked at topmost speed. When the first man had handed in his solution another problem was read out, with the result that the slower men missed many of the questions. At night in the rooms of one of the moderators more difficult work was set, in which the race for speed was not so great, and men had a choice of problems offered them.

The results were published on the fourth day; and, at not quite twenty years of age, Henry Martyn found that his darling ambition had been realized, and he was senior wrangler. His first sensation was keen disappointment. His father was not there to glory in the news. "I obtained my highest wishes," he says, "but was surprised to find that I had grasped a shadow." Be that as it may, he did later find much seductive pleasure in the sense of distinction, and in the subtle tone of regard that crept into the voices of university officials when they talked to one at once so young and so distinguished.

Cambridge had given to her young son her highest honors,

but at the cost of a diligence that cut him off from many of the richer interests of life. She had given him a formal intellectual training; she had yet in store for him that training in the humanities which only comes of friendship and of fruitful meditation.

Chapter 4

FELLOW OF ST. JOHN'S

I have seen a great deal of him, have studied his sentiments and heard his opinion on subjects of literature and taste; and upon the whole, I venture to pronounce that his mind is well informed, his enjoyment of books exceedingly great, his imagination lively, his observations just and correct, and his taste delicate and pure. . . . His person can hardly be called handsome, till the expression of his eyes, which are uncommonly good, and the general sweetness of his countenance, is perceived. At present I know him well that I think him really handsome; or at least almost so.—JANE AUSTEN, *Sense and Sensibility.*

Oh dear Sir, do not think it enough to live at the rate of common Christians. . . . And oh, dear Sir, let me beseech you frequently to attend to the great and precious duties of secret fasting and prayer.—*Letter of* DAVID BRAINERD.

THE ORDEAL of the degree examination was followed two months later by what was then considered the still more searching test of the examination for the Smith's Prizes, in which less was required of the reproduction of book-work, and more of mathematical thought. Martyn held his own and went home at Easter to receive the congratulations of his old schoolmaster and

all the Cornish cousinry, as senior wrangler and first Smith's
Prizeman of a brilliant year.

Only Sally was dissatisfied and told him so. Cambridge
meant little to her, and her brother's religion meant much; in
this she was not content with his rate of progress.

He returned to Cambridge to take pupils and prepare for
the examination for a fellowship that was an almost certain
reward of such distinctions as his.

This second stage of Martyn's Cambridge life was less
crowded with relentless tasks and richer in friendship and in
growth than his undergraduate days. Martyn was never by
nature a mathematician only. A friend writes:[1] "His mathematical acquisitions clearly left him without a rival of his own
age: and yet, to have known only the employment of his more
free and unfettered moments would have led to the conclusion
that poetry and the classics were his predominant passions."

We have no record of what was the poetry on which he
slaked his thirst for beauty until a few years later, when we find
him steeped in the older traditions. For with all his transcendent abilities, Martyn was no originator in literary thought.
The intellectual realm in which he was to come into his own
was the then little explored field of the comparative philology
of Eastern languages. In regard to English literature he was
content to be a finely appreciative follower of the taste of his
own day, sometimes too of the day just before his, for Blair's
Grave gave him "much pleasure." He was at Cambridge in
those days just before the "Renascence of Wonder" when men
had on them a great industry for compilations, and were busy
over encyclopedias,[2] periodicals full of facts, and public lectures packed with information. But they had also a fresh and
genuine interest in landscapes of the common countryside, and

---

[1] Archdeacon C. J. Horne quoted by Sargent, p. 439.
[2] The *Encyclopaedia Britannica* was first published in 1771.

Marianne Dashwood must possess "every book that tells her how to admire an old, twisted tree."

This taste, so largely due to the loving subtlety with which Cowper drew his bird-haunted shrubberies and placid reaches of the Ouse, was one of the deepest in Martyn's nature; for he, like the poet of his own religious school, knew the relief of escape from his own too eager emotions to quiet fields and waters.

The recognized versifier of the clan of cousins and cousinly friends in Cornwall was Fortescue Hitchins,[3] a boy three years younger than Martyn, whose home with his grandfather, the Rev. Malachy Hitchins of Marazion, had been one of the favorite haunts of Henry's boyhood. Fortescue Hitchins wrote and published by subscription verses full of local landscapes, Cornish shores and sea-birds.

> My steps the barren sands
> (Though barren not unpleasing) oft invite,
> Where not a trace is seen, save the light print
> Of sea-bird . . .
> . . . So smooth the sea,
> It seems a mirror of ethereal blue,
> Dappled with varied plumage. O'er its plain
> Swift wheels the timid sanderling, gregarious,
> Nimble, alert, and mingling on the shore
> With dotterell and plover.

For this type of quiet verse-making, Martyn's appetite was keen. "Some of Fortescue's poems," he says, "set me into a pensive meditation on the happy mornings I had passed near Kea." He would often rest his own mind by composing verses as he walked into the country round Cambridge.

Always, too, there were the immortals and he tells us that he read now "some choruses of Sophocles," or again, "Euripides till very late," and confesses that just before he left for India he allowed himself an Aeschylus and a Pindar, not with-

---

[3] Later a solicitor at St. Ives and compiler of a *History of Cornwall*.

out scruples as to whether he should afford the price.

There was more space now in Martyn's Cambridge life for friendship, and Charles Simeon drew him into closer intimacy and would often ask him to drink tea when they would sit together, Simeon erect in his high chair under that "beautiful old painting of the Crucifixion" which he hoped they would hang before him on his deathbed, and quietly rubbing his hands together, as was his way in moments of placid enjoyment, while he talked with one so eagerly and so respectfully responsive.

To Simeon Martyn owed many of the friendships of these years, and above all his very beautiful intimacy with John Sargent of King's, who had taken his degree with Martyn but was not personally known to him till Simeon's introduction.

Young Sargent, heir of a Sussex squire, had shown at Eton "a decided superiority in the manly sports of the playground, with high classical attainments." When he came up to Cambridge he was one of the only two gownsmen whom Simeon's eye had been unable to quell, a fact which the latter did not fail to appreciate. And when conviction entered the soul of the young rioter, and Sargent placed himself on the side of the "serious" undergraduates, Charles Simeon welcomed him to a lifelong friendship.

Through the pen of his son-in-law[4] we see Sargent as a man of gracious charm. Both he and Martyn "belonged to a school of Attic elegance which is declining amongst us—a school of men who studied the classics, not as a means by which to obtain distinction, nor merely to acquire in the knowledge of another language a key to fresh mental attainments, but for their own sweetness. These were men whose whole spirit breathed of classical refinement."

---

[4] Bishop Samuel Wilberforce who wrote a short memoir of Sargent as an introduction to the *Journals* of Henry Martyn. The details given about him are largely from this sketch.

"A friend indeed" Martyn called Sargent, writing to Sally in September 1801, "and one who has made much about the same advances in religion as myself." For one so sensitive as Martyn, this was a wholesome friendship, for though none ever possessed "a softer touch" than Sargent, he was "frank and sparkling," with "a perpetual spring of holy, guileless gaiety." As yet he was a young disciple, but he was growing towards that freedom and spontaneity as of a child at home in his father's house, which his son-in-law shows as one of the dominant notes in his religious life, a rare note in those days of rather portentous solemnity.

It might be from mingling in the sports and merriments of childhood; it might be from the excitement of intellectual conversation; that he was called upon to turn his attention at once to holy things. The transition was effected in a moment. It was natural and reverend; free from anything of sternness; and impressing upon everyone the evident truth that his religion was no gloomy system of prohibitions and restraint.

To these two friends Charles Simeon sounded a call. To them as to all the choice youth whom he gathered into the inner circle of his friendship it was his way to speak again and again of "the transcendent excellence of the Christian ministry." But in Sargent and in Martyn the words of their leader roused very different feelings.

Sargent who "seemed scarcely able to comprehend the pleasure of owning anything unless he could give it to another" was destined to become a substantial Sussex landowner. He carried in the year 1801 the spirit of a son of Francis in the year 1210. "Could I have been assured that it was God's will that I should serve Him as a minister, were it to preach to the wild Indians," he told a friend, "*nothing* should stand in my way." But parental orders were distinct. He was to go to the Temple and "follow the profession of the law" as a valuable training for the future head of a landed family.

With intense pain of spirit, after being "tossed about for a long time" he decided that Simeon's call was not for him, and bent to the parental will as to discipline from his divine Master. The effect of the self-conquest was manifest to his friends. "Sargent seems to be outstripping us all," wrote Martyn. But Sargent himself was chiefly conscious of the difficulties of his new course. "Do not forget I beseech you," he wrote, "to pray for me, that the love of Jesus may attend me, and His right hand lead me through the perils of the profession I am entering."

In Martyn's mind, Charles Simeon's exhortations had struck a very different and a jarring note. "Few could surpass him," wrote Sargent of his friend, "in an exquisite relish for the various and refined enjoyments of a social and literary life." His university honors placed him in a position to choose his path, and the very profession from which Sargent shrank seemed to Martyn alluring, as a path to money, position and studious leisure. "I could not consent," he says, "to be poor for Christ's sake." He knew the humiliation served out to Simeon's friends in clerical life, and had seen how, if Simeon were absent, his curate was left with a perfectly impossible burden of duty because no cleric in the town or university would demean himself by serving in that notorious parish.

But Martyn's attitude to life was changing, in part through Sargent's friendship, and still more through great draughts of Bible reading and solitary prayer in green places by the Cambridge river during the long vacation of 1801. That summer marks an epoch in his life. "Not until then," he said, "had I ever experienced any real pleasure in religion." The taste which grew in him then for solitude, and especially for solitude out of doors, went with him through life.

In the pages of his Cambridge journal we can trace how the desire grew upon him for the Companionship which he found in that solitude in which he was never alone. In that journal we are allowed to watch with a rare intimacy the growth of a saint. "My object in making this journal," he says, "is to accustom myself to self-examination, and to give my experience a visible form, so as to leave a stronger impression on the memory, and thus to improve my soul in holiness; for the review of such a lasting testimony will serve the double purpose of conviction and consolation." Whatever we may think of the value of such a plan, Martyn's scrupulously transparent journal, written without a shred of self-excuse, as in the sight of God and all His angels, is perhaps the most remarkable human document left by the Church of his day, ranked by Dr. George Smith among "the great spiritual autobiographies of Catholic literature."

Entry after entry like those which follow serves to give us a glimpse of the growing taste for solitude, a solitude at first full of conscious effort, but into which there stole the sense of a Presence so sweet that all earthly joys went less to that communion.

I walked in the fields and endeavoured to consider my ways, and to lift up my heart to God.

Walked to the hawthorn hedge. . . . I devoted myself to Him solemnly, and trust that when tempted to sin I shall remember this walk.

Had a sweet, supporting sense of God's presence in the evening, when I walked by moonlight.

I determined to give all the rest of the day to acts of devotion without going into hall to dinner. So I retired to the garden.

During my walk, my mind was too much engaged in the composition of poetry, which I found to leave me far short of that sweetness I seemed in a frame to enjoy. Yet on the spot where I have often found the presence of God, the spirit of prayer returned.

My imagination takes to itself wings and flies to some wilderness where I may hold converse in solitude with God.

Was empty and tired for want of being alone.

Let me but ply heart-work in secret, let me but walk alone in communion with God, and I shall surely be able to offer Him sacrifices more pure.

From the church I walked to our garden, where I was alone an hour, I trust with Christ.

The sudden appearance of evil thoughts made me very unhappy, but I found refuge in God. O may the Lord . . . make me to find in Himself, the source and centre of beauty, a sweet and satisfied delight.

What is this world, what is religious company, what is anything to me without God? They become a bustle and a crowd when I lose sight of Him. The most dreary wilderness would appear paradise with a little of His presence.

A man cannot yield himself to such Companionship without being molded by it, and the Martyn who thought that he "could not consent to be poor for Christ's sake" found himself writing to Sally in September 1801:

The soul that has truly experienced the love of God will not stay meanly inquiring how much he shall do, and thus limit his service; but will be earnestly seeking more and more to know the will of our heavenly Father that he may be enabled to do it.

He did not reach his final decision as to the choice of a career until the long vacation of 1802. That summer, after a walking tour in Wales, he spent a Cornish holiday in sister Laura's married home, a lovable white house called Woodbury on the winding banks of the Fal Estuary. Here where the curlews called and the steep woods met the lapping water, he wandered alone with the Book of the Prophet Isaiah, passing "some of the sweetest moments of his life." When he returned to Cambridge his mind was made up. He would seek ordination and accept an invitation from Charles Simeon to become his curate. The decision was not easy to announce in Cambridge, as his journal shows.

Was ashamed to confess to ———— that I was to be Simeon's curate, a despicable fear of man.

Five months before reaching this determination Martyn had obtained his fellowship (April 5, 1802), and had followed it up by winning the first of the only university prizes open to middle bachelors, the Members' Prize for a Latin essay which he must declaim in public. Sargent says that "men of great classical celebrity" contested it with him. We can only wonder the more at the ease of the stride with which, after three years of close mathematical work, he returned to the classics that he loved.

The new fellow, in rooms in the corner of the lovely second court of St. John's, lived a life at once sociable and solitary. Men found him accessible, for with all his love of pretty manners he was remarkable, an old schoolfellow tells us, for "simplicity and ease." The *Journal* shows a large acquaintance and it shows too that the men who climbed his staircase had a way of staying to talk long, and sometimes longer than he liked.

Interrupted by R. who stayed till nine. Our conversation was on mathematics.

Some of my acquaintance drank wine with me. I was more careful about offending them by overmuch strictness than of offending God by conformity to the world.

From seven to twelve wasted by repeated calls of friends.

Insensibly passed the whole time in talking about music.

I had promised to walk with ——— which was perfectly hateful to me at this time, when I had such need of being alone with God.

For he was living now in two worlds and the man who at one moment had all heaven before his eyes, at another was terribly mortified because "fear of man" kept him from saying grace when two visitors from Clare Hall came to breakfast. The *Journal* shows him always accessible to younger men in need of help with mathematics, and his schoolfellow, Dr. Carlyon, had memories of running to Martyn's room in trouble over the

Eleventh Book of Newton and watching him push aside a massive Bible, pick up an odd sheet of paper and with a few miraculous lines sweep away all his difficulties.

As fellow, Martyn took his share in conducting the college examinations, then largely oral; at different times he examined in Butler, Locke, Xenophon, Juvenal and Euripides. It cost him a good deal of nervous *malaise* to examine before his brother fellows. He "doubted of his fitness," but when it came to the point examined "with great ease to myself and clearness," and found the "attention and respect" of the fellows after his performance in hall "remarkable." Yet here again he was living in two worlds. "There was something of a sacred impression on my mind during the examination in hall; several of the poetical images in Virgil in which they had been examining, especially those taken from nature, together with the sight of the moon rising over the venerable walls, and sending its light through the painted glass, turned away my thoughts from present things and raised them to God." Did any trembling candidate wonder at a sudden and other-worldly illumination in the face of the man who was examining him "with great ease and clearness"?

And did the dining fellows catch a strange light on his face in hall at times like that when the conversation at their table was of "stones falling from the moon," and "my imagination began to ascend among the shining worlds hung in the midst of space, and to glance from one to another; and my heart bounded at the thought that I was going a much surer way to behold the glories of the Creator hereafter, than by giving up my time to speculations about them"?

Those were the years when men expected Bonaparte to sail across the Channel, and the loyal university formed its volunteer corps with "a grave uniform," dark blue jacket, black stock, grey trousers and short black gaiters. So clad, Martyn **used to drill the fellows, perhaps as the youngest and most** active member of that learned body. One would like to know whether Mr. Catton came down from the observatory tower to present arms at his former pupil's bidding. The drills took place on Sidney Piece (now the Master's Garden) or on Parker's Piece, and sometimes there was a field day at Cherry Hinton chalk-pits. Martyn wrote to Sargent that he was passing his summer "amid the din of arms. I give our drilling this lofty title."

With all his share in college life and work, Martyn yet gave the impression to his colleagues of one who had his being in another world, and they resented it as men always resent the involuntary absorption of the artist or the saint.

> On preparing to go out B. called upon me, and our conversation lasted till near dinner time. He thought that by immoderate seclusion I deadened those fine feelings that we should cultivate, and neglected the active duties of life: that a thorough and universal change of heart and life was not necessary to make us Christians, of whom there might be all degrees, as of everything else. His amazing volubility left me unable to say anything.

Martyn on his part found their tastes as mysterious as they found his gauche and bizarre:

> It sometimes appeared astonishing that men of like passions with myself, of the same bodies, of the same minds, alike in every other respect, knew and saw nothing of that blessed and adorable Being in whom my soul findeth all its happiness, but were living a sort of life which to me would be worse than annihilation.

Under such circumstances that matchless combination room of St. John's with its bossy ceiling and its long row of Tudor windows was not always a place of joy for Martyn. Sometimes, indeed, after an intellectual triumph this very junior fellow found there "respect and admiration" from which he shrank as "dangerous"; but there were other days on which the Johnians had great relish from a little mockery of their resident "Methodist." Martyn must have provided plenty of scope for wit; like Charles Simeon in the early years after his conversion, he found it necessary to cut himself off from much that a maturer disciple could have enjoyed without danger. "I was tinder and did not like to go near sparks," Simeon would explain in later years. To the immature disciple it was a question of entering into life were it blind or halt or maimed; but to the genial souls in the combination room such young severity must have seemed delicious. "Went into the combination room after dinner, where some of those present kept me constantly employed by asking me questions to make me speak against the usual amusements of men."

So he walked among them uncomprehended and often uncomprehending, with that involuntary aloofness of the poet or the saint, and yet equally with a new yearning towards every human soul, that would lead him at the end of a long day's work to read aloud to his bedmaker. It is a strange picture of the rapt young scholar by the lamp, reading St. Luke to the frowzy old lady who could not read for herself. Did she catch the meaning of his ministrations, or did she twiddle her thumbs and possess her soul in patience under the unaccountableness of her gentleman's new whim?

This new-found care of the once fastidious Martyn for the souls of dull and shabby personages was immensely strengthened when in the autumn of 1802 he read the life of David Brainerd[5] and found his hero. He who would know Martyn must ask what manner of man was that Brainerd who called out his depths of admiration.

Martyn's hero was born at Hartford, Connecticut, in 1718, of a Puritan family that named him David and his brothers Hezekiah, Nehemiah, John and Israel. Surrounded by the influences that commonly went with a choice of names in which

---

[5] *An Account of the Life of David Brainerd* by Jonathan Edwards, Edinburgh, 1798.

the Old Testament held so heavy a predominance, and suffering from a wretched constitution and the loss of both parents before he was fourteen, young David hardly surprises us when he writes: "I was, I think from my youth something sober, and inclined rather to melancholy than the contrary extreme; but do not remember anything of conviction of sin, worthy of remark, till I was, I believe, about seven or eight years of age."

Yet for this boy, bred in so dour a school, there was in store an evangelical experience that might be recorded of one of the mystics of Catholicism. It came to him on a "Sabbath evening" in July of 1739 when he was twenty-one. He was, he tells us,

> walking in the solitary place where I was brought to see myself lost and helpless . . . endeavouring to pray (though being as I thought very stupid and senseless) for near half an hour (and by this time the sun was about half an hour high as I remember), then as I was walking in a thick dark grove *unspeakable glory* seemed to open to the view and apprehension of my soul. I do not mean any external brightness, for I saw no such thing; nor do I intend any imagination of a body of light, somewhere away in the third heavens, or anything of that nature; but it was a new inward apprehension or view that I had of God, such as I never had before, nor anything which had the least resemblance of it. I stood and wondered and admired. . . .
>
> My soul was so captivated with the excellency, loveliness, greatness and other perfections of God, that I was even swallowed up in Him; at least to that degree that I had no thought (as I remember) at first about my own salvation, and scarce reflected that there was such a creature as myself. . . . At this time the *way of salvation* opened to me with such infinite wisdom, suitableness and excellency, that I wondered I should ever think of any other way of salvation; was amazed that I had not dropt my own contrivances, and complied with this lovely, blessed and excellent way before.

In turning over the yellow leaves of the life of Martyn's hero, one finds that this son of Calvinistic Independents, this

Nonconformist minister of the mid-eighteenth century, was a saint spiritually akin to Francis and to Raymond Lull, to all the bearers of the stigmata and all the great spiritual lovers throughout the ages.

> In the forenoon, [says Brainerd] while I was looking on the Sacramental elements, and thinking that Jesus Christ would soon be "set forth crucified before me," my soul was filled with light and love, so that I was almost in an estacy; ... and I felt at the same time an exceeding tenderness and most fervent love towards all mankind.

Henceforth this Christocentric love for men was one of the marks of David Brainerd:

> God enabled me so to agonize in prayer, that I was quite wet with sweat, though in the shade, and the wind cool. My soul was drawn out very much for the world; I grasped for multitudes of souls.

> The language of my thoughts and disposition (although I spoke no words) now were, Here I am, Lord, send me to the ends of the earth; send me to the rough, the savage Pagans of the wilderness; send me from all that is called comfort in earth ... send me even to death itself if it be but in Thy service and to Thy kingdom.

To the wilderness he was sent, little strength and little taste as he had for it. A hillside which for Martyn's generation would have been "romantic" was for Brainerd and his fellow settlers, who thought of it in terms of weary and dangerous travel, "a hideous mountain." Into the "hideous and howling wilderness" Brainerd was sent to be the missionary and shepherd of the Indian tribes pushed backwards by advancing settlers. "My Indians," "my poor Indians," or "my dear little flock" he called them, gave them his heart and lived for them under conditions that to him were hateful. His diet as he told his brother John was "mostly of hasty pudding, boiled corn, and bread baked in the ashes and sometimes a little meat and butter.

My lodging is a little heap of straw, laid upon some boards, a little way from the ground, for it is a log room, without any floor that I lodge in." For his Indians he made apostolic journeys to camps on the Susquehanna River, himself fast dying of consumption.

> Near night, my beast that I rode upon hung one of her legs in the rocks, and fell down under me. . . . She broke her leg; and being in such a hideous place, and near thirty miles from any house . . . was obliged to kill her, and to prosecute my way on foot . . . just at dark we kindled a fire, cut up a few bushes, and made a shelter over our heads to save us from the frost, which was very hard that night.

When Brainerd died at the age of thirty, having spent his last night on earth in "very proper discourse" with brother John concerning "the interest of religion among the Indians," the forest round his settlement was full of leafy cells into which his Indian Christians would steal at dawn for secret prayer.

This was the life that made an irresistible appeal to Martyn in the days when, by all accepted canons of taste around him, he should have been listening to the dulcet tones of that divine of whom George III said that he "wished every youth in the kingdom might possess a copy of the Bible and of Blair." Blair, whose "fortune was easy," "lived much in the style of a gentleman" and wrote in a corresponding style. So much did the age enjoy his ornate and measured periods that he received £600 a volume for his sermons. His address to youth was conciliatory: and we feel no incongruity at finding extracts from his sermons bound up with Chesterfield's *Advice to his Son* and Rochefoucauld's *Maxims* as a gift for the young.

"While some by wise and steady conduct," says this most urbane of mentors, "attain distinction in the world, and pass their days with comfort and honour; others of the same rank, by mean and vicious behaviour, forfeit the advantages of their birth, involve themselves in much misery, and end in being a disgrace to their friends, and a burden on society. . . . Shall

happiness grow up to you of its own accord, and solicit your
acceptance, when, to the rest of mankind it is the fruit of long
cultivation, and the acquisition of labour and care? Deceive not
yourselves with such arrogant hopes. Whatever be your rank,
Providence will not, for your sake, reverse its established order.
By listening to wise admonitions, and tempering the vivacity
of youth with a proper mixture of serious thought you may
ensure cheerfulness for the rest of your life. We call you not
to renounce pleasure but enjoy it in safety. Instead of abridging
it, we exhort you to pursue it on an extensive plan. We propose
measures for securing its possession and for prolonging its
duration."[6]

In an age of Blairdom, Martyn preferred his Brainerd
sleeping on the ground by the Susquehanna River, waking in
a cold sweat, spitting blood, dragging himself on, listening unseen to the pow-wows of medicine men, teaching Indians to
fence their corn by day and to answer the questions of his cate-
chism by night, battling against a strain of morbid melancholy,
consumed with a longing "to be a flame of fire in the divine
service."

So Martyn pored alone over the chronicle of "the fatigues
and perils of another journey to Susquehanna," the very river
of dreams where, but a few years since, young Coleridge of
Jesus College, Cambridge, with Robert Southey of Balliol College, Oxford, had planned a "social colony." That "Pantisoc-
racy" where all selfishness was to be proscribed made a glorious
theme for the glorious talk of young republican poets. But
"Mr. C.'s" cooler friends could not ascertain that he had received any specific information respecting this notable river.
'It was a grand river'; but there were many other grand and
noble rivers in America; and the preference given to the Susquehanna, seemed to arise solely from its imposing name."[7]

[6] Blair's *Sermons*, Vol. 1, Sermon XI.
[7] Joseph Cottle, *Reminiscences of Coleridge and Southey*, p. 22.

For Henry Martyn and his hero the Susquehanna was no river of vague ideal beauties. The contemplation of the wayfarer of Christ roused in Martyn, Sargent tells us, "a holy emulation," and pointed the way to the hardest struggle he had yet known. Again and again the name of Brainerd finds its way into the *Journal*:

> I thought of David Brainerd, and ardently desired his devotedness to God and holy breathings of soul.

> Read David Brainerd to-day and yesterday, and find as usual my spirit greatly benefited by it. I long to be like him; let me forget the world and be swallowed up in a desire to glorify God.

> The rest of the evening in conversing and writing letters. My heart was not in visible disorder during all this, but it is not the spiritual life that Brainerd led.

> Read Brainerd. I feel my heart knit to this dear man, and really rejoice to think of meeting him in heaven.

It was to Simeon the leader that Martyn owed the suggestion of the path by which he was to follow Brainerd. Charles Simeon had been one of those "Methodist" clergy to whom Grant and Brown wrote in 1787 of their proposed mission to Bengal. "We understand that such matters lie very near your heart," they had said. Simeon's ardent mind had caught fire, and from that moment, as he lived his industrious days in Cambridge colleges and lanes, his eyes had been set towards the East. India did lie very near his heart. To Martyn on his return from Cornwall in 1802 with the resolution to be ordained, he said some eager words about the good done "by *one* missionary in India," the immortal cobbler Dr. Carey, whose *Periodical Accounts* from Serampore were earnestly followed by Simeon.

Martyn listened to his leader; then he read Brainerd; the appeal of Simeon's words and of Brainerd's life lived together in his mind through the autumn of 1802; against them were all the inclinations of his nature. When the last leaves were falling from the elms in the fellows' garden "he was at length fixed in a resolution to imitate Brainerd's example." And he proposed to do it by offering himself as a missionary to the tiny new society formed in London by some of Simeon's acquaintance under the title of "The Society for Missions to Africa and the East."[8]

Martyn's decision startled his world almost as much as if he had proposed a flight to the moon; and not the least surprised people were the committe of the little missionary society gathered in the study of a London rectory. Since their foundation in 1799 no Englishman had offered to serve them as a foreign missionary, and in the month when Martyn sent his enquiry (November 1802), they had interviewed two young German pietists, an interview not without its difficulties, since neither the committee nor the candidates knew many words of the other party's language. The Germans had been accepted as "catechists" for West Africa and sent to Clapham to learn a little English.[9] The secretary of the committee now received an astonishing enquiry about service from a young scholar who, as far as university preferments were concerned, had the ball at his feet.

Both in Cambridge and in Cornwall Martyn's step was regarded as fantastic and absurd.

> Walked out in the evening in great tranquility and on my return met with Mr. C., with whom I was obliged to walk an hour longer. He thought it a most improper step for me to leave the university to preach to the ignorant heathen, which any person could do.

Such was the university opinion of the missionary vocation. In Cornwall it was much the same:

> Breakfasted with ————, he presently entered into the

---

[8] Known today as the Church Missionary Society. The group who formed it were friends of Simeon and invited him to become a "country member."

[9] See Eugene Stock, *History of the Church Missionary Society*, I. 83.

highest points of the Calvinistic scheme . . . my heart was much frozen by the conversation; he had but a slight opinion of missionary work, though he has, I know, great affection for me. . . . Dined at ————'s who used every argument to dissuade me from going to India.

To Sally he confided, "The thought that I might be unceasingly employed in the same kind of work, amongst poor ignorant people, is what my proud spirit revolts at. To be obliged to submit to a thousand uncomfortable things that must happen to me whether as a minister or a missionary is what the flesh cannot endure."

Even Sally was not encouraging. Perhaps she was beginning to be absorbed in her own love affair. At all events she does not seem to have realized that Henry was no longer the flighty schoolboy for whom she used to pray. "Received a letter from my sister in which she expressed her opinion of my unfitness for the work." She told him that he was lacking in "that deep and solid experience necessary for a missionary."

Martyn was half inclined to agree with her and the *Journal* shows a picture of steady self-discipline, "to fit me for a long life of warfare and constant self-denial."

How mortally do I hate the thought, yet certainly I will do the will of God, if I be cut piece-meal.

I resolved on my knees to live a life of far more self-denial than I had ever yet done, and to begin with little things. Accordingly I ate my breakfast standing at a distance from the fire, and stood reading at the window during the morning, though the thermometer stood at freezing-point. . . . I rejoiced that God had made this life a time of trial. To climb the steep ascent, to run, to fight, to wrestle was the desire of my heart.

Chapter 5

A CURACY AMONG THE EVANGELICALS

Read Mr. Edward's piece on the affections again and again.—
Letter of DAVID BRAINERD.

That great man, Jonathan Edwards.—HENRY MARTYN's *Journal*.

Many spirits are abroad, more are issuing from the pit; the
credentials which they display are the precious gifts of mind,
beauty, richness, depth, originalty. Christian, look hard at them
with Martin in silence, and ask them for the print of the nails.—
J. H. NEWMAN, *The Church of the Fathers*.

We must speak out. Their *Christianity* is *not* Christianity. It
wants the radical principle. It is mainly defective in all the grand
constituents.—WILLIAM WILBERFORCE, *A Practical View of
Christianity*.

ON AN October morning in 1803, Henry Martyn hired a gig
and bowled out of Cambridge through the autumn lanes to Ely,
to be examined by the Bishop's chaplain, and to be ordained
next day in the Cathedral. He went into the Bishop's chapel,
and kneeling there before his examination felt "great shame at
having come so confidently to offer myself for the ministry
of the Lord Jesus Christ with so much ignorance and unholi-
ness." The examination of candidates for ordination in 1803

was an almost casual affair, and Martyn's preparation, mental and spiritual, had been left to his own devices.

Rarely did a candidate present himself with mind more soaked in Holy Scripture, or who took with a more awful reverence "authority to read the Gospel in the Church of God and to preach the same." Three times daily in his college rooms he bathed his soul in Holy Writ; and on walks to Lolworth or Shelford, or on solitary rides he learned whole books by heart. The details in the *Journal* show that his imagination, jealously watched and repressed in some directions, had free play here:

> I addressed myself with earnest prayer and a strong desire to know and learn the Epistle to the Romans in the Greek.
>
> Read the Psalms with a bright light shining upon them.
>
> Read the Acts this morning with great delight. I love to dwell in sacred scenes other than those which pass before me, and especially those in which the men of God are concerned.
>
> Read at night the first three chapters of the Revelation, and found them as usual very searching and awful.
>
> Read the latter end of Revelation, and so very lively was the impression on my mind, that I was often in tears. So awful, so awakening was this book to me.

But the book that was above all the home of his spirit and to which, perhaps insensibly, he returned the most, was the prophecy of Isaiah:

> Hoped to enjoy some of the peace and joy I used to feel in reading Isaiah but was interrupted. [Or again] In great sorrow I read some of Isaiah.

It was his lifelong love, and in the great Bible that he took with him to India this book more than any other is interlined, in his free and delicate penmanship, with readings from the Septuagint or Hebrew.

Butler and Paley he read as the indispensable apologists of

his day; and on them the examining chaplain set most of his questions.

But Martyn had also browsed in experimental divinity. He had found for himself St. Augustine's *Confessions,* then strangely out of fashion, and dismissed a generation later by Macaulay as "an interesting book marred in places by the style of a field preacher," but calling to the deeps in Martyn. William Law: "rather a favourite of mine" ... "Rose at half after five according to the impulse I received from reading Law." Bishop Hopkin's[1] sermons: "Never did I read such energetic language." But above all other divines the man of Martyn's heart, at whose name examining chaplains would have shuddered, was one Jonathan Edwards, born in Connecticut in the days of good Queen Anne, and educated at "Yale College," bred up a Calvinist and ordained a Presbyterian minister, a man whose books show him "a seer oppressed by his tremendous faith."

There was room in Edwards at one and the same moment for an awful sense of sin, a passion of adoration and a terribly lucid intellectual view of the universe.

> My wickedness as I am in myself, has long appeared to me perfectly ineffable, and infinitely swallowing up all thought and imagination, like an infinite deluge, or infinite mountains over my head. I know not how to express better what my sins appear to me to be, than by heaping infinite upon infinite and multiplying infinite by infinite. I go about very often for these many years with such expressions in my mind, and in my mouth "Infinite upon Infinite! Infinite upon Infinite!"

Yet this burdened soul bore about with him what he called "a sort of inward, sheer delight in God."

---

[1] 1634-1690, Bishop of Derry. He won the appreciation of the early evangelicals. Doddridge remarks of him in his *Lectures on Preaching:* "His motto *aut suaviter aut vi* well answers to his works. Yet he trusts most to the latter. He awakes awfully."

I often used to sit and view the moon for a long time; and so in the day time, spent much time in viewing the clouds and sky, to behold the sweet glory of God in these things. . . . And scarce anything, among all the works of nature, was so sweet to me as thunder and lightening . . . it rejoiced me. I felt God at the first appearance of a thunderstorm.

This vivid, emotional nature so congenial to Martyn was joined with a lucid, systematizing mind. Before going to his first cure, Edwards recorded among his resolutions: "Resolved, when I think of any Theorem in Divinity to be solved, immediately to do what I can towards solving it if Circumstances don't hinder." And so there came thundering out of the wilderness books to which Martyn turned again and again as the most satisfying body of divinity: Jonathan Edwards on *The Great Christian Doctrine of Original Sin Defended,* virile, incisive, terrible. Jonathan Edwards on *The History of Redemption,* clear-cut and all but debonair. But above all Jonathan Edwards, *Concerning Religious Affections,* as searching in its scrutiny of human motive as the discipline of any monastic confessor.

Such reading was Martyn's preparation for the ministry. The examining chaplain gave him a test in New Testament Greek, in theological Latin, with some questions in Christian evidences, and set him free.

After leaving the palace I was in very low spirits. I had now nothing to think of but the weight and diffculty of the work which lay before me.

His depression was not helped by finding the other candidates flippant at dinner; good enough boys perhaps, sent by their fathers for ordination to a family living, without a thought of the mysteries profaned. Martyn begged one of them in a quiet moment "to read the ordination service," and he "was much affected."

Next morning

At half-past ten we went to the cathedral. During the ordination and Sacramental services I sought in vain for a humble heavenly mind. The outward shew which tended to inspire solemnity affected me more than the faith of Christ's presence, giving me the commission to preach the gospel.

With inward struggle, then, Martyn's ministry began, and with struggle it continued. Without other training than a resident fellowship in the university, he was thrust as Simeon's curate into the care of the little parish of Lolworth four miles out of Cambridge. There, among his country folk, or in the almshouses and lanes of the city where Simeon set him to visit, he felt "a mere schoolboy" with words and manner smacking of college rather than of life, and perhaps hiding from his hearers the very realities he was struggling to express.

H. and my other friends complained of my speaking too low and with too little elocution. These things, with the difficulty I had found in making sermons, and the poorness of them, made me appear exceedingly contemptible to myself. I began to see (and amazing is it to say) for the first time, that I must be content to take my place among men of second-rate abilities.

C. told me I was far above the comprehension of people in general. Nothing pains and grieves me more than this, for I had rather be a preacher of the Gospel among the poor, and to the poor, so as to be understood by them, than be anything else upon earth.

Later, Mr. Cecil of St. John's, Bedford Row, added his brisk advice:

Brother Martyn, you are a humble man, and would gain regard in private life; but to gain public attention you must force yourself into a more marked and expressive manner.

Mr. Cecil has been taking a great deal of pains with me. My insipid inanimate manner in the pulpit, he says, is intolerable. Sir, said he, it is cupola-painting, not miniature, that must be the aim of a man that harangues a multitude.

Diligent pastoral visiting was the rule for Simeon's curates, and it was no easy rule to Martyn. "It is my will rather to sit down, to please myself with reading, and let the world perish."

The work of visiting the people of Cambridge and reading to and praying with them appeared hateful to me.

Yet day after day he was driven out from the congenial world of books by a sense of terrible responsibility. It is clear that he often stayed too long in a sick-room, but he left his people with no possible doubt that someone cared for their souls. The *Journal* is full of vignettes.

He was lying in his clothes and hat, on the bed, dying: his wife was cleaning the room as if nothing was the matter; and on the threshold was the daughter, about thirty-three years old, who had been deranged thirteen years. Her mother said that the poor creature sometimes talked of religion: so I asked her, several times, before I could arrest her attention, Who came into the world to save sinners? After several wild looks she hastily answered, "Christ," and then talked on as before. The dying man was almost insensible to anything I could say.

Wished for nothing but to be doing the work of Christ and went in this frame to visit the woman and her son. The room was so exceedingly offensive that I could scarcely endure it for an instant, yet by care I was able to continue for about half an hour.

Went to see a poor young woman, who after a life of sin, appears to be in a dying state, though only seventeen; she was in too much pain to attend to me much, and so I withdrew, affected almost to tears. My heart was ready to burst when I thought of the man who had seduced her.

After church called at two of the cottages. In one the man, the father of a large family, and in the other the mother . . . told me in the course of conversation that they

used the belief as their favourite prayer at night. I was perfectly shocked.

All his life Martyn would be "perfectly shocked" at what
another man would meet with a rueful smile. All his friends
note in him a certain "simplicity" which always credited others
with the spiritual standards of his own life, and left him unshielded against many a rude encounter with things as they
were.

There is no denying the fact that these years in Simeon's
parish were years of overwork. College life and interests went
on as before, and to these were added the cure of Lolworth, with
cottage visiting and catechizing in the school ("I seem able
to instruct children"), and a share of the work in Trinity parish,
sermons, weekday services, visits to hospital, almshouses, workhouse, sickbeds and meetings of "Societies" for Bible study.

> The incessant employment of my thoughts about the
> necessary business of my life, parishes, pupils, sermons,
> sick, leave far too little time for my private meditations;
> so that I know little of God and my soul. Resolved I would
> gain some hours from my usual sleep if there were no other
> way.

Martyn's reward and relaxation after work was the grammar of some Eastern language. A grammar was to him what a
novel is to the ordinary tired mortal:

> Finished the Bengalee[2] grammar which I began yester-
> day.

> Wasted much time in looking over an Arabic grammar.

> Finding myself in great stupidity I took up the Hindoo-
> stanee grammar, that the time might not pass away without
> any profit.

> Very unwillingly left Bengalee for writing sermon.

Thus greedily and by snatches, as a delightful relaxation,

---

[2] Here as elsewhere in quotations from Martyn or others of his day their
spelling of oriental words is preserved; perhaps it may help to place them
in their setting as pioneer workers before the days of comparative phonetics.

Martyn worked on Persian and Arabic, Gilchrist's *Hindustani Dictionary and Reader* (a pioneer work) and Halhed's *Bengali Grammar* for which the first printed type ever made in that script was punched with his own hands by Sir Charles Wilkins, the orientalist who under Warren Hastings first made Britain aware of the treasures hidden in Sanskrit literature.

The friends who allowed, nay encouraged, Martyn at an all but intolerable strain, to forsake scholarship for a busy parochial round were men whose gifts lay along the lines of the more active duties. Charles Simeon, essentially an organizer, had found his ideal senior curate, and perhaps the most intimate friend of his life, in Thomas Thomason, a mathematical tutor who learned to dread "the mathematical religion prevalent at Cambridge," and turned for leadership to that intrepid figure in Trinity Church with his forward-pushing chin and his warm urgency of manner. To Simeon Thomason gave as a personal friend an almost filial care, and as a curate all the support of the reliable, unresting diligence of himself and his good wife.

Martyn went often to Thomason's home at Shelford to talk in the riverside garden with Simeon and his host. He would come away full of self-abasement at the sight of Thomason's unfussed diligence, and the piety of his orderly household. For all their love to him the group that he left under the chestnut trees at Shelford did not realize the half of the effort at which he was doing the pastoral duties so delightful to themselves.

So Martyn, Cornish, imaginative, scholarly, took his place among men who for all their solid abilities half agreed with old John Newton (still living in London and laying down the law with homely shrewdness), that aesthetic interests only stimulated the "depraved nature" of man.

"I think it probable," said Newton to a friend who was admiring sculpture in Rome, "I think it probable from many passages in the Apostle Paul's writings, that he likewise had

a taste capable of admiring and relishing the beauties of painting, sculpture, and architecture...but then he had a higher,
a spiritual, a divine taste, which was greatly shocked and
grieved by the ignorance, idolatry and wickedness which surrounded him, in so much that he could attend to nothing else."

A minister of the gospel, he would say, is better without
"a large stock of other people's dreams and fables."

In the fellowship of such a group, Martyn learned Christ.
If they pointed him to intellectual privation, what was that?

> The pursuits of science [he wrote] and all the vain and
> glittering employments of men seemed a cruel withholding
> from their perishing brethren of that time and exertion
> which might save their souls.

> I was led to think a good while on my deficiency in
> human learning. . . . I cannot but think (though it is not
> easy to do so) that it must be more acceptable to God to
> labour for souls, though the mind remains uninformed.

Such entries in his journal would have been read with
warm approval by old John Newton, and by Charles Simeon
himself. But another side of Henry Martyn struggled for life.
At one moment he renounced earthly beauty as "ensnaring"
and set off to pray by a bed in the workhouse. At another he
gave her a hesitating welcome as a handmaid to worship.

> The music and the sight of a rural scene of solitude had
> the effect of fixing my thoughts on heaven.

> I heard the chant at King's with the same emotions of
> devotion. [We almost feel John Newton stirring uneasily
> in his chair.]

> The sanctity of the place and the music, brought heaven
> and eternal things and the presence of God very near to me.

But with what circumspection he admits her, even as a
handmaid, to the sanctuary and with what jealousy lest his
profane love assume more than the handmaid's place! Henry
Martyn's hymnbook like John Wesley's would have been
prefaced with the caution that "what is of infinitely more mo-

ment than the spirit of poetry is the spirit of piety."

At this moment in his life, like his namesake who slashed at his cloak that the beggar might have half, Martyn was cutting ruthlessly at his own intellectual and aesthetic life, for the sake of the souls of the poor. Like his leader Simeon, he observed days of fasting and abstinence, but his true fast was that which he imposed on his intellectual and artistic appetites. Yet even as he crushed back his desires for beauty he found (with an experience rare among the early evangelicals as his nature of aesthetic hungers was rare amongst them) that his lips were laid at her very source.

> My heart adored the Lord as the author and source of all the intellectual beauty that delighted me; as the creator of all the fair scenes that employ the poet's pen; and as the former of the mind that can find pleasure in beauty. . . . My soul seems labouring still with the mysterious glories of religion. What shall appear to this soul when I die? What shall appear of God's glory while I live? Since I have known God . . . painting, poetry and music, have had charms unknown to me before. I have received what I suppose is a taste for them: for religion has . . . made my mind susceptible of impressions from the sublime and beautiful.

With the unfailing paradox of the gospel, Henry Martyn had lost his life only to find it, heightened and summed up in Christ,

> *Ubi non praevenit rem desiderium*
> *Nec desiderio minus est praemium.*

The *Journal* during the Cambridge curacy shows signs of unwilling preocccupation with legal business. Martyn suddenly learned that the slender fortune left him by his father

---

"Where the desire does not precede the thing itself, the reward is not less than the desire."

was totally lost, and his unmarried sister Sally entirely depend-
ent on him. Dr. Smith tells us of a tradition in the family of
his half-brother John that Henry and his sisters litigated with
them at this time.[3] However that may have been, Henry's plans
were now thrown into confusion. He could not feel justified
in accepting the subsistence allowance of a missionary, and
leaving Sally in distress. Bishop Wilberforce says that for nearly
three years (1803-05) the family financial questions "often
harassed his conscience, engrossing much of his time, and
deeply depressing his spirits." "Unless Providence should see
fit to restore our property," Martyn told Sargent, "I see no possibility of my going out [to India]." But his friends pointed out
another opening.

Charles Grant, from one of the chairs in Leadenhall Street,
was looking anxiously for like-minded chaplains to work with
David Brown in Bengal. The Company's salary would enable
Martyn to support Sally; and the need for good men was great.
"The clergy in Bengal," Sir John Shore had written home in
1795, "are not respectable characters." If they did not die "of
drinking punch in the torrid zone," they were apt to retire
with large fortunes amassed in a surprisingly short time. The
Bishop of Llandaff having refused a chaplaincy when at Cambridge thanked God afterwards for denying him "an opportunity of becoming an Asiatic plunderer."[4]

Martyn was not sanguine. Professor Farish warned him of
the danger of "worldly-mindedness" as a Company's servant.
He read Tennant's *India* and decided that the life would be
odious to the last degree. Then he turned to the Bengali Grammar or to Brainerd's *Life* and was all aflame to go, no matter
how.

---

[3] We know, however, from an appeal published by Charles Simeon after
Henry Martyn's death, that on John's coming to financial disaster Henry
was the chief support of his brother's family.

[4] Bishop Watson, *Anecdotes of his Life*, p. 21.

The business involved interviews in London and visits to the India House. There were journeys to town cn the "Telegraph" coach, which told an incredulous public that it could travel in seven hours from Cambridge to the City. There were visits to Leadenhall Street when Martyn must go past the two gorgeous porters into the very house where sat a clerk with a snuff-colored coat and an unforgettable smile, by name Charles Lamb.

Martyn was ushered into the stately presence of Charles Grant, whose mastery of Indian commerce was making him "the real ruler of the rulers of the east, the Director of the Court of Directors," but who nonetheless met with considerable opposition when he proposed to send men of the "Methodist" taint to India. Between the business interviews there was all London for the Cornishman to see. The slight black-clad figure "called at the booksellers"; visited the British Museum; listened to the Gresham Lecture on music; sat on a bench in St. James's Park beside a poor man "of a very passionate and disappointed spirit," into whose hand he slipped a coin; or went to the New London Tavern in Cheapside to hear a farewell charge given to the two young German missionaries starting for West Africa. "I shook hands and almost wished to go with them, but certainly to go to India."

Another day he stood at the gate of St. James's to see the nobility go to court. The yellow coaches rolled past with turbans and fans, garters and swords, to the dull court of the dull old king, and Martyn standing on the pavement wondered at "such a glare of finery on poor old shrivelled people." But in the streets where the "first gentleman of Europe" set the fashion, temptation waited for Martyn, for "him even," when arch glances were directed at him and buxom charms displayed. He "made a covenant with his eyes," and kept it, throwing himself at once into prayer for the bold hussy or the fine lady who caught his eye. "After asking of God, that she might be as pure and beautiful in her mind and heart as in body, and be a temple of the Holy Ghost.... I dare not harbour a thought of an opposite tendency."

So he saw the streets; but a social circle was waiting too for Simeon's curate, in the rural villas bordering Clapham Common. Charles Grant took him down one afternoon from the India House, giving him upon the road "much information on the state of India" and introducing him, in time for dinner, to William Wilberforce, a wiry bright-eyed figure, with powdered hair, a diamond brooch in his linen, and an eyeglass which he fingered while he talked his unforgettable talk, swift-wheeling as a swallow's flight, described by spell-bound listeners as "vivacious," "radiant," "aerial."

Here Martyn found his welcome in the innermost circle of the men then fighting the slave-trade and slashing indeed at the devil wherever they perceived him, "The first 'friends of the negro,'" Mr. G. K. Chesterton calls them, "whose honest industry and philanthropy were darkened by a religion of sombre smugness, which almost makes one fancy that they loved the negro for his colour, and would have turned away from red or yellow men as needlessly gaudy." The enjoyable sentence tells a half-truth which must be faced, for in their own generation Sydney Smith brought much the same taunt against Martyn's friends.[5] Looked at closely the life on Clapham Common, as compared with other middle-class life of the day, seems in part a home of smugness and in part a gallant escape from it.

If to the dwellers in Clapham villas theirs was the best of

---

[5] In his article on "Indian Missions" in the *Edinburgh Review*, April 1808, in which he is very funny on Brother Carey's piety during sea-sickness, and the "difficulty of the Mission in getting converts shaved" occur these words: "Ennui, wretchedness, melancholy, groans and sighs, are the offerings which these unhappy men make to a Deity who has covered the earth with gay colours, and scattered it with rich perfumes."

all possible Commons, that is small matter for surprise. When the Bishop of London's coach had orders to set a lady down at the nearest public-house rather than be seen to stop at Clapham Rectory, the saints of Clapham were thrown in upon one another by a mild ostracism from outside. But nothing of ennui appears in the most intimate accounts of their life together.

It is true that like the rest of their class they were deeply in love with "our happy establishment," and it is also true that their edifying conversation was often expressed in language of an almost unbearable smugness (hard as the word is to associate with William Wilberforce, that Ariel among the reformers), but what is sometimes forgotten is that the possibly less edifying conversation of countless other middle class homes was expressed in language of equal heaviness. A wave of smugness had swept over the great middle class in Martyn's England, that middle class which knew how to appreciate the solid unimaginative virtue of George III and told him so in New Year Odes:

> Still o'er our fields waves Concord's silken wing,
> Still the Arts flourish, and the Muses sing;
> While moral truth and Faith's celestial ray,
> Adorn, illume and bless, a George's prosp'rous sway.[6]

From this prevailing atmosphere adventurous spirits sought escape. The Prince of Wales led off the rakes: the poets, untamed sons of light, escaped to shimmering horizons and

> . . . Aëreal kisses
> Of shapes that haunt thought's wildernesses.

The group among whom Martyn was now numbered, knowing no key to fairy realms, and never to find linguistic escape or shake off the intellectual trappings of their day and class, yet made a spiritual escape. For insofar as they reached vital contact with One whom no man ever yet accused of smugness,

---

[6] Ode for the New Year 1803 by Henry James Pye, Esq., Poet-Laureate.

they became free of a realm where man was face-to-face with the beauty and the terror of reality. The best known literary work of the circle was Wilberforce's *Practical View of Christianity*. He wrote in prose, and he set out to be "practical"; but when a few men of the solid middle class heard the call to the discipleship taught by the Lake of Galilee, incalculable spiritual forces were let loose and incalculable elements of romance broke in upon the prevailing smugness. "It is probable that Pietism in Germany and the Evangelical movement in England did much to prepare the ground for the reception—perhaps even for the creation—of the new spirit that was coming into poetry."[7]

For Christianity even at Clapham made room in life for spiritual adventure. They spoke smugly, but their souls knew how to worship and to dare. Granville Sharp the ordnance clerk "sat at his desk with a soul as distended as that of a Paladin bestriding his warhorse,"[8] and being persuaded that America was right in her War of Independence threw away his livelihood rather than copy the account of a cargo of munitions which had been used against her. Young Clarkson wrote a Latin essay for a university prize, on the set subject "Is it right to make slaves of other men against their will?" No doubt his periods were smug enough, but he was not the man to shelter under phrases. "If the contents of my essay are true," he cried, "it is time some one should see these calamities to their end," and forthwith threw himself into a lifelong grapple with vested interests and semi-sacred institutions. In Parliament the group were known as "men who looked to the facts of the case and not to the wishes of the minister."[9]

Their interests were far-flung. Now it is a crusade against bull-baiting, now provision for widows of the fallen in the

---

[7] C. E. Vaughan in *The Cambridge Modern History*, Vol. VII, p. 826.
[8] Stephen, *Essays in Ecclesiastical Biography*.
[9] Thevelyan, *Life and Letters of Lord Macaulay*, p. 71.

Napoleonic Wars, now a translation of the Bible into Arabic. Martyn's first evening at Clapham was spent in conversation about India—"They wished me to fill the Church in Calcutta very much,"—and in questioning a Mr. Richard Johnson from New South Wales as to what could be done for the convict center at Botany Bay, left for sixteen years without moral or spiritual care.[10]

So Martyn joined the group and fell like the rest of them under the spell of Wilberforce's voice of rare cadences. That was a red-letter day when he dined alone with Wilberforce at Palace Yard.

> It was very agreeable, as there was no one else. Speaking of the slave trade . . . and found my heart so affected that I could with difficulty refrain from tears. . . . Went with Mr. W. to the House of Commons, where I was surprised and charmed with Mr. Pitt's eloquence.

They introduced him, too, to old John Newton, the friend of Cowper, now the Nestor of the evangelicals, widowed and blind, but with undiminished courage and a pawky humor.

> Breakfasted with the venerable Mr. Newton. . . . He said he had heard of a clever gardener, who would sow the seeds when the meat was put down to roast, and engage to produce a salad by the time it was ready, but the Lord did not sow oaks in this way. . . . When I spoke of the opposition that I should be likely to meet with, he said he supposed Satan would not love me for what I was about to do.

On one of these London visits Martyn, having just reached the age of twenty-four, was ordained priest at the Chapel Royal, St. James's. "A solemn ordinance to me . . . yet very little like what it ought to be." He was now ready at any time to obey a summons to India, but it was not till three months later that he wrote in his journal:

---

[10] Through the influence of Wilberforce with Pitt this same Mr. Johnson was appointed first chaplain to Botany Bay, and Mr. Thornton of Clapham took him to Woolwich and introduced him to a flock of two hundred and fifty convicts on one of the hulks there.

April 2, 1805. Went with Mr. Grant towards the India House. He said that he was that day about to take the necessary steps for bringing forward the business of the chaplains, and that by to-morrow night I should know whether I could go or not.

Next day:

Going to Mr. Grant's I found that the chaplaincies had been agreed to after two hours' debate, and some obloquy thrown upon Mr. Grant by the Chairman for his connexion with Mr. Wilberforce, and *those people*. Mr. Grant said that though my nomination had not taken place, the case was now beyond danger.

Mr. Grant little understood with what hidden distaste the chaplaincy was accepted. "I could have been infinitely better pleased to have gone out as a missionary, poor as the Lord and His apostles," Martyn confided to his journal. There is no doubt that it was true. To the man inspired by David Brainerd the acceptance of a handsome salary and the obligations of government service were no alleviation but an addition to the difficulties of his path.

Martyn decided to leave Cambridge at once and take up his abode in London, serving as temporary curate to Mr. Cecil in Bloomsbury and holding himself in readiness for orders to proceed to India with the summer fleet.

On Palm Sunday five days later, he rode out to Lolworth for the last time and preached his farewell sermon to his country folk. There were partings afterwards at the church door.

An old farmer of a neighbouring parish, as he was taking leave of me, turned aside to shed tears; this affected me more than anything. Rode away with my heart heavy.

At night he must preach his last sermon to Mr. Simeon's crowded congregation at Trinity Church. "I prayed over the whole of my sermon for the evening," he writes. When he stood up he read as his text:

Thou, O Lord of Hosts, God of Israel, hast revealed to

Thy servant saying, I will build thee an house. . . . Now let it please Thee to bless the house of Thy servant, that it may continue for ever before Thee: for Thou, O Lord God, hast spoken it: and with Thy blessing let the house of Thy servant be blessed for ever.[11]

The listeners felt the poignancy of such words of settled permanence from one passing out from among them after so brief a sojourn, impelled in spirit to some pilgrim course. It was not usual in 1805 for the people to stand as the clergy left the church, but that night, when Martyn went out, the kneeling people rose as one man and turned to watch his figure down the aisle.

---

[11] I Chronicles 17:25-27.

Chapter 6

THE LOVER

I find a pleasing mournfulness of spirit tonight.—Lydia Grenfell's *Diary*, November 19, 1803.

Passed a happy morning reading Edwards on the Affections.—
Lydia Grenfell's *Diary*, November 15, 1804.

On monday in Holy Week 1805, Martyn left Cambridge.
"A great many," he says, "accompanied me to the coach which
took me up at the end of the town; it was a thick, misty morning, so the University, with its towers and spires, was out of
sight in an instant."

The Cambridge chapter was ended, but there was another
farewell which cost him more; for Henry Martyn was in love.

He had discovered it nine months before, during a summer visit to Cornwall, when although he did not know how
soon the way to India might be opened, he regarded himself
as among his own folk for the last time. It was a crowded visit.
He must say goodby to his sisters and to all the clan of cousins
and cousinly friends. He must preach too in the churches
which they opened to him, though not in the church of his
baptism, since he was deeply tainted with "Methodism," and

96

his old schoolmaster, hitherto proud of his pupil, now led the outcry against his pernicious views.[1]

It was not permitted me to occupy the pulpit of my native town. . . . The clergy seemed to have united to exclude me from their churches, so that I must now be contented with my brother-in-law's two little churches about five miles from Truro.

Kenwyn, which had welcomed John Wesley, had a welcome for Henry Martyn, and when he preached there in the church among the trees through whose branches you peer down over the Truro housetops, the people of the city came up the hill to hear him. "The church at Kenwyn was quite full, many outside, and many obliged to go away. At first beginning the service I felt very uneasy from the number of people gazing, but my peace soon returned."

Another church was open to Martyn in the ancient town of Marazion that looks sleepily from among its yellow sea poppies to St. Michael's Mount, the trysting place of Cornish legend and Cornish history. Marazion church was then a chapel-of-ease under the care of Martyn's cousin Malachy Hitchins, who lived two miles away on a wooded hilltop beside the church of St. Hilary with its whitewashed spire, a landmark to the ships that made for Falmouth or Penzance. Here in the Vicarage garden with Cousin Tom Hitchens a few years older than himself "all the happier hours" of Martyn's boyhood had been spent.

---

[1] The heated feelings of the day are hard to picture now. One of the Cornish clergy who speaks of Martyn as "this poor deluded enthusiast" wrote a tract on the Methodists, divided under the following headings:

Ignorance with Itching Ears	Vainglory
Prevarications	Uncharitableness
Lying	Profaneness
Hypocrisy	Uncleanness
Knavery	The Spirit of Family Discord
Contempt of the Regular Clergy	Freakishness and Distraction
An Intractable and Revengeful	and
Spirit	Insanity
Political Restlessness	

Their walks and rides had been shared by a young brood
of Grenfells from a square house in Marazion Street, children
of the Commissary for the States of Holland in the ancient
port of Penzance. When Cousin Tom Hitchens grew up he
married one of the Grenfell maidens, and Tom and his Emma
at Plymouth Dock were among Martyn's dearest friends. The
rest of the Grenfell family were now established in life: the
eldest son, the pride of the house, a Member of Parliament
in Buckinghamshire; the girls, with one exception, settled in
homes of their own in Cornwall, partly, it was said, through
the energies of their stirring and practical mother, Mrs. Mary
Grenfell. The one exception was the youngest daughter Lydia,
whose love story had come to grief, and who now at the ripe
age (very ripe for those days) of thirty was still at home, a
steady annoyance to her matter-of-fact mother because of her
Methodistical leanings and inclination to pious brooding. It
rarely occurred to the matron of the day that a daughter of
thirty was old enough to make her own decisions, and Lydia,
when the maternal fiat went forth, refrained from attending
the Methodist meeting-house that was for her the gate of
heaven, but did not refrain from confiding her yearnings and
sorrows to a religious diary.

Mr. Hitchins asked Henry Martyn to Marazion for old
times' sake, and on the Sunday which he spent there he made
the discovery of his love for Lydia.

> At. St. Hilary Church in the morning, my thoughts
> wandered from the service and I suffered the keenest dis-
> appointment. Miss Lydia Grenfell did not come.... Called
> after tea on Miss Lydia Grenfell and walked with her
> and ———, conversing on spiritual subjects. All the rest of
> the evening and at night I could not keep her out of my
> mind. I felt too plainly that I loved her passionately.

The discovery was overwhelming. It was impossible for a
Henry Martyn to be a lukewarm lover. Yet this new love and

his vocation seemed to him in deadly rivalry. To him the missionary call meant probably hardship and banishment for life. Supposing she could love him, could he involve his Lydia in this?

True, there was the chance of an East Indian chaplaincy; but that was yet in the air. He had lost his patrimony. His family needed his help. What had he to offer a bride, or a bride's very practical mother, unless he were to forsake his missionary vocation, and settle down at Cambridge, or perhaps in a college living? A country rectory with Lydia, and a quiet study, and children in the garden.

But no.

The direct opposition of this to my devotedness to God in the missionary way, excited no small tumult in my mind. . . . At night I continued an hour and a half in prayer, striving against this attachment. . . . One while I was about to triumph, but in a moment my heart had wandered to the beloved idol. I went to bed in great pain, yet still rather superior to the enemy; but in dreams her image returned, and I awoke in the night, with my mind full of her.

His sense of vocation and his love grappled in deadlock. Next morning the call to sacrifice was uppermost. "I again devoted myself to the Lord, and with more of my will than last night." He took horse and rode away from St. Hilary.

But there was yet a month to spend in Cornwall, a month when he was near her, and would hear friends speak of her, when a ride across the hawthorn-dotted uplands brought him to her door. An old friend, knowing nothing of his inner tumult, gave him *Thomas à Kempis* as a parting gift. The book was new to Martyn and daily during that month he read it, sometimes in a cave on the Cornish coast and sometimes late at night, drinking in its spirit of surrender.

At the end of August came his farewell to St. Hilary. Lydia Grenfell's diary on August 26, 1804, tells us that she heard "H.M. preach a precious sermon." Martyn's on the same day omits the sermon but tells of the evening when he "walked with Mr. Grenfell and Lydia up the hill, with the most beautiful prospect of the sea, but I was unhappy from feeling the attachment to Lydia, for I was unwilling to leave her."

The next day was the last. There was a ride to a cottage, printed forever on his memory and referred to again and again. Five miles by wren-haunted lanes or over uplands with the peewits calling and the soft, large sea-winds buffeting, and Lydia at his side.

> Rode with Lydia to an old man, five miles off.... When we arrived the old man was out, but his sister, a blind woman of seventy, was confined to her bed.... Lydia and myself said everything we could to cheer her.... When the old man arrived we formed a little circle before the door, under the trees, and he conversed ... concerning the things of God. I then read Psalm lxxxiv. (How amiable are thy tabernacles, O Lord.) Our ride home was delightful.

> Reading in the afternoon to Lydia alone, from Dr. Watts, there happened to be among other things a prayer on entire preference of God to the creature. Now, thought I, here am I in the presence of God, and my idol. So I used the prayer for myself, and addressed it to God, who answered it I think, for my love was kindled to God and to divine things.... I continued conversing with her, generally with my heart in heaven, but every now and then resting on her. Parted with Lydia, perhaps forever in this life, with a sort of uncertain pain, which I knew would increase to greater violence.

So he walked away "dwelling at large on the excellence of Lydia," and for the kingdom of heaven's sake he had not breathed his love. But it was not therefore unknown. A part of that "holy simplicity" which his friends all attribute to Martyn was a transparency which neither could nor would hide from their eyes the adventures of his heart.

And what of the lady?

Lydia Grenfell, carrying soup to cottages, or transcribing hymns for favored friends, had a heart that brooded on its own love story. The year 1800 when she was twenty-five had been the momentous year of her life. She then became engaged to the man of her heart, a solicitor of Penzance, Mr. Samuel John, "to whom her heart was more closely united than to any earthly object." In the same year too she experienced a conversion, and became a devout believer, drawing her inspiration from the homely warmth of "the people called Methodists." Before the end of the year she had discovered that her betrothed was an impossible scoundrel. She broke off the engagement, but she could not break her love. Her diary shows a mind turned inward upon its own distresses; unguided self-examination run to seed; genuine religion mixed with morbid scruple and brooding sentiment. In a home with her active managing mother there were few demands on her powers. She was only too free to yearn and to renounce with a daily glow of pious sentiment, "hoping for pardon" for her "broken vows" to her betrothed, and blaming herself for every bad story that she heard of him whom she yet loved. Those "broken vows" seemed to her to render any other marriage a spiritual adultery. While Samuel John remained unmarried, Lydia Grenfell told herself that she was bound to maidenhood. Nothing but his marriage could free her.

Six months before Martyn's appearance Mr. John had announced his engagement to a London lady, and Lydia's diary shows that she received her freedom with a pang.

February 25th, 1804. My slumbers last night were distracted on his account, and through the day he has much occupied my thoughts—too much—but now duty will, I trust, compel me to turn from one who will soon be united to another.

March 5th. I now enter into a resolution and engagement from this hour to resist the temptation of employing my thoughts on one whom I must cease to love.

· That summer, to a Lydia daily expecting the undesired freedom that would be hers with her first lover's marriage; solacing herself with abstracts of sermons or with prayers by cottage deathbeds; a Lydia aged thirty and believing that for her romance was over, to such a Lydia came Henry Martyn, transparently and reverentially in love.

July 25th. I was surprised this morning by a visit from H.M.

August 8th. I was surprised again today by a visit from my friend.

There is no doubt that her surprise was genuine. He was remembered as a boy cousin, or all but a cousin, six years younger than herself, a vast chasm of years when boys and girls play together. She knew that he too, a year later than herself, had experienced conversion; and she knew of his Cambridge honors. Tom Hitchins, her sister's husband, and old Mr. Malachy, himself an astronomer, would not fail to blazon forth their cousin's prowess. Now he returned, with the romance upon him of one dedicated to a lonely pilgrimage. And he preached such a sermon as her soul found "precious," and spoke to her with tremulous eagerness of the joys of the life to come. And there was no mistaking the light in his eyes.

But her first love, the habit of years, could not be suddenly replaced by an equal feeling for one who till lately had seemed merely a boy cousin who did well at books. Yet to a woman still starved of affection while her sisters ruled their homes, such reverent devotion was very sweet. She talked it out with Emma, her good sister, connected by marriage with the Martyn family. The upshot of the consultation was that Martyn, passing through Plymouth on his way from Cornwall, was told by Cousin Emma "that his attachment to her sister was not altogether unreturned."

Such news to a Martyn, who for the kingdom of heaven's sake was leaving Cornwall with his love untold, brought "both pleasure and pain."

Next day he went on by coach to Exeter. "My thoughts were almost wholly occupied with Lydia, though not in a spirit of departure from God, for I considered myself as in His hands."

A young attorney on the coach claimed his attention, one who said that he "knew the necessity of a change, but could not begin." While they changed horses the two went into a garden, and sat by some water on the grass slopes reading the Twenty-third Psalm.

Martyn's spirit was regaining buoyancy. As they drove out of Bath, early on a harvest morning, "Nothing seemed desirable but to glorify God." So he returned to his last months under Simeon, telling himself that the love story was over. "My dear Lydia and my duty call me different ways, yet God hath not forsaken me but strengthened me. . . . At chapel my soul ascended to God, and the sight of a picture at the altar, of John the Baptist preaching in the wilderness, animated me exceedingly to devotedness to the life of a missionary."

But a great love refused so soon to be deposed. They gave him an East India chaplaincy with a salary that would keep Sally and a bride as well. And they showed him a letter from David Brown saying, "Let him marry and come out at once." And then there was always that word of Cousin Emma's about an attachment "not altogether unreturned."

Was all this further temptation or was it an indication of his path? Tossed in spirit he wrote through Cousin Emma to beg for the honor of Lydia's correspondence. But no letter came from Lydia. She on her part was waiting with all her old morbid scruple for a letter to say that her first love was safely married. And Mr. John, as if to tantalize her, still deferred his wedding. Martyn was "keenly disappointed at finding no letter

from Lydia," yet inclined to agree with Simeon, himself unmarried, who "said he wished me to be properly a missionary
dead to the world. . . . I thought of my dear Lydia when he
said this."

Between them the saints tore him in pieces with contrary
advice. Mr. Cecil "said I should be acting like a madman if I
went out unmarried. A wife would supply by her comfort and
counsel the entire want of society." "Mr. Atkinson, whose
opinion I revere, was against my marrying." A letter from Mr.
Simeon "immediately convinced me of the expediency of cel-
ibacy." "Mr. Pratt coming in argued strongly on the other side."
"I could attend to nothing else." What lover could?

> My heart was sometimes ready to break with agony, at
> being torn from its dearest idol; and at other times I was
> visited by a few moments of sublime and enraptured joy.
> Such is the conflict: why have my friends mentioned this
> subject? It has torn open old wounds.

The time came to sail, and the celibates had it. He sent to
Emma and to Lydia each a keepsake, "a little *Pilgrim's Progress*
enclosed in the tea-caddy," and set off to join the East India
fleet at Portsmouth, riding on the way to Sargent's Sussex
home to bid his friend goodbye.

> *July 10th*, 1805. I went to Portsmouth, where we ar-
> rived to breakfast, and found friends from Cambridge.

Sargent, newly married, felt that he must see the last of
that lonely figure and rode down from Midhurst to Martyn's
Portsmouth inn, to find him surrounded by "numerous friends"
from Cambridge and London, led by Simeon himself, who
was deeply stirred, and with his usual energy despatched
Bibles for distribution on Martyn's ship, and gave him a keepsake of a massive volume weighing eleven pounds and eleven
ounces from himself, and a silver compass from his Cambridge hearers who arranged that the day of his sailing should
be set apart by them for fast and prayer.

July 16th. The Commodore called at the inn to desire that all persons might be awakened, as the fleet would sail today. We went immediately to the quay; but after waiting five hours, Mr. Simeon took his last leave of me, [at a long farewell it was Simeon's way to take his friend's hand in both of his and raise it to his lips] and the rest accompanied me on board.

A "triumphal occasion," Sargent called the moment of parting.

But even this was not the end of his farewells. "To my no small surprise I found we were bound to Falmouth." The news brought a torturing bliss. He was to see Cornwall again and to come once again within reach of Lydia. Was it that he might win her?

In three days' time the fleet dropped anchor in the great harbor which "braggeth that a hundred sail of ships may anchor within his circuit, and no one of them see the other's top." "I seemed to be entirely at home," said Martyn, "the scene about me was so familiar, and my friends so near." The fleet was delayed day after day. Shore visits were possible, and "after much deliberation" he decided to go to Marazion and tell his love and ask his Lydia if she could bring herself to come to him in India.

He went on the early mail, and did ever another lover in such case find leisure to speak to the coachmen about the welfare of their souls?

I arrived at Marazion in time for breakfast and met my beloved Lydia. In the course of the morning I walked with her ... with much confusion I declared my affection for her, with the intention of learning whether, if I saw it right in India to be married, she would come out; but she would not declare her sentiments. She said that the shortness of arrangement was an obstacle, even if all others were removed.

"She would not declare her sentiments": but she copied a hymn for her lover.

As I was coming on board this morning, and reading Mr. Serle's hymn you wrote out for me, a sudden gust of wind blew it into the sea. I made the boatmen immediately heave to, and recovered it.

To Cousin Emma, Lydia's sister, and so far the encouraging confidante of Henry's love, he wrote:

The consequence of my Marazion journey is, that I am enveloped in gloom. May He give me grace to turn cheerfully to my proper work and business. . . . Another consequence of my journey is, that I love Lydia more than ever.

There were yet one or two more meetings, and at the last a hurried parting, when as he sat reading to his lady and her mother a servant came in with news that the fleet had immediate sailing orders and a horse was at the door that he might catch his ship.

"It came upon me like a thunderbolt. Lydia was evidently painfully affected by it; she came out, that we might be alone at taking leave." There at the door he told her that if it seemed right for him to marry she must not be offended at receiving a letter from India.

"In the great hurry she discovered more of her mind than she intended; she made no objection whatever to coming out." But "you had better go out free," she stipulated, implying, he thought, that the freedom need not be forever. There was no time to ask her to explain herself. He mounted and galloped away, reaching Falmouth by the aid of relays of horses just as his ship was getting under way.

Next morning being Sunday, he held a service on the deck. As he read the words, "But now they desire a better country, that is an heavenly," St. Michael's Mount and St. Hilary spire and trees were fast fading from sight. His letter to Cousin Emma still showed a lover's interest in those receding hills.

Lydia I knew was about that time at St. Hilary. If you have heard from Marazion since Sunday I should be curious to know whether the fleet was observed passing.... Do not forget to tell me as much as you can about Lydia.

The fleet was so long held up in the Cove of Cork that Martyn had Cousin Emma's answer there. Her letter is not preserved. But it told him more of Lydia than she herself had let him know, for it explained that his lady who had said him neither yea nor nay, was still held back by some insuperable obstacle. From later letters it would seem that the obstacle was a double one. Her obstinate scruple against a second engagement before her former lover's marriage, (and the exasperating person delayed his wedding until 1810) was added to the difficulty of obtaining Mrs. Grenfell's consent to her faring forth to the terribly remote East Indies to marry a man as "methodistical" as herself and (who can gainsay the motherly prudence?) showing signs already to observant eyes of the consumptive tendency now making itself seen in both his sisters.

Henry Martyn was ill-prepared for the letter. Lydia's hesitating farewell speech had left him sanguine. But he was loyal to his lady, though his reply to Cousin Emma breathed more serenity than he could always feel.

Whatever others have said, I think that Lydia acts no more than consistently by persevering in her present determination. I confess, therefore, that till this obstacle is removed my path is perfectly clear, and blessed be God! I feel very, very happy in all that my God shall order concerning me.... The Lord teaches me to desire Christ for my all in all ... surely the soul is happy that thus breathes in a medium of love.

Chapter 7

THE NINE MONTHS AT SEA

The ship lurched, did it? ... and pray Mr. Cooper why has heaven granted you two legs with joints at the knees? ... There take that, you contaminating, stage-dubbing, gimlet-carrying quintessence of a bung-hole!—

Mr. Chucks the boatswain in Captain Marryatt's *Peter Simple*.

I am born for God only. Christ is nearer to me than father or mother or sister—a nearer relative, a more intimate friend; and I rejoice to follow Him and to love Him.—*Journal of* HENRY MARTYN on board the *Union* Transport.

THAT SUMMER of 1805 the beacons were in train on all the south coast heights, to give warning in case the French fleet sailed out of Brest for the invasion of England. Sir Home Popham, the Commodore who was to convoy the East India fleet, was held up in Cork Harbour in case his ships were needed to do battle against invaders, and every man in the convoy was given his battle station—Martyn's to be "with the surgeons in the cockpit."

It was August 28 before the convoy stood out to sea, a great fleet of one hundred and fifty sail. All the summer sailing

of both East and West Indiamen were there with their burden
of trade and with the new officials and cadets of the East India
Company; one vessel was a "Botanyman," the *Pitt*, with a load
of one hundred and twenty women convicts for transportation
to the dreadful Bay; and with the merchant vessels passing "on
their lawful occasions" was a fleet of fifty transports carrying
five thousand troops under Sir John Baird, to some unknown
destination. "We are to join in some expedition," Martyn told
the Plymouth cousins, "probably the Cape of Good Hope or
the Brazils."

The Commodore had no great naval force to escort so large
a fleet, for the Admiralty in that summer before Trafalgar was
scraping together ships enough to fit out a fleet for Nelson,
and Mr. Snodgrass, surveyor to the East India Company's shipping, was showing them how to strengthen crazy vessels with
double planking and diagonal bracings that would hold them
together for one more conflict in that great sea year. Sir Home
Popham's whole naval strength for convoying one hundred
and fifty sail was two men-of-war, the *Diadem* and the *Belli-
iqueuse* each of sixty-four guns,[1] and two naval frigates the
Leda and *Narcissus*—no great force even though manned by
"hearty souls ready to fight the devil if so be as he should
hoist the tricolour ensign." Neither the transports nor the
merchantment, however, were quite defenseless. They arre carried a few guns on the chance of a scrap on the high seas with
an enemy privateer.

In spiritual charge of this assemblage of sea-dogs and fighting men ranging from raw village lads to blasphemous veterans,
was Henry Martyn, aged twenty-four, at home in polite literature and in college courts, all delicate ear and sensitive scruple.
Never were flock and shepherd more strangely assorted. He
sailed on the *Union*, a transport carrying a load of treasure and
his Majesty's 59th together with some of the East India Com-

---

[1] Most of the British ships at Trafalgar had 74 guns; the *Victory* had 100.

pany's cadets and their officers. His cabin was stacked with books—commentaries, oriental grammars, works on India and the life of David Brainerd for himself, together with Simeon's parting gift of an enormous Bible, and for the men a store of Scriptures, hymnbooks and tracts.

The Commodore gave Madeira as the first rendezvous of the fleet, and between leaving Cork Harbour on August 28 and reaching Funchal on September 29 Martyn had an epitome of life at sea. Packed with humanity as the little wooden vessel was, she yet meant for Martyn a discipline of loneliness, always one of the marks of his spirit but now first accentuated. For at Cambridge, although in the society of his own college he moved solitary as regards his deepest interests, there was in reserve the delightful intimacy of Sargent and Corrie and Simeon and half a dozen more, to atone for the disdain of the crowd. And at the Fellows' table the men who shrank from his opinions were at least men who shared the same intellectual interests and vocabulary. On the *Union* he felt himself not only friendless in all the deeper sense of friendship but a foreigner, a "raw academic" as he called himself, out of place among men whose dinner talk was all of "regiments and firemen."

It was impossible that a Henry Martyn should not suffer in the first months after leaving England, as he believed, forever. His delicately strung nature had payment to exact for the strain of overwork during his Cambridge curacy, as well as for the strain of loving and leaving his Lydia. He was as homesick as a child, waking "from disturbed dreams, to find myself with a long sea rolling between myself and all that I hold dear in this life." "England had gone, and with it all my peace . . . the pains of memory were all I felt." For Lydia had not given him permission to write. "I cannot write to her," he told Emma Hitchins, "or I should find the greatest relief and pleasure even in transmitting upon paper the assurances of my tenderest love."

Unable to endure the fetid atmosphere below,[2] Martyn

spent the first days of the voyage on deck "standing in the air in a sort of patient stupidity, very sick and cold," longing for the relief of being alone, but surrounded by a crowd, "the soldiers jeering one another and swearing, the drums and fifes constantly playing." The common miseries of seasickness were followed by fever and faintness; but the struggle that was darkening his days was in its essence spiritual. He was torn by conflicting desires. "The world in a peculiar form [he might have said in a gracious feminine form] has a hold upon my soul, and the spiritual conflict is consequently dreadful. . . . I am now in the fire fighting hard."

Next day he wrote again:

Once more I struggled, determined to rise through God, above the body, the flesh and the world, to a life of ardour and devotedness to God.

And the following morning:

Beginning to grow quite outrageous with myself and like a wild bull in a net, I saw plainly this was coming to nothing, and so in utter despair of working any deliverance for myself, I simply cast myself upon Jesus Christ, praying that if it were possible, something of a change might be wrought in my heart.

Relief came to him two days later; but not the relief of a traveler who regains the sheltered pastures where "love is of the valley." "I gave you up entirely," he told Lydia afterwards. The relief that came to Martyn was rather the relief of the traveler who has climbed through clouds to some upland meadow where gentians drink the sunlight of a peak. As the essential struggle had been on the spiritual plane, so was the victory. This evangelical parson on a troopship in Trafalgar year suddenly carries us into the company of all the mystics when they try to tell us of what came to them as they passed through purging pains to the soul's illumination.

---

[2] The air below decks became too foul even for those unsqueamish days, and at intervals one or other of the lower decks was cleared of humans and fires were lighted to purify the atmosphere.

At last the Lord hath appeared for the comfort of His creature [he says]. In prayer launched sweetly into eternity. ... Thy work may be prosecuted best by my soul's remaining in heaven. The transcendent sweetness of the privilege of being always with God would appear to me too great, were it not for the blessed command "Set your affections on things above."

And again:

I seemed at a long distance from the earth and time, and near the blessed God.

Or again:

Separated from my friends and country for ever, there is nothing to distract me from hearing "the voice of my Beloved," and coming away from the world and walking with Him in love, amid the flowers that perfume the air of Paradise.

Looking back in the light of such experience on the struggle he had just passed through, he felt that God had been also in the cloud, and the words of a sermon preached on the poop of the *Union* convey his confidence. "It may be you will still be kept in darkness, but darkness is not always the frown of God; it is only Himself—thy shade on thy right hand."

Meanwhile, whether the chaplain's soul were in heavenly places or in the nethermost hell, men went through with the routine of seafaring days. The sailors of the *Union* threatened mutiny because of the miseries of their diet of salt junk. And there was a night of storm when several sails were torn away and the wind in the rigging above and the clatter on deck made sleep impossible. Men lay awake in the creaking wooden ship, very near to the wailings and demon howls of the wind. At four o'clock in the morning one of the East India Company's officers came and sat shivering in Martyn's cabin "for company." When dawn came, the cabin floor was awash with water, and going up on deck they found that they "were going under bare poles, the sea covered with so thick a mist from the spray and rain that nothing could be seen but the tops of the nearest waves, which seemed to be running even with the windward side of the ship."

The *Union* was the heaviest sailer in the fleet and she dropped out of sight of the rest of the convoy so that she ran considerable risk of capture. Only in port could the other ships share in the chaplain's ministrations, when they sent for him or came in boats with babes to be baptized. At sea the *Union* was his whole parish and earned the title of "a very praying ship."

Martyn's own mess was with the officers of the 59th and East India Company's cadets and writers in the cuddy (small cabin), "pleasant and orderly," but he sought his flock in every corner of their crowded little world. "I have now free access to the soldiers and sailors," he wrote home. A surprising figure he must have been on a transport of the Napoleonic wars, a figure frail and careful of dress, faintly academic in phrase, wincing at a blasphemy, but no coward on his business. "Went below decks," he says, "there was a quarrel amongst the soldiers and sailors; one of the former who was stripped for fighting I went up to." And the tumult ceased, perhaps from sheer surprise, for it was far from usual in 1805 to meet a padre on the orlop deck. This chaplain was everywhere. They found him sitting among pig-tailed sailors on the gun-deck, where the hammocks of the crew were slung, "in the boatswain's berth" oblivious to everything in "a long and close conversation with the carpenter." The seamen ear-ringed and tattooed, packed together, miserably fed, and flogged for robbing a sugar basin, swore with every breath, and their language was quite literally pain and grief to their chaplain. "Every oath they swore was a call on me to help them," he told himself.

The most astonishing conquest that he made on the gun deck was when the chief mate for his sake ceased to swear, and ranged himself beside Martyn as protector and stout friend, telling those who rebelled at the chaplain's ministrations that one day "their consciences would be overhauled." "He is the image of a blunt good-natured seaman," wrote Martyn of this new friend, adding with naïve surprise that they could not converse "very long on religious subjects," since the mate was "so soon out of his depth."

Below the gun deck were the soldiers; and amidships, just under the main hatchway, their wives, one of whom had come aboard as a stowaway at Portsmouth and remained unnoticed in the crowded confusion sharing a single ration with her husband until they reached Madeira, when the Captain found her, forgave her handsomely, and put her on the ration list. Martyn went below every afternoon and amid "the noise of the children, of the married people and the sailors who were all about us, talking as if nothing were going forward," he read aloud to a small group from *The Pilgrim's Progress*. Later, he hit upon the more popular plan of teaching them to sing. His offer to teach the men to read they would have none of. The subalterns of the 59th chose to regard his singing class as "most dangerous," "unfitting the men to be soldiers." (It is possible that Martyn had felt called to remonstrate with the subalterns on the subject of foul language.) Some of the men agreed with them or tried to make the chaplain think so: "B. said he was determined he would never pray, for if he did, he should not be able to fight, that he was a soldier and robbery was his business." The senior officers, however, saw no harm in Martyn's unusual course if it gave him any pleasure; his audience was not so large as to cause any serious fear of the demoralization of the army. For Martyn had neither Sargent's humor nor Simeon's arresting vehemence nor any of the gifts of the street preacher.

It was never easy to him to thread his way through a crowd in the dark and stifling lower decks, and win for himself a hearing from the figures lolling round or busy with domestic concerns. With intense pain he would rouse himself to rebuke some blasphemy, knowing well that such a rebuke was no ingratiating opening for his message, and listening to the snigger that followed his effort in full consciousness of his own shortcomings.

> I do not know how to push things. I have a delicacy about me which no doubt proves ruinous to souls. . . . I do not, that I know of, shrink from any known method of diffusing the light of truth, but I am not ingenious in methods; . . . I want the essence of zeal, which if no way be open will make a way.

Against humanity in the raw, humanity familiar with salt pork and curses, grog and cutlasses and bumboat women, he felt himself "a schoolboy, a raw academic."

"I pictured myself strutting about the streets and walks of Cambridge wrapt in content, thinking myself very amiable and admired." He longed to escape from "the academic contagion," never doubting that his gospel was for the seamen and the Company's Cadets and for his Majesty's 59th, but longing to break through the barriers that education had built between his mind and theirs. "I could have willingly forgotten all I had ever read or learnt, to be a man of the ancient primitive simplicity." "The words of Milner have been much upon my mind, 'to believe, to suffer and to love, was the primitive taste.' I do not know that any uninspired sentence ever affected me so much."

Martyn never found, and never would find his way to the warm heart of a mob. But his presence in the ship, with his refusal of all compromise, proved there, as wherever the clear flame of his spirit passed, a touchstone for other souls. Many of doubtful mind "offended at his sayings" "went back and walked no more with him." Yet here and there "with tears" a rough and hearty seaman or corporal changed his allegiance and began to follow Christ on no easy path. The loyal few, for whom Martyns' cabin was open at all hours, were led on to harder loyalties than they had known before.

One of the cadets' officers, a Mr. Mackenzie, became almost Martyn's shadow, reading with him and sometimes with the surgeon or another "serious" officer, the *Confessions of St. Augustine*, Milner's *Church History*, Leighton's *Commentaries*, or the *Letters of David Brainerd*. Mr. Mackenzie even went below decks to Martyn's hymn-singing, running the gauntlet of much banter in the cuddy afterwards. On his appearance a cheerful subaltern would sing out, "Come now, let's have a little of the humbug," and the cuddy would be indulged with a choice nasal parody of psalm-singing. The cadets whom Mr. Mackenzie commanded were seriously afraid that their officer in turning "Methodist" would try to make them all "melancholy mad." It was Mr. Mackenzie's none-too-easy task to try to explain the saint to the ship's company and the ship's company to the saint. He brought to Martyn the current reports about his preaching: "Martyn is a good scholar but not much of an orator," they said, and Mackenzie told him, "It was a want of easy flow, arising from a want of confidence in his own abilities."

"If it be not remedied," said the disconsolate Martyn, "I am afraid I shall make but a dull preacher to the Indians."

The one service on Sunday was held on the poop, weather permitting, at any hour that seemed good to the authorities. Sometimes Martyn, expecting a service in the morning, would go up to find "the sailors all at work on the poop and the boatswain swearing at them" and Church would not be rigged till five o'clock in the afternoon. Sometimes it was put off till too late—"The sun was down before they rigged the Church"— and the men were piped to hammocks.

Between two and three hundred came to the services but the soldiers were "not very attentive" to the chaplain's preaching. The boatswain's mate told him, to his deep humiliation, that the sermons were too difficult for the young lads among the soldiers. On reading them one finds that, direct and simple as he made his thought, and relentlessly as he made each sentence do its perfect work, Martyn's words and especially his sentence-building have a faintly classical tinge that must have given them an almost foreign ring in the ears of boys from the tail of the plough, who could not sign their names when they took King George's shilling.

His preaching was far too direct and unequivocal to be popular among the officers. "Mr. Martyn sends us to hell every Sunday" was their comment, which considerably surprised the preacher. "Major Davidson told me that I set the duties of religion in so terrific a light that people were revolted. I felt the force of this remark and determined to make more use of the love of God in the gospel." But his audience, used to the comfortable flowing periods of a moral essay, threatened to stay away unless he would preach a sermon "like one of Blair's." Martyn continued his hot-gospelings; his flaming conviction, his all-compelling God-consciousness strangely clad in carefully turned classical sentences. It was as though an Old Testament prophet stood among them on the poop and delivered his burning message of "righteousness, temperance and judgment to come," clad all the while in the black gown and white bands associated with plump velvet pulpit-cushions and afternoon slumber induced by a gently flowing voice and the buzz of a blue-bottle in a window not made to open.

The officers were annoyed and rude at the chaplain's failure, his deliberate failure too, to accomodate his preaching to their wishes. They arranged themselves behind him, ready to walk out at any statement of which they disapproved, and one of them conspicuously "employed himself in feeding the geese."

Such storms were usual enough when one of the "serious" clergy first made his appearance and preached the tremendous doctrine of sin and justification in days which held it "monstrous" that a high-born lady should be told "she had a heart as sinful as the common wretches." The doctrinal storm on the *Union* gradually died away as such storms do, and two of the ringleaders eventually told the chaplain that "he had persuaded them that a religious character was an amiable one." But Martyn was regarded to the end as too severe a preacher. Charles Simeon himself, sharing to the full Martyn's conviction of the exceeding sinfulness of sin, had yet told him that his condemnations were those of a man who saw black against white and did not distinguish the grey of mingled motives in human action. Dean Church perhaps throws light upon this note in Martyn's preaching when, in a suggestive sentence, he points out a likeness between Henry Martyn and Hurrell Froude who, thirty years later, was to be the youngest and shortest-lived figure in the group that led the Oxford Movement (not Oxford Group Movement). Both men, he says, "were made by strong and even merciless self-discipline over a strong and for a long time refractory nature."[3] And he goes on to write of Froude words that might have been set down of Martyn, and go far to explain the severity of his relentless earnestness:

> He "turned his thoughts on that desolate wilderness, his own conscience, and said what he saw there." A man who has had a good deal to conquer in himself, and has gone a good way to conquer it, is not apt to be indulgent to self-deceit or indolence, or even weakness. . . . It was as unbearable to him to pretend not to see a fallacy as soon as it was detected, as it would have been to him to arrive at the right answer of a sum or a problem by tampering with the processes.

Newman who loved him wrote of Froude, "I should say that his power of entering into the minds of others was not equal to his other gifts." Such words are true of Martyn too,

[3] Dean Richard William Church, *The Oxford Movement*, p. 37.

and it follows that both men would rouse opposition where others of less utterly sincere devotion might serve acceptably.

But there are pleasanter pictures of Martyn with his flock, as when he stole unobserved down three ladders to visit the sick in the cockpit, where he had to feel his way to their hammocks, a light being forbidden. "At night," he writes, "got below without being observed, and with some Madeira and water for two of the sick men."

Or as when a corporal stole up to him and pressed into his hand a letter with the confession of spiritual need that he could never make otherwise on the crowded deck, and Martyn sought him out and spent a Sunday evening by his side at the main hatchway "looking out at a raging sea."

Or as in the *Journal* of another day:

> On deck I had some conversation with one of the sergeants, who said with some emotion that many of the men were the better for my coming among them, and that for himself he had been brought up in this persuasion, and now things he had almost forgotten were brought to his mind. At his request I supplied him with a Bible.

The first break in the monotony of sea life was at Funchal, Madeira, where the fleet put in for water, upsetting the whole economy of the island by the demands of its great numbers. "Not a bed or a meal to be had at either of the two inns" and the whole town in the greatest bustle and confusion at having to water one hundred and fifty sail in a few hours. Martyn had letters of introduction to the English community and characteristically enough persuaded one of his island acquaintance to come to his lodging to hear him read aloud the whole of a volume of French sermons in order to criticize his pronunciation "with great care and attention."

It was his first glimpse of foreign parts.

> I went to the great Catholic Church ... the splendour of the church was beyond anything I had conceived ... the few devotees there, while on their knees, would laugh

and talk together. A poor negro woman crossed herself at this time with much fervour and apparent contrition. I thought she might be truly an awakened soul, and longed to be able to speak to her.

Before they set sail, the Captain of the *Union* took Martyn aboard H.M.S. *Diadem* where the Commodore was giving orders to colonels of regiments and captains of vessels about the mysterious destination of the troops. Martyn, pacing the larboard side of the quarter-deck and observing the eager group, coveted for the business of his own campaign "Sir Home's earnestness of manner in expressing himself." When the fleet had sailed, the men learned that San Salvador (now Bahia) Brazil, was the next rendezvous on their tortuous passage to India, but the troops were still in the dark as to where they were to take the field.

The month of October (October 3 to November 12) they spent in crossing the Atlantic, all unaware that during their voyage the French fleet had sailed out of Cadiz to meet the English under Cape Trafalgar. During this month Martyn made strides with Hindustani in which he was to do original and originative work. He had with him Gilchrist's *Grammar* and *Dictionary* and was making himself master of all the roots, but his problem was to compare the language of grammars with the language of life, and to produce books, not indeed forgetful of classic elegance—ere a Martyn forgot that his right hand must forget her cunning—but still less forgetful of the language of common speech. In his claim for the value of the spoken tongue and his delicate care for actual spoken sound, Martyn was a pioneer among oriental scholars. Men of the type of Sir William Jones built their work upon dictionaries and comparison of written roots; Martyn, as much in love as they with such research, had a message for life, and the living language must be his care. The officers of the *Union* saw their most astonishing chaplain sit down among the Lascars and test on them the sentences from his grammar. He found, as might be expected, that the Hindustani of the grammars was "vastly too fine for these men" and too full of Arabic and Persian words. Slowly he made himself better understood: the *Journal* for Trafalgar Day shows Martyn seated on the gun deck, the center of a group of Lascars, and reading aloud

the prayer of Parboter which I had been translating into Hindoostanee. They seemed to understand me perfectly; Cade corrected my pronunciation in a few words, and one or two other words they did not understand, but I was surprised at being able to gain their attention at all.

Later he bore one of them off to his cabin to test his work sentence by sentence and word by word. A Company's official who invited "blacks" to his cabin must be demented, and the officers henceforth gave Martyn up as "a mad enthusiast."

They ran at last into San Salvador after a day spent in battle stations owing to the presence of a strange sail on the horizon. The Captain of the *Union*, which had as usual fallen behind the rest of the fleet, told Martyn "in a great ferment" that he "would rather fight till the ship sunk than strike to a privateer." But the stranger showed no signs of fight, and amid much "furious bellowing" from Captain to pilot, the *Union* made the harbor of San Salvador.

Here Martyn went ashore on a new continent and spent one of the sunniest fortnights of his life. "Nothing but negro slaves," was his first impression, "very good-natured, cheerful looking people."

A slave was sent to gather three roses for me.... A slave in my bedroom washed my feet. I was struck with the degree of abasement expressed in the act; and as he held the foot in the towel with his head bowed down towards it, I remembered the condescension of our blessed Lord.

Looking for a shady spot where he could be alone under the orange trees, Martyn stumbled on to the estate of a Portuguese gentleman, who, charmed with the manners and the learning of the stranger, gave him great and genial hospitality; carried him about through the sunny air in a palanquin, and showed him off to his friends as "one who knew everything, Persian, Arabic, Greek." Martyn, half amused and wholly interested in his new experiences in the pleasant, lazy land was allowed at intervals the solace of time alone in the garden where trees made a shade near water, the ground covered with oranges, like apples on an English orchard floor. Here, in great peace, he crooned over well-loved hymns, read psalms that carried him to Lydia and Cornwall, and prayed aloud in the security that no Brazilian listener could understand his words.

His home letters tell of the "indescribable slops" of Portuguese feasts, and venture playfully to send kind remembrances to Lydia's mother "if she considers me as now at a sufficient distance." They beg for news. To Cousin Emma he writes: "The simplest narrative in the world will delight me,—what texts Cousin Tom preached on—what sick he went to see—and a thousand nameless little occurrences will present a living picture of you to my mind. Can you send me by Mr. Corrie, or by any other means, your profile and Cousin Tom's and Lydia's?"

In the delights of the tropical garden; in genial hours when Señor Antonio, his wife and a slave played cards, and Martyn "sat at the table learning Hindoostanee roots"; in a rapid devouring of the Portuguese grammar; and in Latin discussions, not unheated, with the Franciscan fathers of the place, the pleasant Brazilian interlude flew by; and Martyn was rowed back to the crowded life on board, by white-robed Lascars singing chants in honor of Mohammed.

The fleet stood out to sea and now at last the object of the military expedition was disclosed.

> *December 6th.* Our Captain going aboard the Commodore by a signal, brought back the information that the Cape was our object, that a stout resistance was expected; and that it would be five weeks before we should arrive

thither. The minds of all were set in motion by this account, as few, I believe, expected hard fighting.

The "side show" for which this expedition had been despatched was the wresting from the French (then masters of the "Batavian Republic") of the Dutch settlement of Cape Colony, which, in view of Napoleon's eastward-straining ambition, loomed large as a naval stronghold that was the halfway house to India.

So through strange seas and under other stars than the stars of home, the *Union* carried her load of fighting men to battle. In this, the third stage of her voyage, many of the men went sick. Martyn staggered amongst them, himself down with dysentery. His journal reveals something of the miseries of illness at sea in 1805.

> The ship's steward lay convulsed with a gunner standing by him, holding a burning lamp that would scarcely burn; the air was so bad and the place withal so hot, being directly under the copper, that it was altogether most intolerable.

> Had no service below as I was taken up in going to and fro to the sick, of whom there is now a great number.... The condition of the sick is miserable. I could not stand it till I got some aromatic vinegar.

The Captain himself was stricken down.

> About seven this morning I was sent for by the surgeon to the captain; I saw that he was a dying man; his eyes rolled in his head, ... but he was in general sensible. I began to read the most encouraging passages I could find.... He repeated "Lord, evermore give us this bread." . . . I prayed. ... On my being interrupted by the doctor, he said "Mind him," meaning that he was to attend to me, and shortly died. We bore down to give notice of it to the Commodore.... The *Sarah Christiana*, when she saw our signal, fired minute guns so that the whole scene was very affecting.

When 1806 was three days old, the high lands of the Cape were discovered, yet eighty miles off; "a most stately thing, and the finest cape we saw in the circumference of the earth,"

Sir Francis Drake had called it; seen now with what eager
suspense by cadets who for the first time would go into battle.
Martyn's journal and a letter to Sargent give us a picture of
the deck of the *Union* when she came to anchor in Table Bay
on Saturday night, January 4.

> About sunset the fleet came to an anchor between Rob-
> ber's Island and the land. The instant our anchor was down,
> a signal was given for the 59th regiment to prepare to land.
> Our men were soon ready and received thirty-six rounds
> of ball cartridge; before the three boats were lowered down
> and fitted it was two o'clock; I stayed up to see them off. The
> privates were keeping up their spirits by affecting to joke
> about the approach of danger, and the ladies sitting in the
> cold night upon the grating of the after-hatchway over-
> whelmed with grief.

Martyn, although an official chaplain of the East India
Company's troops, was left on deck with the women. Señor
Domingo in Brazil had already put him to shame by asking "if
the soldiers had a minister to attend them in their dying moments, to instruct and administer consolation"; and Martyn
"hardly knew what to say to explain such neglect amongst the
Protestants," at which his Portuguese friend was shrugging his
shoulders in horror. He was now left to strain his eyes in following his men as they were rallied among the flowery heaths
and myrtle bushes near the shore, and as they marched, breast-
ing the Blue Mountains to meet the Dutch resistance, ranged
"with twenty-three pieces of cannon" between them and the
town. He heard the artillery speak and "it seemed as if the
mountain itself were torn by intestine convulsions." He could
see his men rush down the hill to meet the Dutch, and then,
as the enemy who had stood fire were broken by a bayonet
charge, Martyn escaped from the *Union* and got ashore to his
men. On the sandy beach he came first upon the cadets of
his own ship who had made a shelter of bushes and straw and
hailed him in to eat with them. But he did not stay long, for

two wounded Highlanders walking into the lines brought news of a number of wounded lying out along the army's line of march. A party with "slings and barrows" went in search and Martyn was off with them six miles through the soft burning sand dotted with heath and geranium.

We were attracted by seeing some English soldiers; wounded men of the 24th; three were mortally wounded. One who was shot through the lungs was spitting blood. The surgeon desired me to spread a greatcoat over him as they left him. As I did this I talked to him a little of the blessed Gospel.

The wounded were being carried into a Boer farmhouse.

All whom we approached cried out instantly for water. One poor Hottentot...lay with extraordinary patience under his wound on the burning sand; I did what I could to make his position comfortable, and laid near him some bread which I found on the ground. Another Hottentot lay struggling with his mouth in the dust and the blood flowing out of it, cursing the Dutch in English....While the surgeon went back to get his instrument in hopes of saving the man's life, a Highland soldier came up, and asked me in a rough tone, "Who are you?" I told him an Englishman, he said, "No, no, you are French," and was going to present his musket. As I saw he was rather intoxicated, and might in mere wantonness fire, I went up to him and told him that if he liked he might take me prisoner to the English Army, but that I was certainly an English clergyman. The man was pacified at last. The surgeon on his return found the thigh of the poor Hottentot broken and therefore left him to die. Oh! that ambitious men at home could see the agonies of dying men left on the field.

Cape Town surrendered January 10. About five the Commodore fired a gun which was answered by the other men-of-war. "On looking out for the cause, we saw the British flag flying on the Dutch fort.... I prayed that the capture of the Cape might be for the advancement of Christ's kingdom."

The fleet lingered nearly a month at the Cape and Martyn took shore lodgings, rejoiced in "honest English apples and pears, tea and bread and butter for breakfast," and came into personal contact with one of his Cambridge heroes, Dr. Vanderkemp, the old Dutch missionary to Kaffraria whose report he had found so "infinitely entertaining" that he "could read nothing else while it lasted."

From the moment of his arrival in South Africa, Martyn had been "anxiously enquiring about Dr. Vanderkemp. At last, to my no small delight, heard that he was now in Cape Town. But it was long before I could find him. At length I did. He was standing outside of the house, silently looking up at the stars. A great number of black people were sitting around. On my introducing myself he led me in and called for Mr. Read."

From the exuberance of Martyn's delight at meeting men who shared the same allegiance, we gather how great had been the repression and loneliness of the months at sea. "I was beyond measure delighted." "I hardly knew what to do." He visited them daily, and with the younger man, Mr. Read, he was "so charmed...that I fancied myself in company with David Brainerd." Mr. Read in a bush station among the Hottentots had often been reduced to penury. At such times, he told Martyn, "it seemed to be suggested to him, 'If thou wilt be my servant, be contented to fare in this way: if not, go and fare better.' His mind was thus satisfied to remain God's missionary." "Walking home I asked Dr. Vanderkemp if he had ever repented of his undertaking. 'No,' said the old man, smiling, 'and I would not exchange my work for a kingdom.' Dear Dr. Vanderkemp gave me a Syriac Testament as a remembrance of him."

So passed a month and the East India fleet was once more ready to sail. Before leaving Africa, Martyn went with two or three friends up Table Mountain; and wandering away from his party he scrambled up the kloof (deep glen) alone. At the end of the last steep pull he came upon a little hollow, green and decked with flame-colored blossoms waving in the breeze. "It seemed to be an emblem of the beauty and peacefulness of heaven as it shall open upon the soul." He left the kloof and stood alone on the roof of the world, looking from sea to sea, "where there was neither noise nor smaller objects to draw off my attention. One might be said to look round the world from this promontory." Gazing out eastward over the watery road to India, the calmness of wide spaces came into his soul. "I felt commanded to wait in silence and see how God would bring His promises to pass."

None of the travelers found it easy to go back to the close-packed life of their voyagings: "A gloom seemed to hang upon all the passengers, at beginning so long a trip as from hence to India, after the weariness of so long a voyage." They set sail February 9, 1806, shortly before Martyn's twenty-fifth birthday, and seven months after leaving England, and they plunged at once into storms and seasickness. Martyn propped up in his cabin a water-color of St. Hilary Vicarage, and longed for a picture of Lydia. But there was a quietness dwelling on his spirit:

I pray that this may be my state, neither to be anxious to escape from this stormy sea that was round the Cape, nor to change the tedious scene of the ship for Madras... but to glorify God where I am and where He puts me.

A change was coming over his experience. During the first months of his voyage, along with the acceptance of loneliness and rebuff there had come to him moments of illumination and escape, which he could only describe as "walking with my Beloved amid the flowers of Paradise."

Now as he left South Africa his climbing soul made fresh discovery. Such moments of ecstasy, like sunlit peaks, were not the summit he was seeking, but only outlying bulwarks of "those shining tablelands."

"I perceived for the first time the difference between sensible sweetness in religion, and the really valuable attainments." He dwelt first with surprise, but later with consent, on a stern sentence of Leighton. "Mortify all affections towards inward sensible spiritual delight in grace, and the following of devotion with sensible sweetness in the lower faculties or powers of the soul, which are in no wise real sanctity or holiness in themselves, but certain gifts of God to help our infirmity." Strong meat for strong climbers this, and no milk for babes. "For the many that come to Bethlehem there be few that go on to Calvary."

The last stage of the *Union's* voyage was the weariest. The ship was several times becalmed in the Indian Ocean and people grew fretful in the heat and tedious delay. It is curious to see the moral ascendancy which Martyn had insensibly won over the men he sailed with. There was little peace for his Hindustani grammar, he was "much teased [vexed with importunity] with the accusations of the Captain, the commander of the troops, the sick, etc. all of whom complain of and abuse one another to me," and was constantly in request to mediate quarrels between the cadets and their officers, or between the King's officers and the Company's. As the delays lengthened, the new Captain confided in Martyn his fears that the provisions might not hold out. Sickness continued among the men and there was no diet fit for invalids. Martyn sent down to them his own allowance of Madeira and water. Coffee gave out, then tea. There was no fresh meat to spare and Martyn's own helping went, when he could manage it, to the convalescents, while he ate salt junk himself.

Read Hindoostanee; the gale of wind continuing and much water flying over the sides, all the hatches were shut down, so that there was perfect darkness below; however I visited the sick man, being obliged to feel my way to him. I am always surprised at the perfect contentment in which they seem to lie. This man was swinging in his hammock in darkness, and heat, and damp, without a creature to speak to him, and in a burning fever.

B. still delirious and dying fast; the first thing he said
to me when I visited him this afternoon was, "Mr. Martyn,
what will you choose for a kingdom?" ... All I can get from
breakfast and at night I thought it right to give to Beasant,
who is still on the borders of the grave from ... want of
proper meat after the weakening effect of his disease. . . .
Among the sick whom I went to afterwards I found but
one sensible.

Word was brought to me this morning that Beasant
had just died. He was crawling upon his hands and knees
to his breakfast, when he was taken worse and died as they
were lifting him into his hammock.

Martyn was himself a sick man with constant headache,
dysentery and "a distressing sensation of shortness of breath,"
contending too against "nervous irritability." And how he did
contend, through those torpid days when nerves were raw, forever putting himself to some new fence, soul and body tensely
trained for the enterprise in India that was never far from his
thoughts.

In general I find, that, in beginning to pray, I transport
myself in imagination to some solitary spot ... and there
fancy myself praying. The bad consequence of this is that
when I open my eyes and am conversant with the things
around me, I am distressed and unable to maintain such a
sense of God's presence; imagination seems to be a sort of
help like music. . . . Yet I feel that I ought to learn to live
without it.

Began to pray for the setting up of God's kingdom ...
especially in India. . . . My whole soul wrestled with God.
I knew not how to leave off.

After two months at sea Martyn, coming on deck early from
his sleepless cabin, "saw the island of Ceylon bearing west
three or four leagues. . . . The smell from the land was exceedingly fragrant." All spirits rose and on April 25 at sunlight, the
Union anchored in the Madras roads. Martyn, amid a white-
clad chattering crowd, went ashore to the country of his

dreams. A round of invitations waited for him, a kindly welcome from the chaplain, Dr. Kerr, and pleasant words of approval from the Governor, Lord William Bentinck, before
whom he preached. But already his heart was given to the East.
"While the turbaned Asiatics waited upon us at dinner I could
not help feeling as if we had got into their places"; he was
perhaps the first Englishman in India to think just that
thought. He engaged a servant who "could speak Hindustani,"
and escaping from the European settlement walked out with
him by field paths to his native village. "Here all was Indian;
no vestige of anything European." Martyn, for the first time
alone in the East, felt now the power of the spiritual force
against which his life was hurled. The man who stood there
in the village street, though frail of body, was a young athlete
in the spiritual realm. It was no untrained soul that felt there
the "power of the air," and shuddered

> as if in the dominions of the prince of darkness. I fancy the
> frown of God to be visible ... the veil of the covering cast
> over all nations seems thicker here; the fiends of darkness
> seem to sit in sullen repose in this land.

The battle was set.

Chapter 8

CALCUTTA, 1806

The mornings are so pleasant in the garden. Very early, at about three in the morning, the Bheem-raj, a little bird, begins his song; half an hour afterwards, all the bushes and trees burst into melody...and the gay little humming-birds, with their brilliant colours, dive into the flowers for honey, with busy twitters. Oh, it is so cool and pleasant in the morning till ten o'clock, when the warmth increases; from noon to about four in the afternoon, all is quite still, except some lone woodpecker tapping at some far-off tree.—*Letter of* TORU DUTT *from Garden House, Calcutta, April 25th*, 1875.

He often said to us there was no spot in the world so dear to him as Calcutta.—MRS. THOMASON *of* HENRY MARTYN.

As THE UNION slowly made sail up the Hooghly, her sea-worn passengers feasting their eyes on the low tranquil shore, she was met by the *Charlotte* yacht out of Calcutta, sent by the Company to relieve her of her load of Government treasure. Martyn went aboard the yacht, hoping that the smaller boat would make Calcutta faster. That evening they lay in Garden Reach, "very beautiful" in the sunset light. Even to the outward eye there were changes since David Brown had entered Garden Reach some twenty years before. The buildings of the

College of Fort William now dominated the stately sweep of the Reach from the north. And beyond them again rose the new Government House, both buildings outward and visible signs of a new dignity that was coming into British life in India. Martyn was to learn on landing of the death of that Governor General who had first come to India in the same year as David Brown, and also of the great minister who trusted him. For the travelers in the *Union* had yet to hear of the death of Pitt and of Cornwallis.[1]

When in David Brown's first year of service Cornwallis came to Calcutta, he brought her no great originative mind but a calm and dignified common sense. He set out to stabilize life in Bengal and finance in Leadenhall Street by creating a permanent land settlement, a conservative Bengali landed class, and a fixed revenue. A man of such clear-cut and limited ideals went far to reach them; and his industrious and honest fight against corruption meant much for India. But he aimed at a stable and static condition, and in the long run the forces of life are against the man who tries to bind instead of to direct them.

Under Cornwallis, the first peer of the realm whom the merchant city had received, orgies of eating and drinking dear to Jos Sedley and his like grew less, and Calcutta assemblies became more discreet and dignified. Church-going, however, was not yet in fashion, and when the Governor General said to David Brown that the new Church of St. John was "a pretty Church, but it had many critics," that worthy desired with a twinkle that it might have more critics on a Sunday.

Sir John Shore's governorship was a pale and timid sequel to that of Cornwallis. Color and vigor came with the next administration—color indeed that appeared on the river in a

---

[1] The Governors General since David Brown's arrival were Cornwallis, 1786, Sir John Shore, 1793, Mornington (afterwards Wellesley), 1798, Cornwallis again 1805, Sir George Barlow, 1805.

state barge of green and gold rowed by twenty boatmen in
scarlet turbans and rose-colored livery. When Wellesley on his
death-bed asked to be buried at Eton, he was making a fitting
request. The outlook that he brought to Calcutta was that of
Eton and the Foreign Office. He saw his work in India as part
of the Napoleonic struggle. There was in his mind no question of Indian independence, but only of a desperate race between the French and British for dominance there.

One of the most fantastic fruits of the French Revolution
had been the planting of a "tree of liberty" in the dominions
of Tipu, Sultan of Mysore, while that autocrat conducted correspondence with the French Directory and enrolled himself in
a republican club as "Citoyen Tipu."

Wellesley (then Mornington), the friend and favorite of
Pitt, came out to India in 1798 conscious that she might be
the scene of a death-grapple with France, which had the islands
of Mauritius and Bourbon for an assembling place. This consciousness grew and was focused with the growth of Napoleon's career. If he took Egypt in his stride and came upon
India inchoate and unprotected, he might indeed become lord
of East and West. But in racing Napoleon, Wellesley set a pace
too great for the directors in Leadenhall Street.

One of their letters complains sadly that "neither His Majesty's ministers nor the Marquis Wellesley appear to wish to
shrink from responsibility." When in 1805 they recalled him
"suspended between admiration and reproach," he left them
responsible for an empire but looking ruefully at their purses,
and summing up the results of his administration as "an increased revenue of five millions, and a debt contracted of
twenty millions sterling. The great accession of territory made
under the same government has necessarily required an increased army, at least so long as the power of France pre-
dominates."[2]

---

[2] Chatfield's *Hindostan*, 1808, p. 123.

They recalled him, but not before he had left his mark on Calcutta. On reaching Bengal he had not disguised his horror at what he found. "When I arrived there it was in a disgraceful and a lamentable state." He put Calcutta into training as the capital of an empire and introduced a new magnificence into the life of the dazzled city. Government House rose, with a stately entrance and ceremonial stairway. It was opened with a breakfast to seven hundred people. Functions must now be attended in full dress (white linen had sufficed before) and no longer were there hookahs in attendance at the Supreme Council. In the general tightening up of easy-going ways, Wellesley expressed himself as shocked to find that divine service was never held at his suburban residence of Barrackpore. He was no friend to any sort of laxity, and decided to turn church-going into one of the official functions of Calcutta life. He made David Brown senior chaplain and helped him to choose the lessons for a most novel function in Calcutta, a thanksgiving service after the defeat of Citizen Tipu, to which Wellesley came, and his great soldier brother, in state through streets lined with troops. The service was held in St. John's Church with a sentry and his firelock at the door, and servants bearing the gold and silver maces of all the officials. After the fashion of the day when the state wished to pay its compliments to religion, the Governor General ordered Dr. Buchanan's sermon to be printed and circulated. Calcutta had never seen such doings; for as Burke said, "The Europeans were commonly unbaptized in their passage to India." "You may easily conceive," wrote the preacher, "the astonishment of men at these religious proceedings. However, all was silence and deep acquiescence. It became fashionable to say that religion was a very proper thing."[3] Society began to come to church. Good David Brown, serene and faithful under patronage as under

---

[3] See Hough, *Christianity in India*, IX. 1.

contempt, would now find the streets around St. John's blocked up on Sunday morning with coaches and lacquered palanquins.

The Governor General, "the marvelous little man" as his subordinates loved to call him, with his unfailing flair for the right man, now saw in David Brown and in Claudius Buchanan who had joined him in 1797, the very leaders needed for a scheme that was to alter the face of Indian administration. Writers who came out at sixteen were not, in Lord Wellesley's opinion, qualified to govern an empire, and in 1800 he sent home his "Notes on the necessity of a special collegiate training of civil servants," marked out a noble site on Garden Reach, put up a worthy building, gathered together upwards of one hundred learned teachers of eastern languages, law and literature, and placed this whole "College of Fort William" under the provostship (the very name breathing his love for Eton) of David Brown.

The Vice-Provost was Claudius Buchanan, a man of restless intellect, who had run away from the home of his boyhood with a fiddle for his sole means of support, and now after strange courses had become the most statesmanlike ecclesiastic of the East, and Wellesley's trusted chaplain. The professor of Bengali was a yet more remarkable man, William Carey, blent of genius and faith, the one-time cobbler and Baptist minister in Midland villages, now translator of the New Testament into Bengali, and the man who established the literary form in workaday prose of that tongue whose poetry has today become one of the joys of the whole earth.

Carey was living at Serampore under Danish protection because of the Company's ban on missionaries. But Wellesley foresaw that Bengali must one day replace the foreign Persian as the language of justice, and he determined that Bengali should be taught in the new college. When Brown and Buchanan vouched for Carey as the one man capable of superintending the Bengali studies, Wellesley choked back his suspicions (the local press not knowing what a "Baptist" might be had put about that Carey and his colleagues were Romish priests in the pay of Napoleon) and called forth Carey from his seclusion to be professor of Sanskrit and Bengali.

Wellesley was gone when Martyn came. They sent out Cornwallis to reverse his policy, and Cornwallis was towed up the river in Wellesley's state barge, a dying man. Sir George Barlow now held the reins, but that notable trio at the college were still working together and turning out men who would leave their mark on India.

To a Calcutta under Sir George Barlow's rule, and in the inevitable tide of reaction that followed the withdrawal of Wellesley's imperious hand, Martyn went ashore at daylight on May 16, 1806, and asked for David Brown. He was fifteen miles away at his suburban home, Aldeen. His colleague Buchanan had sailed out of the Hooghly as Martyn entered it, and so it came about that the first man to welcome Martyn to Bengal was William Carey. With him, so different in upbringing, so like in gifts and apostolic spirit, Martyn sat down to his first breakfast without "the smell of the ship." Carey bald-headed, unassuming, almost uncouth in manner, had no small talk, but he never failed to take fire, like Martyn himself, if the talk turned to missions.

> With him I breakfasted, and joined with him in worship, which was in Bengalee, for the advantage of a few servants, who sat however perfectly unmoved. I could not help contrasting them with the slaves and Hottentots at Cape Town whose hearts seemed to burn within them. After breakfast Carey began to translate with a Pundit from a Sanskrit manuscript.

A chit from Mr. Brown during the morning put his Calcutta house at Martyn's disposal—the chaplain's rooms adjoining St. John's Church. There in the heart of the city, where the moving shadow of the spire still marks the glaring hours, Martyn retired for solitude and prayer. There too on that first day he was hunted out by "Mr. Brown's moonshi, a Brahmin" who "came in and disputed with me two hours about the Gospel." The solitude of that beginning, broken only by the arguments of the learned visitor, are a strange foreshadowing of what was to come.

Mr. Brown soon came to Calcutta and bore Martyn out to his home at Aldeen, buried in foliage of mango, teak and bamboo, with green lawns (since broken up into tanks for the Howrah Water Works) that sloped down to the river and made a playground for his flock of children. Here at the large family table where, whoever might come, motherly Mrs. Brown always made room for one guest more, Martyn found his Indian home. Of David Brown he always spoke as a father, and Mr. Brown wrote later to a friend that "Martyn lived five months with me, and a more heavenly-minded young man I never saw." It was pure joy to Martyn after work to romp with children. A friend[4] tells us that "when he relaxed from his labours in the presence of friends it was to play and laugh like an innocent, happy child, more especially if children were present to play and laugh with him." Into that grave journal of his there creeps a line that tells much, when he writes of returning to Aldeen with "children jumping and shouting and convoying me in troops to the house. They are a lovely family indeed."

As a "griffin" or new arrival in Calcutta, Martyn had calls to pay, and as a new official of the Company he must go to Government House and be presented to Sir George Barlow, who had an unhappy and repellent coldness of manner that often won him personal dislike and does not seem to have been more successful with Martyn than with others. "After waiting a considerable time in a crowd of military men, an aide-de-camp presented me to Sir G. Barlow, who after one or two trifling questions passed on." At a later levee, Martyn received "great attention" but was no more able to like the Governor.

---

[4] Mrs. Sherwood.

Martyn began at once to preach for David Brown at the Old Mission Church, and his Calcutta friends did their best to keep him there, carrying their appeals "farther than mere civility." Congenial as his new friends were, the thought of staying in Calcutta chafed his spirit. He knew that three of the six chaplains for the Company's fifty-three stations in Bengal were planted there, together with the group of Baptist missionaries under Carey's leadership at Serampore; and with a true instinct he felt that Calcutta was dominantly European, a foreign merchant settlement upon the mudheaps. He set his heart on a chaplaincy at one of the great inland centers of population.

> Brown and Buchanan wish to keep me here, as I expected, and the Governor accedes to their wishes. I have a great many reasons for not liking this; I almost think that to be prevented going among the heathen as a missionary would break my heart. Whether it be self-will or aught else, I cannot yet rightly ascertain. . . . I feel pressed in spirit to do something for God. . . . I have hitherto lived to little purpose more like a clod than a servant of God; now let me burn out for God.

> Amid the want of activity and decision so remarkable among the friends of religion here I must begin at last to act for myself, though I am no more qualified than a child. At present this is the state of things, I wish to fix at Benares. . . . If not I must endeavour to be fixed at Patna as civil chaplain. . . . I shall endeavour to have an audience of the Governor-General.

His home while he waited for the decision about his station was in a pagoda in David Brown's Aldeen garden, overhanging the broad river. It was a weird place of vaulted cells, its bricks carven with many-armed figures of Hindu gods. Once it had been the shrine of a little black figure wafted there by unseen powers, the idol Radhabullub; but the waters of the sacred river lapped closer and closer to the shrine, until it stood within the sacred limit (three-hundred feet from either bank) where no Brahmin may eat or take a gift. Then Radhabullub left his shrine and retreated, with his conch shells, his cymbals and his offerings, to a grove beyond the sacred limit. The forsaken temple, added by David Brown to Aldeen garden ground, was made by him an oratory. This eerie home of crumbling masonry and creeping vegetation now became Martyn's cell. He reveled in the sense of solitude, the twittering birds, or the moonlight lying placid on the lawns; but to the Cornish saint, as to St. Antony in the Egyptian tomb, haunting evil powers were not far from the sometime shrine.

My habitation, assigned me by Mr. Brown, is a pagoda in his grounds, on the edge of the river. Thither I retired at night, and really felt something like superstitious dread, at being in a place once inhabited as it were by devils, but yet felt disposed to be triumphantly joyful, that the temple where they were worshipped was become Christ's oratory. I prayed out aloud to my God, and the echoes returned from the vaulted roof. . . . I like my dwelling much, it is so retired and free from noise; it has so many recesses and cells that I can hardly find my way in and out.

Here on a platform built over the placid lapping river, Henry Martyn wrote his sermons for Calcutta congregations and almost grudged the time they cost. For the English of Calcutta had David Brown to their shepherd, and he was constrained to press on to the unshepherded. Here too he flung himself greedily on Bengali and Persian and Hindustani, with a Brahmin and a Moslem teacher with whom he would sit for hours as they introduced him for the first time to long winding oriental arguments upon religion, interminable as the flow of the river under his pagoda. In Hindustani especially he had made gigantic strides, and could now point out to his teacher mistakes in a translation of Genesis. Sometimes he took boat down to the College of Fort William for lessons in oriental penmanship, learning Hindustani roots in the boat as he went,

and returning perhaps in the evening with a crowd of the
Aldeen children in the boat, singing across the sunset water.

Here in the pagoda, too, he made new friendships. Five
minutes' walk along the river bank brought him to the apostolic
settlement of Carey, Marshman and Ward, the immortal trio
of Serampore missionaries. He found his way there on his first
day with David Brown.

> In the cool of the evening we walked to the mission
> house, a few hundred yards off, and I at last saw the place
> about which I have so long read with pleasure; I was intro-
> duced to all the missionaries. We sat down about one hun-
> dred and fifty to tea, at several long tables in an immense
> room. After this there was evening service in another room
> adjoining, by Mr. Ward. . . . With Mr. Marshman alone
> I had much conversation.

And John Clark Marshman became more than them all the
friend of Henry Martyn. He was the son of a Wiltshire weaver,
and in boyhood had often walked a dozen miles for the loan
of a book. Now in his Serampore house Martyn found "many
agreeable sights"; one pundit was translating Scripture into
Sanskrit, another into Gujerati, and a table was covered with
materials for a Chinese Dictionary. Pacing up and down Mr.
Brown's garden paths at night, Martyn and Marshman ce-
mented their friendship. Martyn entered keenly into all the
joys and sorrows of the Serampore community: the tragic night
when they were all agog to welcome Mr. Chamberlain and his
wife, only to find that Mrs. Chamberlain had died on the boat:
the Greek Testament lectures to younger missionaries: the
preachings to wayside groups under banyan trees, or to immense crowds at fair-time: or the night (when Martyn could
not sleep for indignation) of the news that Sir George Barlow,
not content with the ban on missionaries in British territory,
had forbidden the captain of an American vessel to land two
who were bound for Serampore under the protection of the
King of Denmark.

In long evenings of talk beside the river the friends would touch on deeper questions. "He is a most lively sanguine missionary," Martyn wrote of Marshman, "and made my heart burn within me." His friend tried to persuade Martyn to stay, for the present at least, in the Bible factory that the dauntless men of Serampore had established in their house for the translation of Holy Scripture into all the main tongues of the East. The work was after Martyn's own heart. He coveted for it the scholarship of Cambridge. Why, he asked Sargent, should it be left to men "who cannot in ten years supply the want of what we gain by a classical education?" But he was perfectly convinced that the call to stay in or near Calcutta was not the call for him.

A yet dearer friend came to the pagoda, a junior of Cambridge days, Daniel Corrie, afterwards Bishop of Madras. That plain-faced, genial person, adoring children and adored by them, fighting down the claims of rare social popularity, had recorded his desire to "become the world's fool for the sake of Christ"; and inspired by Simeon, but still more by Martyn, now followed his friend to an Indian chaplaincy. As he lay in the Hooghly, a note came to him to say that Martyn was awaiting him at the College of Fort William.

"I set off immediately," says Corrie, "and was received by him with lively demonstrations of joy." It was pure delight to Martyn to see that genial expansive countenance again, and to introduce his friend to David Brown. ("A sensible, determined pious man," was Corrie's comment in his journal.) Martyn as guide to Calcutta took the newcomer for a drive on the dusty "Course" that evening, "as if I meant to exhibit my reinforcement."

Corrie found Martyn eating his heart out at delay in Calcutta. The sights around him were burning themselves into his spirit, as not unsimilar sights had stirred the spirit of St. Paul. From his pagoda he could watch the crowds who climbed the ghat to worship Radhabullub. Into his prayers or his translation work there broke the clang of gongs, with drums or conch shells from the god's new shrine—"detestable music" to him. He went to visit the temple:

The way up to it was by a flight of steps on each side. The people to the number of about fifty were standing on the outside, and playing the instruments. In the centre of the building was the idol, a little ugly black image, about two feet high, with a few lights burning round him. At intervals they prostrated themselves with their foreheads to the earth. I shivered at being in the neighbourhood of hell.

Again, he went to see the great Juggernaut car in procession near Aldeen. When the car stopped at a neighboring shrine "the god, with one or two attending deities, was let down by ropes, muffled up in red cloths." Holy water was poured over the image, and Martyn heard the great shout of the one hundred and fifty thousand people who stood with uplifted hands to watch this ceremony.

Before the stumps of images, for they were not better, some of the people prostrated themselves, striking the ground twice with their foreheads. This excited more horror in me than I can well express. . . . I thought that if I had words I would preach to the multitudes all day if I lost my life for it.

Corrie, more than most of Martyn's friends, entered into his haunting sense of the evil "power of the air." He tells of one evening when he was dining at Aldeen, and their eyes were attracted by a flame that rose and quivered on the opposite bank of the river.

We soon perceived that it was a funeral pile, on which the wife was burning with the dead body of her husband . . . by the light of the flames we could discover a great crowd of people, their horrid noise, and senseless music, joined with the testimony of some of the servants, convinced us that our apprehensions were founded on fact. The noise continued until ten o'clock, and the fire was kept burning till that time. My mind was struck with horror and pity. On going out to walk with Martyn to the pagoda, the noise so unnatural, so little calculated to excite joy, raised in my mind an awful sense of the presence and influence of evil spirits.

So Martyn waited in Calcutta, constrained in spirit, reading the life of St. Francis Xavier "exceedingly roused at the astonishing example of that great man," and raising in the city just such a storm as he had excited on the *Union* by his uncompromising sermons. At the Old Mission Church his earnestness was deeply acceptable, but St. John's was a scene of trial. It still stands much as Martyn saw it, in the heart of Calcutta with Zoffany's queer altarpiece of the Last Supper, drawn with all the faces taken from old Calcutta characters. Those Sunday morning services at which Martyn sometimes preached before Sir George Barlow and his staff were all but government functions. In side galleries (now pulled down) sat the great ones of Calcutta; the Governor General on one side, facing the judges of the supreme court on the other. Behind the judges on the north, as being the cooler side, sat the government ladies who had come in palanquins, wearing caps or turbans of sufficient gorgeousness to flaunt under the Governor's very eye. Lesser folk were ranged on chairs on the blue marble floor below. Here, before all the great ones of that little world, the new chaplain stood up to preach.

I knew what I was to be on my guard against—and therefore, that I might not have my mind full of idle thoughts about the opinions of men, I prayed both before and after, that the word might be for the conversion of souls, and that I might feel indifferent except on this score. The sermon excited no small ferment; however, after some looks of surprise and whispering, the congregation became attentive and serious.

Afterwards the storm burst: two other chaplains of the Company felt it their duty to preach counter-blasts in which they even appealed by name to their new colleague to turn from doctrines so "inconsistent, extravagant and absurd," and described him (he sitting in the church the while) as "one of those who understand neither what they say nor whereof they affirm." Even to a man of Martyn's humility such orations were not altogether easy to listen to, and it is a very gracious gesture of his spirit that he describes in a rather stilted sentence when he says, "I rejoiced at having the Sacrament of the Lord's Supper afterwards, the solemnities of that blessed ordinance sweetly tended to soothe the asperities and dissipate the contempt which was rising. I think I administered the cup to —— and —— [the opposing chaplains] with sincere goodwill." The storm was at its height when Corrie landed and we have the comment of the man who had the art of disarming opposition on his friend who so often aroused it:

> A great opposition, I find, is raised against Martyn and the principles he preaches. . . . At three o'clock Martyn preached from Rom. iii. 21-23, the most impressive and best composition I ever heard. The disposition of love and goodwill which appeared in him must have had great effect; and the calmness and firmness with which he spoke raised in me great wonder.

Perhaps the authorities were not relucant to send their firebrand chaplain out of Calcutta; be that as it may, his summons came at last to an upcountry station, and on September 14, 1806, he wrote to Sargent, "I am this day appointed to Dinapore in the neighbourhood of Patna."

Patna was in those days some six weeks from Calcutta, traveling by a leisurely houseboat towed against the stream. The Browns, and indeed the whole friendly Calcutta group who had hoped to keep Martyn amongst them, quailed at the thought of sending him out alone. He had already shown them his helplessness in sickness, when it was his way to stagger on where a wiser man would have yielded. They dreaded the effect of solitude on his tense nature, and while they told him their kindly fears, the phantom form of Lydia was once more haunting his every thought.

July 12th, 1806. Found Europe letters. . . . My letters were from Lydia, T. H. and Emma, Mr. Simeon and Sargent. All their first letters had been taken in the Bell Packet. I longed to see Lydia's. . . . The one I did receive from her was very animating. . . . Mr. Simeon's letter contained her praises, and even he seemed to regret that I had gone without her.

Oh, the pity of it! A letter from Lydia. She had sent him off to the ends of the earth with "the half of a broken hope for pillow at night" and with no leave to correspond with her. In her own eyes she was not free to marry, for Mr. John's wedding had never taken place. Had she been wise she would have let ill alone. But Lydia, for all her real goodness, was not of the heroic build. She could not (as she thought) accept Henry's love; nor could she bear to let it go entirely out of her life, and a few months after Martyn's departure she began sending letters after him. A series of six she despatched, of which the first had been lost at sea. Sisterly or cousinly letters she would have called them, but they served to rouse in Martyn all his buried hopes. What lover would not have found it "animating" to be told that his lady prayed for him many times every day? Was not his Lydia giving him now the answer that she was not ready to give in the moment of hurried parting? Martyn took the letter to David Brown who certainly understood from it that the lady was to be won if she were not won already. His fatherly heart rejoiced at the prospect of care and sympathy for his young saint, so determined to strike out a lonely course. After such a consultation Martyn's journal says that Mr. Brown "strongly recommended the measure of endeavouring to bring her here, and was clear that my future situation in the country would be such as to make it necessary to be married."

A letter from Colonel Sandys, which he opened afterwards, spoke in the highest terms of her. . . . Sat up late with

Mr. Brown, considering the same subject . . . and it dwelt so much on my mind, that I got hardly any sleep the whole night.

Next day:

Mr. Brown's arguments appear so strong that my mind is almost made up to send for Lydia.

So it came to pass that Martyn sat down in the pagoda to write his first love letter:

July 29th, 1806. Much of this morning taken up in writing to Lydia. . . . Staid up till midnight in finishing the letter to Lydia.

It was very long, as the letter would be of one hitherto pent up in silence and at last able to write his love. There was much to be said too, for this was a letter with a definite proposal that she should break through all her timidities and come to him. His pen flew on after the last boat had splashed homeward on the river and the night was broken only by the wash of water or the sudden cry of a bird. But it was no unrestrained pen, the letter breathes a discipline of spirit remarkable in any lover, but learned only at severest cost by so passionate a soul.

MY DEAREST LYDIA,—

. . . I wish to assure you that I am not acting without much consideration and prayer, while I at last sit down to request you to come out to me in India.

. . . A few weeks ago we received your welcome letter, and others from Mr. Simeon and Colonel Sandys, both of whom spoke of you in reference to me. . . . Mr. Simeon seemed in his letter to me to regret that he had so strongly dissuaded me from thinking about you at the time of my leaving England. . . . Mr. Brown became very earnest for me to endeavour to prevail upon you. Your letter to me perfectly delighted him and induced him to say that you would be the greatest aid to the mission I could possibly meet with. . . . Now with a safe conscience and the enjoyment of the divine presence I calmly and deliberately make the proposal to you. . . . If He shall forbid it, I think, that by

His grace, I shall even then be contented. . . . It can be nothing but a sacrifice on your part.

There follow assurances about the voyage and the climate,
so dreadful and so unknown to the Cornish friends; his salary
will keep her in comfort, and there will be English ladies at
hand. Can she be ready to sail in the February fleet? (The
impatience of the lover made him over-sanguine about dates.
Lydia did not receive his letter until March.) She is to come
out as "guest to Mr. Brown" in any ship where there is a lady
of high rank in the service to chaperon her. And will she take
Gilchrist's *Indian Strangers' Guide*[5] on the voyage? (a work
in which she could learn to read in romanized character such
Hindustani sentences as "Hand me the tooth-brush and powder," "I want a palanquin and bearers," "Brush the curtains
well that no mosquitoes may remain.")

Then, as it drew on to midnight and the long letter must
come to a close, the lover in the ghostly pagoda allowed himself
to speak.

> You say in your letter that *frequently every day* you
> remember my worthless name before the throne of grace.
> This instance of extraordinary and undeserved kindness
> draws my heart towards you with a tenderness which I
> cannot describe. Dearest Lydia, in the sweet and fond ex-
> pectation of your being given to me by God, and of the hap-
> piness which I humbly hope you yourself might enjoy here,
> I find a pleasure in breathing out my assurance of ardent
> love.

To his vivid imagination, his Lydia was almost there. "As
soon as she arrives on the river," he wrote to Simeon, "Mrs.
Brown (a most sensible and zealous woman) will go down
fifty or sixty miles to bring her up, so that she will not have the
least trouble." "I please myself with the idea of visiting these
places the next time in company with Lydia, and of walking

---

[5] *The Strangers' East Indian Guide to the Hindoostanee or Grand Popular Language of India (improperly called Moors)*, by J. Gilchrist.

with her morning and evening on these delightful banks." "Everything I see or do is a source of pleasure."

Her letters meanwhile only buoyed up his hopes. "My dearest Lydia's assurances of her love are grateful to my heart." But she was yet in Cornwall, and the immediate business was to send Henry Martyn off alone to his new station.

The Aldeen family and the Serampore missionaries came to the pagoda for a farewell meeting. They told him that they were "alarmed about the solitariness of his future life." At that moment he could hardly know alarm. The strange interaction of body, mind and spirit were producing in him something more like exultation. Warmth and sunshine had for the moment stayed or seemed to stay the tendency to disease. Hope had flooded the heart of the lover. And the disciple saw before him at last the longed-for task allotted to him by his Master's hand. So, while they sang and prayed under the echoing vault, he was exultant: "My soul never before had such divine enjoyment . . . my joy was too great for my body. I was in actual pain. . . . How sweet to walk with Jesus—to love Him and to die for Him."

Next morning he took a houseboat and passed away from the Aldeen garden and the community at Calcutta that would so gladly have kept him in their midst.

Chapter 9

DINAPORE

No man (not an Anabaptist) will, we presume, contend that it is our duty to lay before them so fully and emphatically the scheme of the gospel as to make them rise up in the dead of the night and shoot their instructors through the head. If conversion be the greatest of all objects, the possession of the country to be converted is the only means, in this instance, by which that conversion can be accomplished.—SYDNEY SMITH's view of Indian Missions, from the *Edinburgh Review, April,* 1808.

Let me be torn to pieces, and my dear Lydia torn from me; or let me labour for fifty years amidst scorn, and never seeing one soul converted; . . . Though the heathen rage and the English people imagine a vain thing, the Lord Jesus, who controls all events is my friend, my master, my God, my all.—HENRY MARTYN's view of his life-work on arrival at Dinapore, *December,* 1806.

FOUR OF THE Calcutta friends brought Martyn on his way up the river, till bad weather turned them back, and he was left for six weeks of leisurely travel alone with his Moslem language teacher and his company of servants and boatmen. All day they towed the boat up-stream and at sunset made her fast and lighted cooking fires on the bank.

149

Cut off as he was from all but Indian scenes, the river became his teacher as she bore him slowly through the teeming land. She scowled at first and showed him her angry face in such a storm as that of which Tagore wrote[1] that it "droned like a giant snake-charmer's pipe, and to its rhythm swayed hundreds and thousands of crested waves, like so many hooded snakes."

I was rather anxious about your little boat the day you left me, [wrote Martyn to Mr. Brown] it blew so violently. As soon as you were out of sight, the men laid down the rope and would not track any more for the day. They were about to put back into a nullah [a tributary water-course, the refuge of small craft during river storms] but found that preoccupied by so many boats, that we were obliged to lie on the naked shore, exposed to the direct stream and wind. The budgerow made a good deal of water by beating about on the ground.

But in general the houseboat passed placidly on the face of a full and gliding stream between banks that showed Martyn in an endless picture the life of Bengal in pleasant October days: muddy children splashing at the waterside; sesame or towering hemp plants standing tall against the sky; cotton pods bursting milky-white; rustling winds swaying water-rice sown on the river silt; colored groups where women stood in the water bathing and washing clothes; bamboo stakes hung with fishing nets spread out to dry; "sweet fields dressed in living green" where the new-sown wheat was springing; clusters of thatched roofs among shivering bamboos or plantains; each village of those days guarded by its own absurd mud fort; paddy birds standing in line where mud and water meet; and over all the wheeling kites watching the river life with the keen eye of hunger.

Through the sunny hours when the servants liked to roll themselves in cotton sheets and sleep on the roof of the house-

---

[1] In *Glimpses of Indian Life*.

boat, Martyn sat at his books, sometimes with his teacher at
Hindustani and Bengali, sometimes alone at Sanskrit.

> Tell Marshman with my affectionate remembrances that
> I have seriously begun the Sanscrit grammar, but I cannot
> say whereabouts I am in it, being enveloped at present in a
> thick cloud with the exceptions, limitations, anomalies, etc.

> Sanscrit sleeps a little, though I am daily more convinced
> of the need of it in order to know the country Hindoostanee.

Hindustani he was making more and more his own as
Carey had made Bengali. He brought to the language already
some knowledge of Persian and Arabic from which on the one
side it traced descent, and he was now adding Sanskrit, its
parent on the other side, and so fitting himself for a critical
mastery of its form and vocabulary. Already, after six months
in the country, he could write to Marshman at Serampore with
a list of mistakes in one of their Hindustani tracts.

He brought also the delicate ear that was quick to detect
changes of dialect as he passed from village to village on the
Hooghly and the Ganges. So the river days glided by. "Reading hard all day." "Employed all the day in translating, in
which work the time passes away pleasantly and rapidly. The
cold mornings and evenings begin to be very severe."

At sunset when the gaily painted "budgerow" was moored,
the boatmen in little circles round their supper fires smoked
cocoanut hookahs or told interminable tales. And Martyn went
ashore for exercise sometimes with his gun, bringing home
snipe or minas "enough to make a change with the curry";
sometimes with New Testaments or some of the leaflets printed
at Serampore. He would plunge into villages where no "sahib"
had been seen before, scaring away graceful companies of
women as they came up from the river with dripping saris,
the household waterpots balanced against their flanks.

One day he was shown the fresh footprint of a tiger;
another day the trail of wild buffaloes was on the path. The
Journal is full of glimpses of the myriad life of India.

Went ashore and ascended an eminence to look at the ruins of a mosque. The grave of a Mussalman[2] warrior killed in battle, and a room over it, were in perfect preservation; and lamps are lighted there every night. We saw a few more of the hill-people, one of whom had a bow and arrows; they were in a hurry to be gone; and went off, men, women and children, into their native woods. As I was entering the boat, I happened to touch with my stick the brass pot of one of the Hindoos, in which rice was boiling. So defiled are we in their sight, that the pollution passed from my hand, through the stick and the brass to the meat. He rose and threw it all away.

He talked with all and sundry, testing his Hindusta wherever he could find a friendly soul ready to chat with him

All ran away when they saw me, except one poor old woman who was ill, and begged. Though she spoke clearly enough, I could scarcely understand one of her words, so that I have quite a new language to learn. When she received half a rupee, she was mute with astonishment.

People in general were shy of taking his books, but one when he had given away some New Testaments he wrote

My fame arrived here before me, and some men had travelled on from the spring, having heard that Sahib was giving away copies of the Ramayuna! I told them it was not the Ramayuna, but something better, and parted with as many as I could spare. One poor fellow who was selling gun-rods followed the budgerow along the walls of the fort; and finding an opportunity got on board, and begged and intreated me for one, even with tears. As I hesitated, having given as many as I could spare for one place, he prostrated himself on the earth, and placed his forehead in the dust at which I felt an indescribable horror, so I could not hold out. When he got it he clasped it with rapture, still thinking it to be the Ramayuna.

---

[2] Martyn writes Mussalman where we write Moslem or more correct Muslim.

So gliding through the teeming land he came at last to Patna and its European suburbs of Dinapore (military) and Bankipore (civil), his new parish, the whole stretching for fourteen miles along the bank of the river which here is two miles wide.

By an early and all-but-forgotten statute of the East India Company it was the duty of their chaplains to teach the natives at their stations, and Henry Martyn, eager as he was for the task, "was almost overwhelmed" at the sight of "the immense multitudes" in this the second city of Bengal—"the multitudes at the waterside prodigious."

He left the houseboat for barrack quarters and surveyed the work before him. "I have now made my calls and delivered my letters, and the result of my observations upon whom and what I have seen is that I stand alone," he wrote to the Aldeen friends. The East India Company's troops, of which two regiments were stationed at Dinapore, were a reckless fighting force of adventurers from many European nations, and ne'er-do-wells from English families. Others besides Martyn found them "disdainful and abandoned." There was no church, and he was expected to conduct service at the drumhead, either in a barrack room with no seats or in one of the two squares of the cantonments, with no shade from the Indian sun. "After seeing the European regiment drawn up I felt as I used to feel on board ship."

The civilians at Bankipore had never had a service and were embarrassed when the new chaplain offered to come and give them one, more especially as the judge had married a Moselm wife, abandoned his faith and built a mosque to please her, which Martyn found on his first call decked out with flags and lanterns for a Moslem feast. But little desirous as his countrymen seemed to be of his services for themselves, they approved still less of his intercourse with the people of the great Indian city.

They seem to hate to see me associating at all with the natives, and one gave me a hint a few days ago about taking my exercise on foot. But if our Lord had always travelled about in His palanquin, the poor woman, who was healed by touching the hem of His garment might have perished.

Or countrymen, when speaking of the natives, said as they usually do, that they cannot be converted, and if they could, they would be worse than they are. Though I have observed before now, that the English are not in the way of knowing much about the natives, yet the number of difficulties they mentioned proved another source of discouragement to me.

Martyn annoyed the General "by what I said about the natives." In those days of preposterous superiority the chaplain dared to believe that "these men are not all fools, and that all ingenuity and clearness of reasoning are not confined to England and Europe. I seem to feel that these descendants of Ham are as dear to God as the haughty sons of Japheth."

When he entered Patna itself he speedily found that "haughty son of Japheth" though he were, he was met with equal racial hauteur on the part of a population chafing under the new rule of western aliens, and cherishing memories of the days not so long ago, when Mir Kasim, to avenge commercial injustice, had a hundred and fifty Europeans done to death in their city.[3]

Patna was in India the home of those most formidable Puritans of Islam, the fanatical sect of Wahabis; it was a city full of growling rumor. Martyn was greeted with scowls.

The thought of interrupting a crowd of busy people like those at Patna, whose every day is a market day, with a message about eternity, without command of language, sufficient to explain and defend myself, and so of becoming the scorn of the rabble without doing them good, was offensive to my pride. The manifest disaffection of the people, and

---

[3] The Patna massacre, 1762.

the contempt with which they eyed me confirmed my dread.

England appears almost a heaven upon earth because there one is not viewed as an unjust intruder.

Altogether his new parish presented no rosy prospect. But Martyn did not ask for roses. He found work to his hand in the hospital and the incessant funerals of a station where one regiment on arriving lost fifteen men in fourteen days. The sick men were sometimes ribald, but at other times Martyn "was much comforted to hear that the men had great love for him." His barrack quarters, as the General had warned him, became untenable in the heat, and he thereupon moved to a bungalow in the smaller cantonment square, which seemed to him too sumptuous for a missionary, but which he forever filled with a strange assortment of language teachers, scribes, and poverty-stricken guests. The house was probably tenantless because in the rains it was flooded and cut off from the barracks by a stagnant pond.

Martyn, now master of a house, set aside the big central room and verandas for a church, retaining only the use of the smaller rooms.[4] He had forms set out (though superior persons sent their servants before service with their own chairs and footstools), and a table behind which he stood. He begged from the General the help of the band to lead hymns and chants. The men were paraded, the station merchants drove up, the ladies were handed in from their palanquins by officers, the soldiers' wives in white dresses and mob caps came across the dusty square under painted umbrellas, and Martyn at his table, with the light filtering through the double green lattices behind him, saw before him, as he told David Brown, a larger congregation and one in far greater need of instruction in the Christian faith than would have been his had he stayed at the Calcutta mission church.

But he was not content with a flock that came indeed to

---

[4] See Harriet Wainwright, *A Sermon Against Calumny*.

his service, but took no further notice of religion. At Dinapore as everywhere his presence was a touchstone; souls here and there accepted his standards and mounted his steep path. Martyn yearned over such and wrestled on their behalf. A Major and his wife who made a marked change of life had to face the music:

> The Major was telling me yesterday, almost with tears, of the sneers he met with from nearly all for his religion. ... He longs to be in England to follow religion unmolested.
>
> I learnt from him that on Sunday evening at the General's he had been bantered on the late change that had taken place in him with regard to religion. I felt such love to him that I could have laid down my life for him.

It was no easier for the men. Martyn put his house at the disposal of the "serious" soldiers twice a week, and never failed to meet the tiny group, for whom sometimes a fair linen cloth was spread and a Communion held in his veranda. They were not more than about a half dozen hardy souls who could gather at any one time. "Six soldiers came last night. To escape as much as possible the taunts of their wicked companions, they go out of their barracks in opposite directions to come to me."

For one part of Martyn's flock in the cantonments no pastoral care had ever yet been shown. With each European regiment of the East India Company there came a half-recognized following of Portuguese and Indian women of the camp. Military regulations forbade Martyn to give Christian marriage to these women and the soldiers. Yet many of the unions with them were lifelong and faithful; and in barracks full of nameless vice made on the whole for better living among men who were not, like the King's regiments, looking forward to a return from foreign service to their English sweethearts. Since marriage was against the regulations, it became one of the hardest tests for Martyn's "serious" soldiers to give their women an allowance and cease to live with them. The camp women, nominally Roman Catholic or Moslem, but virtually ignorant of all

faiths, had become an institution in cantonment life. For good
or evil they were there and quite unshepherded and Martyn
could not leave them without care.

I signified to the Colonel that I was ready to minister in
the country language to the native women belonging to his
soldiers of the European regiment, which he approved, but
told me it was my business to find them an order and not
his. So I issued my command to the sergeant-major to give
public notice that there would be divine service in the native
language on the morrow. The morrow came and . . . 200
women. Instead of the lessons I began Matthew. I could
not keep myself from attempting to expound a little, and
but a little.

The women come, I fear, rather because it is the wish
of their masters. The conversion of any of such despised
people is never likely perhaps to be of any extensive use in
regard to the natives at large; but they are a people com-
mitted to me by God, and as dear to Him as others; and next
in order after the English, they come within the expanding
circle of action.

"The expanding circle of action"—so in a single phrase he
reveals his outlook. His first step beyond the cantonments was
the setting up of four little primary schools in Patna and its
neighborhood. The well-greased urchins squatted more or less
contentedly, writing the Persian character in the sand or on
wooden slates and singing out the name of the letter as they
did so. "Thus they learn both to read and to write at the same
time." For such scholars as mastered the art of reading, Martyn
prepared in Hindustani the Sermon on the Mount and a little
book of the Parables of Christ with explanations, his own first
effort at Hindustani composition, corrected again and again
with loving and scrupulous care under the eye of his several
teachers.

I went on to Patna to see how matters stood with respect
to the school. Its situation is highly favourable, near an old
gate now in the midst of the city, and where three ways

meet. . . . The people immediately gathered round me in great numbers. I told them that what they understood by making people Christians was not my intention; I wished the children to be taught to fear God and to become good men. . . . The General observed to me one morning, that that school of mine made a very good appearance from the road; "but," said he, "you will make no proselytes." If that be all the opposition he makes I shall not much mind.

Such little schools, together with the habit of welcoming Indian friends to their houses, earned for Martyn and his friend Corrie (now stationed above him at the rock fortress of Chunar overhanging the Ganges) the title of "the black chaplains."

Martyn and Corrie wrote to one another once a week, sending up and down the river accounts of language difficulties, refractory schoolmasters, children's progress, or quaint ecclesiastical adventures in neglected communities where all manner of questions crept in about baptism, marriage and Christian burial, that had to be solved on the spot by the isolated young chaplains, in a country where there was no bishop, and David Brown himself, whom Martyn's letters call "the patriarch," was only in deacon's orders. Those unfettered weekly letters reveal, as more official documents could not, the single-heartedness of the men who wrote.

I trust we shall . ∴ . keep our eyes fixed on the fiery, cloudy pillar [wrote Martyn]. If you see it move when I do not, you will give me the signal, and I will strike my tent and go forward.

Second only to Corrie's letters and occasional visits, as the joy of Martyn's life, was a budget that came periodically from Calcutta. Buchanan with the mind of an ecclesiastical strategist and Brown with the care of a father for his isolated juniors, started together a kind of clerical club for keeping in touch with such chaplains as cared to study the whole Christian position in India. Each man was to send a monthly report of his own task; and other documents of interest were circulated with these, such as Buchanan's researches on the ancient Syrian Churches in the South, or the Latin correspondence which Martyn set up with the Roman Catholic fathers of the Propaganda. The group planned together to supplement the work at Serampore in Bible translation, and collected books on oriental tongues. Martyn heard of the club—"The Associated Clergy" they called it—with enthusiasm.

What a gratification it would be to me to lean my head across your long table to hear what you and your colleagues are planning. But I hope you will send me constant intelligence. Your wish to hear from me can never equal my desire for your letters. The Lord love you and yours.

Among the clerical details of the letters that went down to Aldeen, messages creep in for the children of the house that more than any other was home to him. "Dear little Hannah." "Dear child! Give my love to her." "Tell James and Charles that I expect to find them great scholars when next I see them." "So you intend the new little one for me; I accept the boon with pleasure."

Sorely did he need these Indian friendships, for home letters were few and distressing. His sister Laura died of consumption, and Sally though happily married (so happily that she did not often write to Henry) was also in poor health. And at last the answer came from Lydia. It came to one who dreamed at night of her coming, who after a day "hard at Arabic Grammar" sat at his door looking across the dusty barrack square with his heart at St. Hilary and Marazion, and who "hastened on the alterations" in his comfortless house and garden to make it fit for her.

October 24, 1807. An unhappy day; received at last a letter from Lydia, in which she refuses to come because her mother will not consent to it.

He began a letter to her at once:

My Dear Lydia,—

Though my heart is bursting with grief and disappoint-

ment, I write not to blame you. . . . You condemn yourself
for having given me, though unintentionally, encourage-
ment to believe that my attachment was returned. Perhaps
you have. I have read your former letters with feelings less
sanguine since the receipt of the last, and am still not surprised at the interpretation I put upon them. . . .

You do not assign among your reasons for refusal a want
of regard to me. . . . On the contrary you say that "*present
circumstances seen to you to forbid my indulging expectations.*" . . . Let me say I must be contented to wait till you
feel that the way is clear. . . . If there were no reason for
your coming here, and the contest were only between Mrs.
Grenfell and me, that is between her happiness and mine,
I would urge nothing further, but resign you to her. But I
have considered that there are many things that might
reconcile her to a separation from you (if indeed a separation is necessary, for if she would come along with you, I
should rejoice the more). First she does not depend on you
alone for the comfort of her declining years. She is surrounded by friends. She has a greater number of sons and
daughters honourably established in the world than falls
to the lot of most parents—all of whom would be happy in
having her amongst them. Again, if a person worthy of your
hand, and settled in England, were to offer himself, Mrs.
Grenfell would not have insuperable objections though it
did deprive her of her daughter. . . .

But the more I write and the more I think of you, the
more my affection warms, and I should feel it difficult to
keep my pen from expressions that might not be acceptable
to you.

Farewell! dearest, most beloved Lydia, remember your
faithful and ever affectionate

                                        H. MARTYN.

To David Brown:

It is as I feared. She refuses to come because her mother
will not give her consent. Sir, you must not wonder at my
pale looks when I receive so many hard blows on my heart.

... The queen's ware on its way out to me can be sold at an outcry or sent to Corrie. I do not want queen's ware or anything else now.

Was Mrs. Grenfell then so obdurate a parent? Or was Lydia only half in love with the man and half with the romance of being loved by him? A niece of Lydia tells us that the maternal opposition was real. "The connexion with the Martyns was distasteful" to Mrs. Grenfell who did not feel the families equally matched. And she adds, "I should say that my [great] aunt's ideas of paternal authority, up to middle life even, were extreme, as I well remember her expressing them."

An entry in Lydia's diary for May 20, 1806, is revealing:

My chief concern now is lest I should have given too much reason for my dear friend's hoping I might yet be prevailed on to attend to his request, and I feel the restraint stronger than ever, that having before promised, I am not free to marry. I paint the scene of his return, and whichever way I take, nothing but misery and guilt seems to await me.... Thou knowest these consequences of my regard for Thy dear saint were not intended by me, and that when first I regarded him otherwise than as a Christian brother, I believed myself free to do so, imagining him I first loved *united to another!*"

Charles Simeon, when he knew that Martyn's proposal had been sent home, took horse and rode into Cornwall, the erect precise old bachelor, a most quaint ambassador of love. But Lydia had already written her refusal when Simeon came. "May the Lord comfort me by him," her diary said as she prepared to meet him. She was edified by seeing "how a Christian lives." But the hope of his journey had not been her comfort so much as Henry Martyn's, and he came away depressed. Lydia admitted that she had "entered into a correspondence with Henry Martyn and expressed too freely her regard," but she once more paraded her scruple about Mr. John. He was not yet married and she was not free.

Simeon brushed it away and told her no objection was insuperable except her mother's prohibition, and that he was not disposed to regard as everlasting.

But he rode back depressed to Cambridge and sent out to India a letter which Martyn also found depressing; while Lydia, with her gift for prolonging emotional situations, wrote another letter "to bid him a last farewell."

It was well for Martyn that the greatest task of his life had just begun to fill his thoughts. The "Associated Clergy" in their desire for Bible translation had sent to him to ask if he would make a New Testament in Hindustani, the existing one being "unintelligible to the vulgar," and also a satisfactory version in Persian, since neither that of Mr. Colebrook, the great Sanskrit scholar, nor of the Serampore missionaries, had quite the idiomatic freedom that was needed. Already Martyn's uncomfortable church-like house was filled with strangely assorted guests who hung about him, now a learned Moslem from Patna, now a Roman Catholic father from the Propaganda, now a Jew from Babylon, now an Armenian from Jerusalem ("a very agreeable Armenian padre in a black little cassock exactly such as we wear, or ought to wear. I feel almost ashamed of my secular appearance before these very venerable and appropriate figures"), now a Prussian sergeant anxious about his soul. The strangest of them all was now to be added to the establishment—Sabat, as he called him, a wild Arab with a wild history whom Mr. Brown was despatching to be his assistant in translation work. The work was to be his joy and delight and Sabat an engrossing care, so that the Martyn of these days, his whole being concentrated on one end, undistracted by hope of human solace, moves in a strange calm, finding rest in toil, like the sleep of a spinning top.

"He wishes, if it please God," wrote Corrie on a visit in September, 1808, "to be spared on account of the translations, but with great earnestness he said, 'I wish to have my whole soul swallowed up in the will of God.'"[5]

And now at last a "budgerow" was coming up the Ganges bringing one who saw in vivid colors and knew how to write down what she saw.

Mrs. Sherwood, wife of the paymaster of the King's 53rd, had been a story-writer from her childhood and went about the world with a seeing eye and a warm, compassionate heart. Her *Fairchild Family* was to make her a nursery classic, but to her gossiping autobiography the Church owes all its most vivid pictures of Henry Martyn in India.

The chaplain at their last station, one of the "Associated Clergy," had given Mr. Sherwood a note for Martyn which he hurried to present on arrival, leaving his wife in the boat.

Mr. Martyn received Mr. Sherwood not as a stranger but as a brother. . . . As the sun was already low, he must needs walk back with him to see me. I perfectly remember the figure of that simple-hearted and holy young man, when he entered our budgerow. He was dressed in white, and looked very pale, which however was nothing singular in India; his hair, a light brown, was raised from his forehead which was a remarkably fine one. His features were not regular, but the expression was so luminous, so intellectual, so affectionate, so beaming with Divine charity, that no one could have looked at his features and thought of their shape or form,—the out-beaming of his soul would absorb the attention of every observer. There was a very decided air, too, of the gentleman about Mr. Martyn, and a perfection of manners which, from his extreme attention to all minute civilities, might seem almost inconsistent with the general bent of his thoughts to the most serious subjects. He was as remarkable for ease as for cheerfulness, and in these particulars his *Journal* does not give a graphic account of this blessed child of God. . . .

5 *Memoirs of Daniel Corrie*, p. 118.

Mr. Martyn invited us to visit him at his quarters at Dinapore, and we agreed to accept his invitation the next day. Mr. Martyn's house was destitute of every comfort, though he had multitudes of people about him. I had been troubled with a pain in my face, and there was not such a thing as a pillow in the house. I could not find anything to lay my head on at night but a bolster, stuffed as hard as a pin-cushion. We had not, as is normal in India, brought our own bedding from the boats. Our kind friend had given us his room; but I could get no rest. After breakfast Mr. Martyn had family prayers, which he commenced by singing a hymn. He had a rich, deep voice, and a fine taste for vocal music. After singing he read a chapter, explained parts of it and prayed extempore. Afterwards he withdrew to his studies. The conversion of the natives and the building up of the Kingdom of Christ were the great objects for which alone that child of God seemed to exist. It was chiefly while walking with him on the Plain, on the Saturday and Sunday evenings, that he opened his heart to us.

This however I can never forget, that Henry Martyn was one of the very few persons whom I have ever met who appeared never to be drawn away from one leading and prevailing object of interest. He did not appear like one who felt the necessity of contending with the world and denying himself its delights.[6]

She little guessed the struggles that had been the price of serenity for the man whom she described as "walking in this turbulent world with peace in his mind and charity in his heart."

---

[6] *Life of Mrs. Sherwood, chiefly autobiographical*, 1854, p. 340, etc.

Chapter 10

THE LINGUIST

There is a book printed at the Hirkara Press, called Celtic derivatives—this I want; also grammars and dictionaries of all the languages of the earth. I have one or both in Latin, Greek, French, Italian, Portuguese, Dutch, Hebrew, Rabbinical Hebrew, Chaldee, Syriac, Ethiopic, Samaritan, Arabic, Persian, Sanscrit, Bengalee, Hindoostanee.—HENRY MARTYN to DAVID BROWN, *October*, 1809.

Christianity has been, as it were, a great searchlight flung across the expanse of the religions; and in its blaze all the coarse, unclean and superstitious elements of the old faiths stood out, quite early, in painful vividness. India shuddered. . . . But the same light which exposed all the grossness gradually enabled men to distinguish the nobler and more spiritual elements in the religions.— J. N. FARQUHAR, *Modern Religious Movements in India*.

DURING Martyn's months in Calcutta he had missed meeting one of her most impressive personalities, Claudius Buchanan, the Vice-Provost of Fort William College.

After penniless wanderings with a violin, this sturdy and ambitious person had found his religion and his education among the evangelicals, who sent him to Cambridge. Amongst these men who laid all their stress on the religion of the heart, Buchanan bore a nature fitted for the career of a medieval prince-bishop. At home he might have been a notable prelate with the ear of statesmen, or, if the reproach of his religious school had debarred him from preferment, a redoubtable party polemic, an honest dealer of shrewd and smashing blows. In India, where he became Wellesley's trusted chaplain, the vast sweep of the problems of a continent delighted him, but the position of the handful of chaplains as an unconsidered appendage of the East India Company caused him grave distress.

His most placid period was during the few years that followed the opening of the College of Fort William, when under Wellesley's approving eye, he bent his great powers to the working out of its ambitious curriculum, and returned in the evening to a little wife for whom his rather condescending courtship had meant entrance into a wider world both of spirit and of intellect.

"It is a new Gospel to me," wrote the bride after listening to his instructions (and Buchanan was a luminous and inspiring teacher), "and I seem to live in a new world, differing far more from my old world than India differs from England." She could not admire him enough, and he approved of her. "Mrs. Buchanan is not yet nineteen," he wrote; "she has had a very proper education for my wife. She has docility of disposition, sweetness of temper, and a strong passion for retired life."[1] Under "my Mary's care," Claudius Buchanan spent some contented years, his days busy with college organization, his leisure occupied with schemes for the Church in India. He gave munificently from his salary to provide prizes in home universities and schools for odes or essays on subjects connected with Christianity in the East. To his Mary it was all most wonderful. But she died, and there passed from her rugged husband's life a touch of mellowing softness. He was in danger of hardening into the ecclesiastical strategist. He found, he tells us, "some consolation in writing a few lines to her memory in

[1] Pearson, *Memoirs of Claudius Buchanan*, p. 195.

the Hebrew, Syriac, Greek and Latin languages which I inscribed on a leaf of her own Bible."

That done he turned to survey India and her needs. In 1805 he published his *Memoir of the Expediency of an Ecclesiastical Establishment in British India.* After a clear and succinct statement of existing conditions he suggested as Grant and Brown had suggested before him) that India stood in dire need of an extension of "our happy establishment." If today lovers of India are out of love with the yoking of church and state, it must at least be acknowledged that Buchanan's proposals were daring in days when there were but three Anglican Church buildings in India, one in each presidency.[2]

"An archbishop is wanted for India," he wrote, "a sacred and exalted character, surrounded by his bishops, of ample revenue and extensive sway."

The sentence gives a picture of his mind, courageous, political, with a curious trust in externals.

As Martyn sailed up the Hooghly, Buchanan had passed down it, borne southwards on a survey whose wide sweep delighted his heart. He was on his way to enquire into the state of the Christian Church in South India and describe, in his *Christian Researches in India,* the ancient and then little known Syrian Church in Travancore.[3] When he returned his chests were stuffed with manuscripts and his head seething with schemes for Bible translation. He inspired David Brown, and together they started the club known as "The Associated Clergy" and inspired their brethren. Martyn in Dinapore gave his heartfelt admiration to the sweep of Dr. Buchanan's intellect and responded gratefully to the vigor of his leadership.

I feel bound to bless our God for the arrival of Dr.

---

[2] Three churches served by official chaplains of the Company. The Old Mission Church in Calcutta was an unofficial fourth.

[3] So late as 1831, a clergyman in Cornwall could write that "the Syrian Christians and their good Bishop are said to have no existence but in Buchanan's imagination."

Buchanan. To him I beg my kindest love, congratulations
on his personal preservation and thanks in the name of the
whole church for those MSS. he has brought away. My
expectation dwells on the lids of those chests; who knows
how important the acquisition of them may be?

It is a thought that has lately occurred to me that if Dr.
Buchanan is disposed to add another to his acts of munifi-
cence, he might revive Arabic and Oriental literature in Cambridge by establishing an annual prize there—Arabic and
Persian Bibles will soon have to undergo a rapid succession
of editions in England, and it is therefore desirable that
many persons should be at hand qualified to superintend the
printing of them.

Read Dr. Buchanan's correspondence with indescribable
joy. It will read like a romance in England and the people
of God will be in an ecstasy. But while so many things are
calling us to look abroad into the earth, may the people of
God mind their own hearts.

Letters now began to come up the river to Dinapore telling Martyn that Brown and Buchanan had comprehensive
schemes for "a British Propaganda for uniting all the talents
and industry in India." He could not at first get from his leaders
all the details of so grand a scheme, but they told him that his
part was to study Hindustani, Persian and Arabic. He obeyed.

Since your first letter, [he replied to David Brown]
commanding me to change my studies, the dust has been
collecting on Mr. Carey's great grammar, [Carey's Sanskrit
grammar was a work of one thousand pages] and the time
formerly devoted to Sanscrit is given to Persian and Hebrew.
I am too shallow in both of these to touch the Arabic yet.
In Hindoostanee translations I begin to feel my ground,
and can go on much faster than one moonshee can follow.
I have some thoughts of engaging another. . . . You have left
me still in the dark respecting the new Propaganda, but
I see enough to rejoice in the zeal that animates you all;
and in time I hope to catch the flame, and with you to
become a living sacrifice.

You can command me in any service which you can prove to be most favourable to the interests of Zion.

It was in June, 1807, that the definite proposal came to him from David Brown that he should translate the New Testament into Hindustani (or Urdu) and supervise translations into Persian and Arabic, with the help of two men whom they would send to him as specialists in these languages, Mirza Muhammad Fitrat of Benares and Nathaniel Sabat, an Arab educated at Baghdad.

David Brown enclosed a letter of Claudius Buchanan, which with Martyn's comment on it throws a curious sidelight on two characters:

In a note of Dr. Buchanan's to Mr. Brown, which he sent me is this: "We shall give to Martyn Mirza and Sabat, and announce to the world three versions of Scripture in Arabic, Persian and Hindoostanee, and a threefold cord is not easily broken." This plan of placing the two with me I accord to, as it seems to be the will of God; but annunciations I abhor, except the annunciation of Christ to the Gentiles.

So with diffidence, Martyn accepted the task hardly realizing at first that it might involve a situation of some little delicacy with his friends the Baptist missionaries at Serampore. Those men of heroic industry had taken for their province the translation and printing of the Scriptures in all the great tongues of India, Burma and China. The vastness of the task undertaken at Serampore can only be seen when it is realized that most of the missionaries there were self-taught in Greek and Hebrew; some of them only learning those tongues in India for the sake of the translations.

What men so handicapped produced is almost miraculous. In the face of their actual achievements anything seemed possible, and it was hard for them to realize all that was involved in a critical mastery of Greek or Hebrew, or the tentative nature of all first translations made by foreigners.

The friendship between the Baptist missionaries and the Anglican chaplains was real. "I believe you will not find many in England who have less bigotry and more friendship,"[4] wrote Carey of David Brown and Claudius Buchanan. Nonetheless, there was a little gallantly suppressed sore feeling in Serampore when the chaplains, in starting a Calcutta branch of the new Bible Society, made it clear that not all of the translations of the Society would of necessity be made at Serampore. There was a little tendency to resent the fact that official chaplains had the ear of the government while the Serampore mission was there on sufferance, and a little natural irritation at the rather lordly tone of Claudius Buchanan's announcements.

But Martyn in his distant station, full of appreciative love for the men of Serampore, and of warm friendship for his "brother" Marshman, was unconscious of the slightly strained feelings for the most part so gallantly controlled. He wrote quite freely and critically, as he would have written of the work of any Cambridge friend, about the quality of their Persian or Hindustani versions; and when his own translations were made, he in his turn showed the scholar's eagerness for all the criticism that his friends could give.

> Marshman sent me, you know, some translations. The general style of the Hinduwee is just adapted to the most general use—it will be understood by millions; but it ought to be done with more care. Many important sentences are wholly lost, from faults in the order or other small mistakes. The errors of the press are also very considerable. Remind them that the more haste the less speed.

Had Martyn been in Calcutta there would have been no misunderstanding. As it was, he learnt with something of a shock that his Serampore friends were chafed a little by Dr. Buchanan's entrusting to so young a "Daniel come to judgment" work which they had expected to see done in Serampore.

---

[4] E. Carey, *Memoir of William Carey*, p. 458.

"Most cordially do I wish to remain in the background to the end of life," he protested, and it was true. But it was too late to draw back from the great enterprise on which he was now launched, and for which his standard was the most exacting.

"Perspicuity is not the only requisite," he wrote; "a certain portion of grace is desirable and dignity indispensable. The Mahometans are more affected with sound than even the Greeks."

That a man of Martyn's critical power should, after so few years in the country, pass with calm assurance his judgment upon the translations of others and himself venture upon work for which he had so high a standard, is in any case remarkable. It is seen to be still more so when the difficulties of Hindustani study in Martyn's day are taken into account.

He found the language neglected of both eastern and western scholars, and on the whole despised by men of letters. A certain number of small phrase books, not without their modern counterparts, had been published to help civilians to talk to their servants. But Gilchrist and Colebrooke, the chief English representatives among the very few students who had done more serious work on Hindustani, poured candid scorn upon these works: "Hadley's insignificant catch-penny publication, a mere Tom Thumb," wrote Gilchrist, whose Grammar and Dictionary were standard books, and who with some complacency christened works of his own by such names as *The Anti-jargonist* or *The Hindee-Roman Orthoepigraphical Ultimatum*.

Martyn found then a great living language, the tongue of sixty millions, a tongue of hybrid origin, and not yet standardized by any universal work of literature.[5] He was making it more and more his own as Carey had made Bengali, and learn-

---

[5] Gilchrist only knew the names of thirty writers in Hindi; but by 1839, Garcin de Tassy had found the names of 750, including some twelfth century chroniclers in verse and some seventeenth century biographies of Hindu saints; but in pure literature the great mass of work was translation from Persian, Sanskrit or Arabic rather than original writing.

ing it always with reference to life, picking out with his pundit
the most used words in the vocabulary, or fetching in a story-
teller from the bazaar to be his teacher. This language, as yet
a tongue of intercourse rather than of books, he by a prophetic
instinct seized on as a great vehicle for religious truth. Time
has proved him right.

De même qu'en Europe les réformateurs Chrétiens ont
adopté les langues vivantes pour tout ce qui a rapport au
culte et à l'instruction religieuse; ainsi dans l'Inde, les chefs
des sectes modernes hindoues et mussulmanes se sont servis
généralement de l'hindoustani pour propager leur doctrines.
. . . Non seulement ils ont écrit leurs ouvrages en hindoustani, mais les prières que récitent leurs sectateurs, les
hymnes qu'ils chantent, sont en cet idiome.[6]

Just as in Europe, the Christian reformers adopted living languages for all which has to do with worship and religious instruction, so in India, the leaders of the modern
Hindu and Mussulman sects have generally made use of
Hindustani to propagate their doctrines . . . not only have
they written their works in Hindustani, but also the prayers
which their followers recite, and the hymns that they sing
are in this idiom.

All Martyn's critical skill went into his translation. He refused to be hurried.

You chide me for not trusting my Hindoostanee to the
press. I congratulate myself. Last week we began the correction of it: present—a Seid of Delhi, a Poet of Lucknow,
three or four literati of Patna, and Babir Ali in the chair.
Sabat and myself assessors. After four days' hard labour, five
hours each day, we reached to the end of the second chapter,
so when you will have a gospel I do not know.

When even his scrupulous taste was satisfied that the work
might be sent to the printer, its publication was delayed by a
fire at Serampore. And before the book had come into circula-

---

[6] Garcin de Tassy, *Préface de L'Histoire de la Littérature Hindoui et
Hindoustani.*

tion he had passed from India and the world. But he left it as a legacy of price. His patient consultations with Indian scholars had prepared for it a welcome. It was even set as a textbook in Mohammedan schools in Agra. Martyn himself was too scholarly to hope that his work was final. "I have too little faith in the instruments to believe that the first edition will be excellent," he told David Brown. Yet fifty years later it was written of Martyn's work: "All subsequent translations have, as a matter of course, proceeded upon it as a work of excellent skill and learning and rigid fidelity."[7] So he played his part in introducing the "Great Intruder" whose presence has meant so much of upheaval and stir in the spirit and brain of India.

Hour after hour as the work proceeded, Henry Martyn sat in close daily intercourse with Mohammedan scholars, and he learned to know as few men know the Moslem outlook upon life and God. "I read everything I can pick up about the Mohammedans," one of his letters said. But it was in long, eager conversations when dictionaries and reed pens were thrust aside in the interest of the moment, that he gained that astonishing mastery of Moslem ways of thought which won the respect of the doctors of Shiraz.

The conversations, often lasting late into the night, were startling to both parties. Henry Martyn never assumed the superior attitude of the man who cannot be ruffled. It was well seen that he cared with his whole soul for the matters he talked about and the men he talked with. "My tongue is parched," he wrote, "and my hand trembles from the violent onsets I have had this day with moonshee and pundit."

The *Journal* is full of Martyn's notes of conversations. For us they have significance as the first meeting after centuries (Martyn's immediate predecessor as a Christian apologist to Moslem India was a Portuguese Jesuit named Hieronymo

---

[7] Rev. R. C. Mather, LL.D., *Monograph on Hindustani Versions of the Old and New Testaments.*

Xavier, confessor of Christ at the court of the great Akbar) of two gigantic spiritual forces all unguarded and unaware, coming together with a first rude clash, unsoftened by intercourse and interaction of thought.

On the text "the time cometh, that he that killeth you shall think he doeth God service," he allowed and declared the lawfulness of putting infidels to death, and the certainty of salvation to believers dying in battle with infidels; and that it was no more strange than for the magistrate to have power to put an offender to death.

He said that prayer was not a duty among the Mahometans, that reading the numaz was merely the praising of God, and that when a servant after doing his master's service well, thought it a favourable opportunity for asking a favour, so the Moslem after doing his duty might ask of God riches or a son, or, if he liked, for patience in affliction. I have never felt so excited as by this dispute. It followed me all night in my dreams.

In the evening had long disputes with moonshee on the enjoyments of heaven, but I felt bitter mortification at not having command of language. However I was enabled to tell the moonshee one thing which rather confused him, namely, that my chief delight even now in the world was the enjoyment of God's presence.

He said with dreadful bitterness and contempt that after the present generation should pass away, a set of fools would perhaps be born, such as the gospel required.

Mirza said with great earnestness, "Sir, why won't you try to save me?" "Save you?" said I, "I would lay down my life to save your soul: what can I do?" He wished me to go to Phoolwari, the Mussulman college, and there examine the subject with the most learned of their doctors. I told him I had no objection.

So in long intimate talk and in the heat of argument with men who, in spite of themselves, grew to love him and if they sometimes left him in a passion returned again to work with him, Martyn began to learn the religious mind of Islam.

Above all things, [he wrote] *seriousness* in argument with them seems most desirable, for without it they laugh away the clearest proofs. Zeal for making proselytes they are used to and generally attribute to a false motive; but a tender concern manifested for their souls is certainly new to them, and seemingly produces corresponding seriousness in their minds.

But he knew the limitations of argument. "I wish a spirit of enquiry may be excited, but I lay not much stress upon *clear arguments*; the work of God is seldom wrought in this way."

The possibilities of his work in Arabic, the great religious tongue of the Moslem world, fired his imagination. As he began the Arabic New Testament he wrote, "So now, *favente Deo*, we will begin to preach to Arabia, Syria, Persia, India, Tartary, China, half of Africa, all the south coast of the Mediterranean and Turkey, and one tongue shall suffice for them all."

Brown and Buchanan sent to assist him in this work an extraordinary and tormenting character, whom they might have chosen expressly for the discipline of a saint. When Mrs. Sherwood first met him at Henry Martyn's dinner table, she poured out into her diary impressions of "that wild man of the desert":

Every feature in the large disk of Sabat's face was what we should call exaggerated. His eyebrows were arched, black, and strongly pencilled; his eyes dark and round, and from time to time flashing with unsubdued emotion, and ready to kindle to flame on the most trifling occasion. His nose was high, his mouth wide, his teeth large, and looked white in contrast with his bronzed complexion and fierce black mustachios. He was a large and powerful man, and generally wore a skull-cap of rich shawling, or embroidered silk, with circular flaps of the same hanging over each ear.

She expounded the details of his costume, silk attire, dagger, earrings and golden chain, as though she could not satisfy her own interest in that striking figure.

This son of the desert never sat in a chair without contriving to tuck up his legs under him on the seat, in attitude very like a tailor on his board. The only languages which he was able to speak were Persian, Arabic, and a very little bad Hindustani; but what was wanting in the words of this man was more than made up by the loudness with which he uttered them, for he had a voice like roaring thunder.

When that mighty voice first resounded through Martyn's bungalow, Sabat was midway in a wild career. An Arab of the Arabs, after a life of wanderings, passions, remorses, protestations, recantations, he was at last sewn up in a sack and dropped by orders of a Malayan prince to the bottom of the sea. But his last message, the message of a lonely prisoner writing in his own blood, declared that he died in the Christian faith. It had taken the death of one saint and the life of another to win him.

He was first driven to Christianity by remorse. The friend of his youth, with whom he had made the pilgrimage to Mecca, came across an Arabic Bible in Cabul, of all unlikely places, and far from any human teacher became a disciple of Christ. The change in him could not be hid, and he had to fly for his life. He came to Bokhara. Sabat his friend was in the city.

"I had no pity," said Sabat afterwards. "I delivered him up to Morad Shah the king." In the market-place they cut off one of the Christian's hands, Sabat the informer standing by in the crowd that watched. Then they pressed him to recant.

He made no answer [Sabat said afterwards], but looked up steadfastly towards heaven, like Stephen, the first martyr, his eyes streaming with tears. He looked at me, but it was with the countenance of forgiveness. His other hand was then cut off. But he never changed, and when he bowed his head to receive the blow of death all Bokhara seemed to say, "What new thing is this?"

Sabat could not ease himself of his friend's last look. In South India he read for himself the Book that had made a martyr. Then he all but bullied the chaplain, Dr. Kerr, until he gave him baptism. But in sooth, when Martyn first knew him Sabat had gone but a very little way along the Christian path. Martyn welcomed him with eagerness, but soon found that with his coming domestic peace was gone.

Sabat lives and eats with me and goes to his bungalow at night, so that I hope he has no care on his mind. On Sunday morning he went to church with me. While I was in the vestry, a bearer took away his chair from him, saying it was another gentleman's. The Arab took fire and left the church, and when I sent the clerk after him he would not return.

That was the precursor of many storms. At any moment Martyn looking up from his books would find flashing black eyes and a livid countenance glaring at him, while floods of angry Arabic or Persian poured forth in a voice of thunder demanding the instant dismissal of one of the servants or a fellow translator for some insult; or threatening eternal wrath because when he was late for dinner Martyn and his guests sat down without him. Naturally Sabat looms large in Martyn's journal.

Poor Sabat fell into one of his furious passions. I thought of St. James's words, "set on fire of hell." He thirsted for revenge on one of the servants who had offended him. He went and fetched his sword and dagger and with lips trembling with rage vowed he would kill the man.

Sabat has been tolerably quiet this week, but think of the keeper of a lunatic and you see me. After he got home at night he sent a letter complaining of a high crime and misdemeanour in some servant; I sent him a soothing letter and the wild beast fell asleep.

He said he would never live under the same roof with Mirza. Because he knew the servants would at last say, "This belongs to the Hindoostanee moonshee, and this to the Arabian moonshee" thus equalizing him with an Indian, and depriving him of his Arabian honour.

He is angry with me for not hating Mirza too, according

to the Arabian proverb—that a friend is an enemy of his friend's enemy.

Somehow Martyn managed to love his tormentor. "He is very dear to me. When I think of the circumstances of his life, and look upon him, I cannot help considering it as one of the most singular and interesting events of my life that I was brought acquainted with him. Indeed, everything in the East has been interesting to me." He sat with Sabat night after night when he was ill, and handled his tantrums with a gentleness and humility that few men could have shown.

If in any of our disputes I get the better of him, he is stung to the quick and does not forget it for days. So I avoid as much as possible all questions gendering strifes. If he sees anything wrong in me, any appearance of pride or love of grandeur, he tells me of it without ceremony, and thus he is a friend indeed. He describes so well the character of a missionary that I am ashamed of my great house and mean to sell it at the first opportunity and take the smallest quarters I can find.

Most charming is Martyn's humorous tolerance of Sabat's intellectual bombast.

He loves as a Christian brother [Martyn wrote], but as a logician, he holds us all in supreme contempt. He assumes all the province of reasoning as his own by right, and decides every question magisterially. He allows Europeans to know a little about Arithmetic and Navigation, but nothing more. Dear man! I smile to observe his pedantry. Never have I seen such an instance of dogmatical pride, since I heard Dr. Parr preach his Greek sermon at St. Mary's, about the τὸ ὄν.

He looks on the missionaries at Serampore as so many degrees below him in intellect that he says he could write so deeply on a text that not one of them would be able to follow him. So I have challenged him in their name, and to-day he has brought me the first half of his essay or sermon on a text: with some ingenuity it is the most idle display of schoolboy pedantic logic you ever saw.

When a young officer told Martyn that some friends had fooled him about a supposed text in the Bible which said that men should become bears, Sabat rushed into the conversation. "Oh, if there is such an expression in the Word of God it must be true," he said, *"and we will prove it by logic."*[8]

But as the translation proceeded, Martyn found it impossible ever to convince this logician of a flaw in his own work.

> Sabat would often contend for a whole morning [Mrs. Sherwood says] about the meaning of an unimportant word; and Mr. Martyn has not unseldom ordered his palanquin and come over to us, to get out of the sound of the voice of the fierce Ishmaelite.

"If all the Indian moonshees in Calcutta should unite," said Martyn, "I fear Sabat would not value their opinion a straw. 'He did not come from Persia to India to learn Persian.' "

In Arabic, Sabat's grammar needed watchfulness, but his style was nervous and idiomatic. In Persian his writing was more than usually interlarded with Arabic phrases; and Martyn became convinced that it was faulty in style, and that the final New Testament translation in Persian would not be made outside Persia itself.

> Before the second edition of the Arabic what say you, [he wrote to David Brown] to my carrying the first with me to Arabia, having under the other arm the Persian to be examined at Shiraz or Teheran?

So he planned, his mind moving with an almost gay freedom at this beloved task. He speaks with firm assurance, always the master and never the slave of meticulous grammatical details. He criticizes the setting out of Arabic grammar: "What Erpenius has comprehended in a couple of pages Mr. B. has wire-drawn through a folio." He is equally frank over other men's translations. In Arabic—"The New Testament we have, edited by Erpenius, is indescribably bad; it is not a translation

---

but a paraphrase, and that always wrong." Greatly daring, he will even pass independent judgment on the English Authorized Version. "It appears to me that the two royal authors have suffered more from the plebian touch of their interpreters, than even the prophets or any others but Job." Nay, the Martyn of these days is audacious. "The books which you mention I shall expect with impatience. Street's version; Hammond who is a learned man. Horne is all words. Next to oriental translations, my wish and prayer is, that I may live to give a new English version of the Bible from Job to Malachi. Such are some of my modest desires."

A mind like Martyn's could not be incessantly busy with the details of half a dozen languages, without enquiry as to their relation to one another and the nature of all language.

I suppose [he wrote to Corrie] that of all things in the world language is that which submits itself most obsequiously to our examination, and may therefore be understood better than anything else. For we can summon it before us without any trouble, and make it assume any form we please, and turn it upside down and inside out, and yet I must confess the more I look at it the more I am puzzled. I seem to be gazing with stupid wonder at the legerdemain of a conjuror.

In the story of linguistic speculation he stood at a time of change and boundless expectation. The eighteenth century had wondered whether the gift of speech was given to man ready-made or whether it grew. Herder (*Origin of Language,* 1772) supposed that it grew, since nothing direct from the hand of the Almighty could be so illogical and full of caprice as any human speech. Then empire in the East gave a new direction to men's thoughts of language.

Coeurdoux, a French missionary, had sent to the French *Institut* in 1767 a memoir calling attention to the similarity of many Sanskrit words, and some of its flexions, with Latin. And English Sanskrit scholars, Sir Charles Wilkins and Sir William

nes, did their part in creating a tendency to make Sanskrit
e mother of tongues. And so with the new century scholars
ere busy with the genealogy of languages. Men felt that they
ere on the verge of some great and unifying discovery. Mar-
n like the rest was on tiptoe with expectation. He rejected
nskrit speculations and looked on Hebrew, which for Sir
'illiam Jones was "rather an object of veneration than de-
;ht," as the possible norm and fountain of language.

I have been seized with a philological mania again [he
wrote to a friend], and after passing some hours in sleepless
cogitation, was obliged to get up to examine all the Greek
prepositions, and see if I could not derive them all from the
Hebrew.

I am glad you take a liking to Hebrew. It transports me
at present. My speculations occupy me night and day....
I carry these thoughts to bed with me, and there am I all
night long in my dreams tracing etymologies, and measuring
the power of some Hebrew letter.

I sit hours alone, contemplating this mysterious language. I sometimes say in my vain heart, I will either make
a deep cut in the mine of philology or I will do nothing.

How do you go on in Hebrew? Though my duty calls
me to other languages, I am perpetually speculating on that,
and the nature of language in general. It goes against the
grain with me now to read a little Arabic or Greek, as much
as it once did to cram a proposition I did not understand.
How or by what magic is it, that we convey our thoughts to
one another with such ease and accuracy? Lately I was
called on duty to a distant station, the way to which was
chiefly on the river. There, far removed from noise, and
everything European, I glided along, speculating with as
much subtilty as the visionary γυμνοσοφοι [ill-clad hermits]
who pursue their reveries on the banks. These hermits
literally forsake the world; they build a little hut close to
the margin of the river and there they sit and muse....
It is probable that for some time to come, as long as I am

engaged in translation, my thoughts will be rather tinged with philology.... But on my own mind I perceive that I must keep a tight rein. I beg your prayers that after having begun in the Spirit I may not leave off in the flesh.

Truly love is better than knowledge. Much as I long to know what I seek after, I would rather have the smallest portion of humility and love than the knowledge of an arch-angel.

Chapter 11

CAWNPORE

This, sir, is a climate which tries the mind like a furnace. Deterioration seems inherent in Indian existence.—LETTER *of* CLAUDIUS BUCHANAN *from Barrackpore.*

There was a hollow, fearful whistling, like human voices, in the blast; and Mr. Martyn said, "It was often in his mind, that the prince of the power of the air was permitted to inflict, not only all storms and tempests, but all diseases and sufferings on man in the flesh."—MRS. SHERWOOD's *Autobiography.*

THE burning winds of the spring in Cawnpore were blowing, and the Sherwood family stationed there with the 53rd Regiment were existing as best they might. Every outer door was shut, and behind grass screens they sat almost in darkness, under the punkah in the central hall as the most endurable place. Captain Sherwood had his table with account books and journal before him. In a side room was the family's faithful factotum, Sergeant Clarke, copying manuscripts. In another side room a silent ayah chewed and chewed as she kept guard over the white-faced baby on the floor with her toys—the

---

[1] Mrs. Sherwood is virtually the writer of this chapter. All the quotations from her are taken from her autobiography, *Life of Mrs. Sherwood, chiefly autobiographical,* 1854.

motherless Sally rescued by Mrs. Sherwood from starvation and now creeping back to life.

The Sherwoods had no little child of their own in the spring of 1809; the two babies born to them in India had died like primroses in an oven: but the motherly woman had hopes of another child in her nursery after the rains. Meanwhile the hot days dragged on wearily. Mrs. Sherwood lay on the sofa, a table beside her, with pen and ink and any books she could lay hold of. "Somebody lent me *Robinson Crusoe,* and Mr. Sherwood picked up an old copy of Sir Charles Grandison." On a tiny chair by that sofa, with a tiny table beside it, sat the demurest of little quiet girls, the orphan, Annie Childe, another babe whom Mrs. Sherwood had rescued as a little drugged starveling from a heartless nurse. Cared for and daintily clad, she looked "a delicate little lady," and passed the long hot days placidly enough at Mrs. Sherwood's side.

"I had my orphan, my little Annie, always by me. . . . I had given her a good-sized box, painted green, with a lock and key. She was the neatest of all neat little people, somewhat faddy and particular. She was the child of all others to live with an ancient grandmother. Annie's treasures were few, but they were all contained in her green box. She never wanted occupation: she was either dressing her doll or finding pretty verses in her Bible, marking the places with an infinitude of minute pieces of paper."

They were sitting so on the morning of May 30, 1809, the silence only broken by the click of the punkah and the moaning of the hot wind outside, when, the lady tells us, "We suddenly heard the quick steps of many bearers. Mr. Sherwood ran out to the leeward of the house, and exclaimed, 'Mr. Martyn!'

"The next moment I saw him lead in that excellent man, and saw our visitor, a moment afterwards, fall down in a fainting fit. . . . In his fainting state Mr. Martyn could not have retired to the sleeping-room which we caused to be prepared immediately for him, because we had no means of cooling any sleeping room so thoroughly as we could the hall. We therefore had a couch set for him in the hall. There he was laid, and very ill he was for a day or two. The hot winds left us and we had a close suffocating calm. Mr. Martyn could not lift his head from the couch."

Martyn had been transferred by the military authorities from Dinapore to Cawnpore in April 1809, at the hottest moment of the year. He left Sabat and his pretty wife Ameena (a couple who spent their time together in noisy quarrels) to come up by water with all the household goods, and he set out by palanquin, saying goodby to Dinapore with some regret.

> Preparation for departure does not disturb and disorder me as it used to do. The little things of this world come more as matters of course. Still I find it necessary to repeat often in the day, "Thou wilt keep him in perfect peace whose mind is staid on Thee." My men seem to be in a more flourishing state than they have yet been. About thirty attend every night. I have had a delightful party this week of six young men who I hope will prove to be true soldiers of Christ.

That three-hundred-mile palanquin journey in the heat was an absurdity. "I transported myself with such rapidity to this place, that I nearly transported myself out of the world," he told David Brown. At first he traveled by night only. But Mrs. Sherwood explains that between Allahabad and Cawnpore there was no halting-place, and Martyn when he fainted in her hall had been traveling for two days and two nights without a pause, slung in a palanquin that could do nothing to keep out winds that burnt like fire from a furnace.

She took care of him, and he had one of his rare glimpses of domestic life.

"When Mr. Martyn got a little better he became very cheerful, and seemed quite happy with us all about him. He commonly lay on his couch in the hall during the morning, with many books near to his hand, and amongst these always a Hebrew Bible and a Greek Testament. Soon, very soon, he began to talk to me of what was passing in his mind, calling to me at my table to tell me his thoughts.

"In a very few days he had discerned the sweet qualities of the orphan Annie, and had so encouraged her to come about him that she drew her chair, and her table, and her green box to the vicinity of his couch. She showed him her verses, and consulted him about the adoption of more passages into the number of her favorites. What could have been more beautiful than to see the Senior Wrangler and the almost infant Annie thus conversing together, while the elder seemed to be in no way conscious of any condescension in bringing his mind down to the level of the child's?

"When Mr. Martyn lost the worst symptoms of his illness he used to sing a great deal. He had an uncommonly fine voice and fine ear; he could sing many fine chants, and a vast variety of hymns and psalms. He would insist upon it that I should sing with him, and he taught me many tunes, all of which were afterwards brought into requisition; and when fatigued himself, he made me sit by his couch and practise these hymns."

And so the good woman mothered him, knowing that she had found a saint, but a little concerned because he did not seem "very distinct in all his religious views" (there is no indistinctness about the views of the writer of the *Fairchild Family*), and because of a certain vague trustfulness over money. He sent off a coolie to draw for him long arrears of salary, involving the payment to the messenger of some hundreds of pounds counted out in silver into cotton bags. "Mr. Martyn said in a quiet voice to us, 'The coolie does not come with my money. I was thinking this morning how rich I should be; and now I should not wonder in the least if he has run off and taken my treasure with him.' 'What!' we exclaimed. 'Surely you have not sent a common coolie for your pay?' 'I have,' he replied."

The money arrived; and Martyn was at a loss to understand his friends' concern about it.

But he was now recovering and must get to the work of his new station. His first impressions, outside the Sherwoods' bungalow, were not cheering.

> I do not like this place at all. There is no church, not so much as the fly of a tent; what to do I know not, except to address Lord Minto in a private letter.

> I feel fixed at the last place where I shall ever live in India, and sometimes look with interest at the road that leads to Cabul and Candahar [Kabul and Kandahar, both in Afghanistan].... I hear of a Mrs. A. as one who is religious, and is even suspected of singing Psalms of a Sunday. Such flagrant violations of established rules seem to mark her for one of our fraternity.

His first service in Cawnpore, himself still a tottering convalescent, was held out of doors on the parade on May 14.

> Two officers dropped down, and some of the men. They wondered how I could go through the fatigue. When I looked at the other end of the square which they had formed, I gave up all hopes of making myself heard, but it seems they did hear. There are above a hundred men in the hospital. What time shall I find for doing half what ought to be done?

Already he had made friends, as was his way in every place, with a small group of "serious" soldiers. Mrs. Sherwood takes up her pen again:

"As soon as Mr. Martyn could in any way exert himself, he made acquaintance with some of the pious men of the regiment (the same poor men whom I have mentioned before, who used to meet in ravines, in huts, in woods and in every wild and secret place they could find, to read and pray and sing); and he invited them to come to him in our house, Mr. Sherwood making no objection. The time first fixed was an evening after parade, and in consequence they all appeared at the appointed hour, each carrying their *mora* (a low seat), and their books tied up in pocket-handkerchiefs. In this very unmilitary fashion they were all met in a body by some officers. It was with some difficulty that Mr. Sherwood could divert the storm of displeasure.... These poor good men were received by Mr. Martyn in his own apartment; and a most joyful meeting he had with them. We did not join the party, but we heard them praying and singing and the sound was very sweet. Mr. Martyn then promised them that when he had got a house he would set aside a room for them, where they might come every evening."

Martyn bought a house near the Sepoy lines. "Now, Cawnpore is about one of the most dusty places in the world," said Mrs. Sherwood, who disapproved his choice, "and the Sepoy lines are the most dusty part of Cawnpore." His compound was not near enough to his friends, but it had its advantages, for its "funereal avenue" of palm trees and aloes that rattled in the hot wind, led not to one bungalow but two. This was admirable. Sabat and the goods arrived, and the Arab and his lady were bestowed in the lesser bungalow, while Martyn inhabited the larger, or such part of it as was not filled with "pious soldiers" reading the Bible, scribes copying translations amidst piles of manuscripts and dictionaries, or a medley of guests who gathered from no one knows where. "A vast number and variety of huts and sheds formed one boundary of the compound; these were concealed by the shrubs. But who would venture to give any account of the heterogeneous population which occupied these buildings? For besides the usual complement of servants found in and about the houses of persons of a certain rank in India, we must add to Mr. Martyn's household a multitude of pundits, munshis, schoolmasters and poor nominal Christians, who hung about him because there was no other to give them a handful of rice for their daily maintenance; and most strange was the murmur which proceeded at times from this ill-assorted and discordant multitude." Such was Mrs. Sherwood's impression of the ménage.

Sabat was as pleased as a child with his new mansion, and work went on apace.

> He is gentle and almost as diligent as I could wish [said Martyn]. Everything seems to please him. His bungalow joins mine, and is very neat; so from morning to night we work together, and the work goes forward. The first two or three days he translated into Arabic and I was his scribe; but this being too fatiguing to me, we have been since that at the Persian.

The spurt did not last long.

> Sabat does not work half hard enough for me. I feel grieved and ashamed that we produce so little, but the fault is not mine. I would never willingly be employed about anything else, but Sabat has no ardour. The smallest difficulty discourages him, the slightest headache is an excuse for shutting up his books, and doing nothing for days.

> Sabat creeps on, and smokes his hookah with great complacency if he gets through a chapter a day. I grieve at this hireling spirit, but for peace sake I have long ceased to say anything.

At sunset the translation was dropped, and the frail linguist, whose ardor had exhausted the energies of his various assistants, went out for exercise. Two evenings in the week he spent with his soldiers. On the others he was apt to gravitate towards that friendly household of the Sherwoods. For the soaring linguist was very human. Mrs. Sherwood took her airing in an open palanquin, wearing "a lace cap with Europe ribbons," while Captain Sherwood rode, and Martyn would often arrive at their bungalow before his hosts returned. "Two or three times a week he used to come on horseback, with the sais running by his side. He sat his horse as if he were not quite aware that he was on horseback, and he generally wore his coat as if it were falling from his shoulders. When he dismounted, his favourite place was in the veranda with a book, till we came in from our airing. And when we returned many a sweet and long discourse we had whilst waiting for our dinner. Mr. Martyn often looked up to the starry heavens, and spoke of those glorious worlds of which we know so little now, but of which we hope to know so much hereafter. He used often to show me the pole-star just above the line of the horizon; and I have seen the moon when almost new looking like a ball of ebony in a silver cup."

In August, 1809, a little daughter was born to the Sherwoods, whom they determined to name after their baby Lucy who had died. When Martyn came for the christening in the cool of the evening, the family had not yet returned from the sunset airing. He told the servants to set in readiness a table and water in a cool corner of the long veranda, not knowing that he had chosen for the christening the very spot where the first little daughter had been laid dying on a mattress to catch what air there was.

"Never can I forget the solemn manner with which Mr. Martyn went through the service, or the beautiful and earnest blessing which he implored for my baby, when he took her in his arms after the service was concluded. I still fancy that I see that child of God as he looked down tenderly on the gentle babe, and then looked upwards."

"This babe in infancy had so peculiar a gentleness of aspect that Mr. Martyn called her Serena." Her parents decided to go down to Calcutta in October and take the advice of the best doctor in India as to whether they could rear her in Cawnpore. They broke up their household in the full expectation that the mother would be sent home to save her baby's life, and two English ladies, one of them Corrie's sister who had arrived to join her brother, took from Mrs. Sherwood the charge of the small orphans she had rescued.

The Sherwoods' last week was spent in Martyn's house. They slept in their houseboats and went to him for breakfast. "In the mornings we all used to set out together, children and servants, to go up from the river to the house, whilst the dew lay yet upon the grass; for it was the beginning of the cold season, and the many aromatic flowers of that southern climate shed their perfume in the air."

The children and ayahs went to rooms set apart for them, and Captain and Mrs. Sherwood went into the hall, where Martyn nearly always had some guest for breakfast. "We often sat long over breakfast." Then Martyn turned to his translation, and the Sherwoods went about their business.

"Mr. Martyn's house was peaceful, holy and cheerful."

At the sunset airing with the day's work done, Martyn enjoyed his friends again, and on their last Sunday he arranged a little chapel with his careful nicety of touch in one of the long verandas, where he gave the Communion to the Sherwoods and to sixteen of his "pious soldiers."

When he had seen them down to their boats for the last time, "blessing our little children," he returned to Cawnpore a lonely man. It is probable that the army society of the place was terrified of Martyn. Otherwise it is hard to explain the gaucherie of their manners to the padre.

> It is extraordinary how much I am left to myself here. In the midst of multitudes I am a solitary.... The pride of my heart has discovered itself very strongly since I entered this new circle. They sometimes take no more notice of me than a dog, at other times vouchsafe a dignified condescension, so that were it not to become all things to all men in order to save some, I should never trouble them with my company. But how then should I be like Christ? I would rather pass my time with children if I had the choice.

In his loneliness his thoughts would not be kept from Lydia. "I love so true that though it is now the fifth year since I parted from the object of my affections, she is as dear to me as ever," he wrote to Cousin Tom Hitchins in that month when the Sherwoods left. Next month (November, 1809) Mr. Simeon's letter brought him news that his sister Sally was dying of consumption. He could not hope that a letter would reach her. He began one impulsively; then turned and wrote instead to her husband: "God make us both from this time live more as pilgrims and strangers upon the earth."

His home letters now let slip the fact that this man with his gigantic plans knew well enough, when he gave it a thought, that the disease which had killed all his near relatives was working in him also. The dusty lines in Cawnpore were trying to him, and he began to confess that every sermon he preached left him in pain. "There is something in the air at the close of the rains so unfavourable that public speaking at that time is a violent strain upon the whole body.... I am sorry to say that my strength for public speaking is almost gone. My ministrations among the Europeans at this station have injured my lungs," he told David Brown.

They were difficult ministrations even for a strong man. Soldiers fainted at the out-of-door parades, and ladies chattered in the General's drawing-room where he went on for a second service. He decided to ask for the use of the billiard room "which is better than the ball-room," but they gave him the riding school instead. "The effluvium was such as would please only the knights of the turf." When the rains came, out-of-door parades had to be scratched. "The General has not yet forwarded to Government the proposal for a church," Martyn wrote after long delay. But he at length prevailed on the authorities to adapt an ordinary bungalow near his own for church services. He watched eagerly over the alterations, but they went slowly. In December, 1809, when every service was leaving him exhausted, Sabat challenged him to add to his labors another sermon, to the strangest congregation that ever gathered to listen to a saint. Beggars of all sorts found their way to Martryn's house, among them crowds of religious mendicants. To save time he gave out that his alms would be given only once a week. The news went round the beggar world, and every Sunday his gates were thrown open to admit a motley crowd, to whom he gave small coins or rice.

Sabat said to me yesterday, "Your beggars are come, why do not you preach to them? it is your duty." I made excuses. But the true cause is shame. I am afraid of exposing myself to the contempt of Sabat, my servants, and the mob, by attempting to speak in a language which I do not speak well. This therefore I desire to keep ever before my mind, that I must get to the Kingdom through great contempt.

Next Sunday:

In the afternoon the beggars came, to the number of above four hundred, and by the help of God, I determined to preach to them though I felt as if I were leading to execution.

There was an open space in his garden, green after the rain, with a raised platform of lime at its center. Here the beggars were seated, and Martyn climbed on to the platform and told them "that he gave with pleasure what alms he could afford, but wished to give them something better—the knowledge of God."

The Sherwoods, encouraged by doctors to remain in India, returned to Cawnpore that December. When Henry Martyn rode to welcome his friends, "he looked, we thought, very ill, and complained of what he called a fire burning in his breast."

But he was full of his new venture with the beggars, though he "looked forward to the next attempt with some dread." Mrs. Sherwood went to see what he was doing. She was amazed.

"No dreams," she said, "or visions excited in the delirium of a raging fever could surpass these realities. They were young and old, male and female, tall and short, athletic and feeble, bloated and wizened; some clothed in abominable rags, some nearly without clothes; some plastered with mud and cow-dung;

others with matted, uncombed locks streaming down to their heels; others with heads bald or scabby; every countenance being hard and fixed, as it were, by the continual indulgence of bad passions; the features having become exaggerated, and the lips blackened with tobacco or blood-red with the juice of the henna.... One little man used to come in a small cart drawn by a bullock. The body and limbs in general of this poor creature were so shrivelled as to give him, with his black skin and large head, the appearance of a gigantic frog. Another had his arm fixed above his head, the nail of the thumb piercing through the palm of the hand. Another, and a very large man, had all his ribs and the bones of his face externally traced with white chalk, which, striking the eye in relief above the dark skin, made him appear as he approached like a moving skeleton.... Such was the view of human nature presented every Sunday evening in Mr. Martyn's compound."

Mrs. Sherwood stood behind Martyn on the raised platform that evening and on many following Sundays.

"We had to make our way through a dense crowd, with a temperature often rising above 92°, whilst the sun poured its burning rays upon us through a lurid haze of dust. So many monstrous and diseased limbs, and hideous faces, were displayed before us and pushed forward for our inspection, that I have often made my way to the *chabootra* with my eyes shut, whilst Mr. Sherwood led me. I still imagine that I hear the calm, distinct, and musical tones of Henry Martyn as he stood raised above the people."

His preaching was as simple as he could make it.

I shuffled and stammered and indeed am persuaded that there were many sentences the poor things did not understand at all. I mentioned Gunga (Ganges), "a good river," but there were others as good. God loves Hindoos, but does He not love others also? He gave them a good river, but to others as good. All are alike before God. This was received with applause. On the work of the fourth day, "Sun and

moon are lamps. Shall I worship a candle in my hand? As a
candle in the house so is the sun in the sky." Applause from
the Mohammedans. There were also hisses, but whether
these betokened displeasure against me or the worship of the
sun, I do not know. I then charged them to worship Gunga
and sun and moon no more, but the honour they used to
give to them, henceforward to give to God their Maker.

They were no dispassionate audience. Often as he preached
bursts of anger would arise, with "shouts and curses and deep
and lengthened groans, hissings and gestures till Mr. Martyn
was compelled to silence. But when the storm passed away
again might he be heard going on where he had left off, in the
same calm, steadfast tone, as if he were incapable of irritation
from the interruption. Mr. Martyn himself assisted in giving
each person his pice (copper) after the address was concluded;
and when he withdrew to his bungalow I have seen him drop
almost fainting on a sofa, for he had, as he often said, a slow
inflammation burning in his chest, and one which he knew
must eventually terminate his existence."

All that spring they watched him tear himself to pieces;
cheerful enough when he came round after a day of translation with the sense of something done, and picked up the baby
Lucy for a game before she went to bed; but plainly enough
a sick man every Sunday when the four services left him half-
fainting with pain and exhaustion.

Accounts of Sally's death reached him in that spring of
1810, and with them an unexpected joy. Lydia told herself that
he had now no sister of his own to correspond with and wrote
offering to take a sister's place if he would accept a correspondence on that basis. He was overjoyed. "My long, long-lost Lydia
has consented to write to me again," he told David Brown.

To her he was explicit about his health.

Study never makes me ill—scarcely ever fatigues me—
but my lungs! death is seated there; it is speaking that kills
me. Nature intended me for chamber-counsel, not for a

pleader at the bar. But the call of Jesus Christ bids me cry
aloud, and spare not.

You know how apt we are to overstep the bounds of
prudence, when there is no kind monitor at hand to warn
us of the consequence.

When the hot winds blew again in April he had to confess
to David Brown and Corrie that taking a service always left
him with pain in his chest and hardly able to speak above a
whisper. The references to his health only occurred casually
in letters crowded with details about the translations.

Old Mirza gives me more satisfaction than anyone in
Cawnpore. He seems to take great pleasure in seeing an
intricate sentence in the Epistles unravelled.

I should be more contented to depart if I had finished
the translation of the Epistles.

Or even the translation is forgotten while the scholar moves
in another world.

He seems to move in a world by himself [he wrote of
St. Paul], and sometimes to utter the unspeakable words
such as my understanding discerneth not; and when I turn
to commentators, I find that I have passed out of the spiritual
to the material world, and have got among men like myself.

But Corrie knew his friend and knew that the health question was serious. "It perhaps would be of importance," he wrote
to David Brown, "to get Martyn to resign the service and give
himself to the translating and printing of the Scriptures. It is
clear that his present labours will bring an early period to his
life: I scarce know how to write it, but so it is."

Corrie took boat for Cawnpore to see for himself what could
be done. He found Martyn every evening, after ever so little
exertion in speaking, reduced to loss of voice, pain in his chest,
and such restless fatigue as kept him awake, or troubled his
sleep with confused and distressing dreams ("was walking with
Lydia, both much affected, and speaking on the things dearest
to us both. I awoke, and behold it was a dream"); yet buoyed

up with hope and plans for his work. "My church is nearly ready for the organ and the bell. . . . My work at present is evidently to translate; hereafter I may itinerate."

"This morning Martyn said he thought a month's silence would entirely restore him." Corrie did what he could. With the General's consent he moved himself and his good sister to Cawnpore to nurse Martyn and take his services for him.

> *July* 31, 1810. On my first arrival [Corrie writes] he recruited greatly for a fortnight, but is now, to say the least, at a stand. He has agreed to go on the river to try the effect of change and solitude. He objects to going to sea at present. ... The truth is he expects the New Testament will soon be done in Arabic. Your applications for Arabic have set him to work anew with an ardour that nothing but death can repress.

For a few months of bliss Martyn became, far more than he was aware, the central figure of a sort of double household. Corrie, that understanding person, was with him, taking services and setting him free for the beloved translation. Miss Corrie was with the Sherwoods, and in the evening there were the ladies to take for an airing. Of those evenings Mrs. Sherwood writes: "I often went out with Mr. Martyn in his gig, during that month, when he used to call either for me or Miss Corrie, and whoever went with him went at the peril of their lives. He never looked where he was driving, but went dashing through thick and thin, being always occupied in reading Hindoostanee by word of mouth, or discussing some text of Scripture. I certainly never expected to have survived a lesson he gave me in his gig, in the midst of the plain at Cawnpore, on the pronunciation of one of the Persian letters."

The two households had so many meals together that they found with amusement that the servants were making common cause, and the same cheese appeared on the table at either house. There were hymn-singings in the bungalow, and evening services for which they went together, "not omitting the children," into the unfinished church near Martyn's house.

"We are inexpressibly happy together," said Corrie, and for a time they thought that Martyn was rallying. He himself, engrossed with the great work and delighted with his friends, was generally far too preoccupied to realize that he was ill. When a bout of pain and faintness gave him pause, and he stopped to realize that the family disease had clutched him, he was probably less concerned about it than any of the circle that watched him anxiously. "He spoke of being in a consumption in the tone in which most people would speak of a legacy," said Corrie.

As he flagged more and more they decided to take him on the river. They hired a pinnace in which to go together. Mrs. Sherwood describes the mornings in the cabin:

"Mr. Martyn sent a quantity of books, and used to take possession of the sofa, with all his books about him. He was often studying Hebrew, and had huge lexicons lying by him. Little Lucy used always to make her way to Mr. Martyn when he was by any means approachable. On one occasion I remember seeing the little one, with her grave yet placid countenance, her silken hair and shoeless feet, step out of the inner room of the pinnace with a little mora, which she set by Mr. Martyn's couch, then mounting on it, she got upon the sofa which was low, and next seated herself on his huge lexicon. He would not suffer her to be disturbed, though he required his book every instant."

Still he flagged, and they told him he must go to sea. He would not believe them at first; but as the Arabic translation drew to a close and criticisms reached him of Sabat's style, he turned seawards eagerly. If they wanted him to go to sea, why not sail to Arabia and make before he died the perfect version of the Arabic New Testament? On August 22, 1810, he wrote to David Brown:

DEAREST SIR,—

Shall I come down, or shall I not? I have an aversion to Calcutta, with all the talking and preaching to which I shall be tempted there; yet you insist upon it, and sooner or later I must pass through you to the sea, or I shall be buried here. ...I want silence and diversion, a little dog to play with; or what would be best of all, a dear little child....Perhaps you could learn when the ships usually sail for Mocha. I have set my heart upon going there; I could be there and back in six months.

H. MARTYN

Two days later another letter followed.

Henceforward I have done with India. Arabia shall hide me till I come forth with an approved New Testament in Arabic. I do not ask your advice because I have made up my mind.

...So now, dear Sir, take measures for transmitting me with the least possible delay, detain me not, for the King's business requires haste. My health in general is good, but the lungs are not strong. One loud dispute brings on pain.

Yours ever affectionately,

HENRY MARTYN.

The General at Cawnpore granted unlimited leave of absence to one whom he probably looked on as a dying man.

Martyn's last day with his friends was a Sunday. They could not take their eyes off him, believing that they should see his face no more. There was a triumphant glow about him, for it was a great day. The new bell was rung for the first time to call the people to the opening service in the church that he had made. "There was a considerable congregation," and Sergeant Clarke in his red coat was parish clerk, and Corrie read the prayers. Martyn stood up to preach his first and last sermon in the new church.

"A bright glow prevailed, a brilliant light shone from his eyes. He was filled with hope and joy. Most eloquent, earnest and affectionate was his address."

But when they went to his bungalow after service he sank fainting on a sofa in the hall. There remained one more effort in Cawnpore, the last act of his ministry there, the sermon to the beggars.

"When the sun began to descend we went over to Mr. Martyn's bungalow to hear his last address to the *fakeers*. It was one of those sickly, hazy, burning evenings. Mr. Martyn nearly fainted again after this effort, and when he got to his house, with his friends about him, he told us that he was afraid he had not been the means of doing the smallest good to any one of the strange people whom he had thus so often addressed."

But Martyn was wrong.

As he preached one of his first sermons to the beggars a group of young men, taking the air in a kiosk on the garden wall, sipping sherbet and smoking, had been struck by the strange proceedings in the English house next door. Down they came from the wall to see what Martyn was about. They pushed through the crowd and stood before him in a row, their arms folded, their turbans slightly tilted on one side and their lips drawn up in a superb sneer. But one of them heard enough to rouse his keenest curiosity. He was a young Moslem, a sheikh of Delhi, a professor of Persian and Arabic, but with the heart of a learner.

That gospel preached to the poor seemed to him something new, and he determined to know more of Martyn's faith. He did not venture direct to the Christian preacher, but made interest with Sabat to be employed as copier of the Persian gospel. He even sought out Martyn's schoolchildren and asked them to repeat their lessons. Then he found a great opportunity when they gave him charge of a complete copy of the Persian New Testament on its way to the bookbinder. He held back till he had read it all, and with the reading came the great decision.

On that last Sunday he was still unknown to Martyn, but Martyn's plans were known to him, and Sheikh Salih was making ready to follow the preacher to Calcutta and ask him there for baptism.[2]

On Monday morning, October 1, 1810, Martyn must leave Cawnpore. "We were all low, very, very low," says Mrs. Sherwood. Corrie, who had struggled to save his friend, was white with the strain of parting. He had found Martyn about to make a bonfire of all his memoranda, but persuaded him to let him keep them under seal against his return, and so saved for the Church that journal by which she knows the mind of Henry Martyn. "His life is beyond all price to us," Corrie wrote. Only Martyn, in a strange serenity, hardly realized their anxiety. He thought that Corrie must have worked too hard, and wrote to him from his boat, "Your pale face as it appeared on Monday morning is still before my eyes, and will not let me be easy till you tell me you are strong and prudent."

So he left them. "I am advised," he told Lydia, "to recruit my strength by rest. So I am come forth with my face towards Calcutta, with an ulterior view to the sea."

---

[2] He was baptized on Whit Sunday, 1811, under the name of Abd el Masih, and became eventually a clergyman and a notable Christian leader.

Chapter 12

TO SHIRAZ

My home
The shimmery-bounded glare,
The gazing fire-hung dome
Of scorching air.

For friend
The dazzling breathing dream,
The strength at last to find
Of Glory Supreme.

From anonymous poem on Saint
John Baptist in ΧΑΡΙΤΕΣΣΙ

Read Ephesians i. It is a chapter I keep in mind every day in
prayer. We cannot believe too much or hope too much.

HENRY MARTYN *to* LYDIA GRENFELL
from Muscat, Arabia

MARTYN's budgerow, paddled from the stern, bore him down
stream to the house that was above all others his Indian home.

"Entered the Hooghly," says his journal for November 25,
1810, "with something of those sensations with which I should
come in sight of the white cliffs of England." At Aldeen he
found the Brown children waiting to convoy him with shouts
to the house, and next morning in the city another long-
expected meeting took place with friends arrived from England.

Thomas Thomason, Simeon's senior curate, that good, serene and diligent person, had been inspired by Martyn's example to break up his home by the riverside at Shelford and to set out in middle life with his calm, methodical wife and their small children, to give the rest of his years to the service of India. Martyn, little if at all conscious how far he had himself inspired both Corrie and Thomason to follow him, hailed the news of his coming with exultation.

Thomason was indeed a notable recruit. His friends had long smiled at his habit in all spare moments of pulling out of his pocket a portion of the Bible. In his own methodical way he had had his Hebrew Old Testament re-bound into sections small enough for pocket use and kept one always at hand. He now brought these years of patient study to the help of the translators in India. On his way out the good scholar was shipwrecked; he rescued each child in a sheet and their mother in a counterpane, but every book that he possessed was lost. Martyn found the family living in the heart of Calcutta, patiently collecting household goods once more, and Thomason catechizing the little English children of the settlement with his own babes—"Fair English children, all of them elegantly dressed, standing round the desk and answering the good man's questions."

The Thomasons were shocked at the change in Martyn. "Dear, dear Martyn arrived," wrote the wife, "and we had the unspeakable delight of seeing his face. He is much altered, is thin and sallow, but he has the same loving heart." He sat on the sofa and picked up the old intercourse with them, even to the point when the steady Thomason felt it necessary to prick the bubble of Martyn's airy speculations. "That obstinate lover of antiquity," Martyn wrote of him in a letter, "whose potent touch has dissolved so many of my fabrics heretofore, that I do not like to submit anything to him which is not proof."

After that first long talk, Thomason sat down to write to

Simeon his impression of the friend so much his junior, who had always been to him both an enigma and an inspiration.

He is on his way to Arabia, where he is going in pursuit of health and knowledge. You know his genius, and what gigantic strides he takes in everything. He has some great plan in his mind of which I am no competent judge; but as far as I do understand it, the object is far too grand for one short life, and much beyond his feeble and exhausted frame. Feeble it is indeed! how fallen and changed! But let us hope that the sea-air may revive him. . . . In all other respects he is exactly the same as he was; he shines in all the dignity of love; and seems to carry about him such a heavenly majesty, as impresses the mind beyond description. But if he talks much, though in a low voice, he sinks, and you are reminded of his being "dust and ashes."

The Martyn of these days seems to have cast a spell over all his friends. They watched him with a kind of awe, as men who dared not interfere. "Can I then bring myself to cut the string and let you go?" wrote David Brown when the Arabian plan was first proposed. "I confess I could not, if your bodily frame were strong, and promised to last for half a century. But as you burn with the intenseness and rapid blaze of heated phosphorus, why should we not make the most of you? Your flame may last as long, and perhaps longer, in Arabia, than in India."

In fulfillment of a five-year-old promise to Simeon, Martyn had his portrait painted in Calcutta.[1] It was "thought a striking likeness," but on seeing it David Brown remarked, "That is not the Martyn who arrived in India, it is Martyn the recluse." Martyn acknowledged the truth of the observation. A man could not live alone with Sabat, battling with illness, stripped of every earthly hope save the perfecting of his gospel, and come out from that seclusion unmarked.

He blamed himself. "It sometimes calls itself deadness to

---

[1] Now in the University Library, Cambridge.

the world," he said, "but I much fear that it is deadness of heart. I am exempt from worldly cares myself and therefore do not feel for others."

The portrait was sent home to the India House, and Charles Simeon went up to London to claim it. His letters from India had left him unprepared for the change in Martyn's face.

> It was opened.... I could not bear to look upon it, but turned away and went to a distance, covering my face, and in spite of every effort to the contrary, crying aloud with anguish.... In seeing how much he is worn I am constrained to call to my relief the thought in *Whose* service he has worn himself so much.[2]

On consultation with the learned in Calcutta, Martyn heard little but praise of his own Hindustani New Testament, but Sabat's work, it seemed, and especially his Persian, stood yet in need of polishing. So Martyn determined to take both Persian and Arabic with him, and to go first to Persia. Afterwards he would travel—who knows where? to Damascus perhaps, he said, for there he might enquire as to ancient Arabic versions; or perhaps to Baghdad or the heart of Arabia itself. But Persia must come first.

"All his imaginations of Persia," Mrs. Sherwood tells us, "were taken from the beautiful descriptions given by the poets. He often spoke of that land as of a land of roses and nightingales, of fresh flowing streams, of sparkling fountains and of breezes laden with perfumes." A lover of Persian poetry, and especially of Sadi, Martyn had certainly been since Cambridge days; but he was no mere visionary, for he had been also a greedy reader of modern travels, such as Scott Waring's account of his visit to Shiraz, written in 1807.[3] Lord Minto, the statesman who had himself sent Sir John Malcolm[4] to

---

[2] Carus, *Life of Charles Simeon*, p. 358.
[3] *A Tour to Sheeraz by the Route of Kazroon and Feerozabad*, by Edward Scott Waring, Esq., of the Bengal Civil Establishment.
[4] See page 211.

Persia, listened to Martyn's statement of the aims of his journey, and gave him leave to proceed; the Armenians of Calcutta wrote a commendation of him to their brethren in Persia, and "a list of places in Mesopotamia, etc., where there were Christians, and the number of them"; and Martyn was ready to set out.

But to find a ship was not easy. He was told that he had best go to Bombay, and from Bombay to Bosra; but having at length found a coasting trader bound for Bombay, he failed to get a passage. He wrote to Corrie:

> The captain of the ship after many excuses has at last refused to take me; on the ground that I might try to convert the Arab sailors, and so cause a mutiny in the ship. So I am half out of heart, and more than half disposed to go to the rightabout, and come back to Cawnpore, for there is no ship to be heard of going to Bombay.

He waited on, preaching every Sunday sermons that left him in pain, and kept awake at night by a hacking cough. They gave him the task of preaching for the Bible Society on the first day of 1811. "Mr. Brown, foreseeing that I should have to stay over New Year's Day, ordered me to preach for the British and Foreign Bible Society. In consequence I prepared an unwieldy sermon, which has just been delivered. None of the great were present."

The sermon is a revelation of the extent to which Martyn had before him in his prayers and plans the needs of all India, "from Meerut to Cape Comorin," and not India only. "Nay," said that sick man to the godly in Calcutta, "Asia must be our care."

Next week he left them and took ship to carry out his own words, having obtained a passage on the boat that was taking Mountstuart Elphinstone to Bombay as the new British Resident at Poona.

Martyn slipped away from his Calcutta friends. "He suddenly vanished" out of their sight they said. To Lydia he explained that "leaving Calcutta was so much like leaving England that I went on board my boat without giving them notice."

> Without taking leave of my too dear friends in Calcutta, I went on board Mr. Elphinstone's pinnace, and began to drop down the river.

He reached the ship at the mouth of the Hooghly in two days. She was an Arab coaster, the property of a merchant of Muscat, who ran her with a country-bred captain, Mr. Kinsay from Madras, an Arab crew and an Abyssinian slave as overseer. No sooner was Martyn aboard the *Ahmoody* than he "began to try his strength" in Arabic conversation with those sailors. But sickness and fatigue overtook him.

> The sea I loathe [he wrote to Corrie], I was scarcely well any part of the voyage, and consequently did little but sit the live-long day upon the poop, looking at the flying fish, and surveying the wide waste of waters blue.

"The most agreeable circumstance" in this voyage of six weeks was, he said, the companionship in "the great cabin" of Mountstuart Elphinstone, of whose "agreeable manners and classical acquirements" he wrote enthusiastically. Throughout life Elphinstone shared Martyn's love of the classics. He had gained it as a small boy in the Edinburgh High School, and in spite of the premature breaking off of that schooling, his chief delight wherever he wandered in the East was to turn to the Greek and Latin poets. At Fort William College he added a love for Eastern literature. It was long since Martyn had met with so omnivorous a reader, and he vastly relished the society of one only a few years older than himself who had already seen responsible service in the Moslem borderlands beyond the fringe of British India. They sat long hours on the poop, or went on shore together to walk in the cinnamon gardens of Ceylon (Martyn sent Lydia a piece of fragrant bark) canvassing many questions about books and men.

One of my fellow passengers [he told Lydia] is Mr. Elphinstone, who was lately ambassador at the court of the King of Cabul, and is now going to be resident at Poona, the capital of the Mahratta empire. So the group is rather interesting.

When sitting on the poop Mr. Elphinstone kindly entertained me with information about India, the politics of which he has had such opportunities of making himself acquainted with.

Mountstuart Elphinstone in his turn enjoyed that voyage and wrote to a friend:

We have in Mr. Martyn an excellent scholar, and one of the mildest, cheerfullest, and pleasantest men I ever saw. He is extremely religious and disputes about the faith with the Nakhoda (the Abyssinian slave), but talks on all subjects, sacred and profane, and makes others laugh as heartily as he could do if he were an infidel. We have people who speak twenty-five languages (not apiece) on the ship.[5]

Or again:

A far better companion than I reckoned on, though my expectations were high...a man of good sense and taste, and simple in his manners and character and cheerful in his conversation.

The coaster crawled round Cape Comorin close to the shore and Martyn, looking up from his Arabic, almost believed himself in Cornwall. He wrote to Lydia describing "the great promontory of India."

At a distance the green waves seemed to wash the foot of the mountain, but on a nearer approach little churches were to be seen, apparently on the beach, with a row of little huts on each side. Was it these maritime situations that recalled to my mind Perran church and town in the way to Gurlyn; or made my thoughts wander on the beach to the

[5] See T. E. Colebrooke, *Life of Mountstuart Elphinstone.* I, p. 231.

east of Lamorran? You do not tell me whether you ever walk there, and imagine the billows that break at your feet to have made their way from India.

They called at Goa where the Portuguese held sway, Martyn on the alert for any information about the extent of the Christian faith in those parts. But, he told David Brown,

this place most miserably disappointed me. I did not care about churches or convents, but I did expect to find men, Bishops and Archbishops, learned friars and scowling inquisitors. Certain it is that though we have been shown all the finery of the churches, not a person have we seen that was able to give us the smallest particle of information.

The Inquisition is still existing at Goa. We were not admitted as far as Dr. Buchanan was to the Hall of Examination.... The priest in waiting acknowledged that they had some prisoners within the walls.... We were told that when the officers of the Inquisition touch an individual and beckon him away, he dare not resist.

Here Martyn stood at the tomb of St. Francis Xavier whose life had inspired him during his first few weeks in India. It was characteristic of him, as it would have been of that other apostolic man by whose grave he stood, that his attention was drawn away from the tomb with its "paintings and figures of bronze done in Italy" when the friar who guided him let fall a chance word about "the grace of God in the heart." Instantly Martyn forgot his sight-seeing and plunged into conversation with his brother in the faith.

So they drew near to Bombay on Martyn's thirtieth birthday, and his journal shows him turning, as was his wont, from the conversation of the great cabin to a higher communing.

I would that all should adore, but especially that I myself should lie prostrate. As for self, contemptible self, I feel myself saying, let it be forgotten for ever, henceforth let Christ live, let Christ reign, let Him be glorified for ever.

In Bombay he found himself a guest at Government House,

and Elphinstone introduced him to good company. For there
were in Bombay two men of parts, who would have made their
mark in any group of intellectuals.

The older man of the two, Sir James Mackintosh, had been
in his young days a friend of revolution and author of *Vindiciae
Gallicae*. But the Mackintosh of middle life, now looked on as
"the lost leader" by the men of drastic political reform, had
repudiated his early views in no uncertain tones. "I abhor,
abjure and for ever renounce the French Revolution, with
its sanguinary history, its abominable principles and for ever
execrable leaders," he wrote, and settled down to practise at
the Bar. Martyn found him as Recorder of Bombay, consoling
himself for exile with a library of the schoolmen and the latest
works of foreign philosophy. When he was stirred by congenial
society no one could resist his good talk, in which a delicious
impertinence just served to remind men of the daring of his
early views.

> Elphinstone introduced me to a young clergyman
> [Mackintosh noted in his journal] called Martyn. He seems
> to be a mild and benevolent enthusiast—a sort of character
> with which I am always half in love. We had the novelty
> of grace before and after dinner, all the company standing.

It is a half-pathetic entry from a man who had once himself
been among the enthusiasts and now sat in Bombay reading
Dean Swift and recording half-benevolent, half-cynical observations on the men who crossed his path. A week later his comment was a little less genial:

> Mr. Martyn, the saint from Calcutta, called here. He
> is a man of acuteness and learning; his meekness is excessive,
> and gives a disagreeable impression of effort to conceal the
> passions of human nature.

Later again he wrote in happier tones:

> Padre Martyn, the saint, dined here in the evening;
> it was a very considerably more pleasant evening than usual;
> he is a mild and ingenious man. We had two or three hours'
> good discussion on grammar and metaphysics.

So we look at the saint through the eyes of a man of the world who "thought that little was to be apprehended and little hoped for from the exertions of missionaries," an attitude which Martyn had met before.

His introduction to the other man of mark in Bombay society was of greater interest to Martyn, since this was a man whose name was a name to conjure with in Persia. Sir John Malcolm, a soldier turned diplomatist, had twice been sent on embassies to establish British trade and prestige in Persia. He talked Persian fluently, "bribed like a king," scattered presents of "watches and pistols; mirrors and toothpicks; filagree boxes and umbrellas; cloths and muslins; with an unlimited supply of sugar, sugar-candy and chintz." In Persia, later travelers took rank in Persian eyes according as they could or could not claim acquaintance with Malcolm Sahib. Martyn found him in Bombay writing his history of Persia and receiving the censure of Leadenhall Street for the cost of his missions.

There was a generous gesture about everything that Malcolm did, since the day when as a twelve-year-old urchin from the Westerkirk parish school, standing before the Directors of the East India Company to demand a cadetship, he had told that august body that were he to meet Hyder Ali he would "cut aff his heid." He now gave Martyn invaluable help, letters of introduction right and left, much Persian information, and a present of a Chaldee missal.

The letter that Malcolm wrote to the British Ambassador in Persia gives one more glimpse of Martyn as he looked to able men, neither prejudiced against "piety" like the military circle in Cawnpore, nor yielding him the spiritual sympathy of the circle at Aldeen. It is the last portrait that has come to us from the pen of a fellow countryman.

> His intention is, I believe, to go by Shiraz, Ispahan [Isfahan] and Kermanshah to Baghdad, and to endeavour on that route to discover some ancient copies of the Gospel, which he and many other saints are persuaded lie hid in the

mountains of Persia. Mr. Martyn also expects to improve himself as an Oriental scholar; he is already an excellent one. His knowledge of Arabic is superior to that of any Englishman in India. He is altogether a very learned and cheerful man, but a great enthusiast in his holy calling.

I have not hesitated to tell him that I thought you would require that he should act with great caution, and not allow his zeal to run away with him. He declares he will not, and he is a man of that character that I must believe. I am satisfied that if ever you see him, you will be pleased with him. He will give you grace before and after dinner, and admonish such of your party as take the Lord's name in vain; but his good sense and great learning will delight you, whilst his constant cheerfulness will add to the hilarity of your party.

The man who added to the hilarity of Malcolm's evening parties was pursuing his own course by day, for there is no confining the man of God in the bounds of one social clique.

"My breath is not at all stronger," he wrote to Corrie, "but I have no doubt it would be if I could flee the haunts of men. At this place I am visited from morning to night by the learned natives, who are drawn here by an Arabic tract, which I was drawing up merely for Sabat to help him in his book."

The friends he made while waiting in Bombay for a ship to the Persian Gulf were the usual motley company. Besides the learned of Islam there was "a rope-maker from London who came and opened his heart and we rejoiced together"; a Parsee poet "he is certainly an ingenious man, and possesses one of the most agreeable qualities a disputant can possess, which is, patience: he never interrupted me; and if I rudely interrupted him, he was silent in a moment"); and a Jew of Bosra, with whom he walked at night by the seaside.

Martyn was given a passage in a ship of the East India Company's navy, sent to cruise in the Persian Gulf against marauding Arab pirates from the coast of Oman. He was to act as chaplain to the European part of the crew of the *Benares*.

In his journal and his letters, especially those to Lydia and to Corrie, "our beloved Daniel in the north," we trace the details of his wanderings. Lydia's proffered letters had never reached him. "When will our correspondence be established? I have been trying to effect it these six years, and it is only yet in train. But I am not yet without hopes that a letter in the beloved hand will yet overtake me somewhere."

I quitted India on Lady Day.... Smooth and light airs left me at liberty to pursue my studies as uninterruptedly as if I were on shore; and more so, as my companions in the great cabin, being sufficient company for each other, and studious and taciturn withal, seldom break my repose. Every day, all day long, I Hebraize.... On the morning of Easter we saw the land of Mekran in Persia.

You will be happy to know that the murderous pirates against whom we were sent, having received notice of our approach, are all got out of the way, so that I am no longer liable to be shot in a battle, or to decapitation after it.

On the Sunday after Easter the *Benares* put into the cove of Muscat for water before pursuing her way up the Gulf to Bushire, and Henry Martyn set foot in Arabia, a land, he said, of "burning, barren rocks. We went through the bazaar, and mounted a hill to look at it, but saw nothing but what was hideous. The town and houses are more mean and filthy than any in India, and in all the environs of the place I counted three trees, date-trees I suppose."

The cove was stifling. Sleep was impossible during the hot nights in shelter of the rocks. But Martyn was about his business.

April 24, 1811. Went with one Englishman, and two Armenians and an Arab who acted as guard and guide, to see a remarkable pass about a mile from the town, and a garden planted by a Hindoo, in a little valley beyond.... The little bit of green in this wilderness seemed to the Arab a great curiosity. I conversed a good deal with him, but particularly with his African slave who was very intelligent about religion.

The talk, as so often happened with Martyn, proved more engrossing than the expedition. The slave followed him down to the landing place and "would not cease from his argument till I left the shore."

So Martyn left Arabian soil. But next day, the ship being still in the cove,

the Arab soldier and his slave came on board to take leave. They asked to see the Gospel. The instant I gave them a copy in Arabic, the poor boy began to read, and carried it off as a great prize.

The *Benares,* having warped out of the stifling cove, was tossed about for days by a north-wester, the more violent of the two prevailing winds that rush up or down the great funnel of the Gulf. On May 21 she came to Bushire, and Henry Martyn landed in Persia at that dilapidated little port surrounded by "a wall with a few bastions which might possibly be a safeguard against the predatory incursions of Horse."[6]

He came into its steamy heat at the hottest season of the year.

"We were hospitably received by the acting Resident. In the evening I walked out by the seaside to recollect myself, to review the past and to look forward to the future."

He at once ordered a Persian costume for travel in the interior, and while it was in making set himself, except when prostrated with headache by the heat of the city, to find out Persian and Arabic opinion on translations of the New Testament.

Learned Mohammedan Arabs enjoyed Sabat's Arabic:

I showed Hosyn, an Arab, the most learned man here, a passage in the New Testament, according to the four versions of Erpenius, English, Polyglot and Sabat. He condemned the three first, but said immediately of Sabat's, "This is good, very good." He read out a chapter in fine style; in short, he gave it unqualified commendation.

---

[6] Scott Waring, *A Tour to Sheeraz,* p. 12.

But learned Persians were not equally pleased with Sabat's work in their language. Already his Persian friend in Bombay had criticized it:

He began about the versions of the New Testament, condemning them all. I asked him whether Sabat's Persian was not much superior? He opened upon a chapter, and pointed out several undeniable errors both in collocation and words, and laughed at some of the Arabic words. When I told him the translator was an Arab who had lived ten years in Persia, he said, an Arab if he live there twenty years, will never speak Persian well.

So the great task remained yet to be done, and Henry Martyn, plunging into Persia, was determined not to come forth again till he brought with him such a version as in all its niceties could satisfy the sensitive Persian ear.

On the night of May 30, 1811, his caravan wound through the sleeping port between blind walls of mud or crumbling stone and set its face towards the distant hills. Martyn had grown a mustache during the voyage; he now "put off the European" and mounted his riding pony in baggy blue trousers and red boots, a conical cap of Astrakhan and a flowing coat. An Armenian servant followed him on a mule and another mule carried his books. For safety they joined a caravan of about thirty beasts carrying baggage to Sir Gore Ouseley, the British Ambassador, then at Shiraz. In that city of poets and lettered men, Martyn could best pursue his object.

They traveled by night, for the heat of day in early June would be intolerable. As they filed out of Bushire on to the sandy plain that stretched for ninety miles between them and the hills that lift the Persian plateau, Martyn felt all the romance of the first starlight journey with a caravan.

When we began to flag and grow sleepy and the kafila was pretty quiet, one of the muleteers on foot began to sing. He sang with a voice so plaintive, that it was impossible not to have one's attention arrested. At the end of the first tune he paused, and nothing was heard but the tinkling of the bells attached to the necks of the mules; every voice was hushed. The first line was enough for me.... The following is perhaps the true translation:

> "Think not that e'er my heart can dwell
>   Contented far from thee;
>   How can the fresh-caught nightingale
>   Enjoy tranquillity?
>
> "Forsake not then thy friend for aught
>   That slanderous tongues can say;
>   The heart that fixes where it ought,
>   No power can rend away."

Thus we went on, and as often as the kafila by their dulness and sleepiness seemed to require it, or perhaps to keep himself awake, he entertained the company and himself with a song. We met two or three other kafilas taking advantage of the night to get on.

Day caught them still on that sweltering plain. And Martyn, who had almost forgotten it, was forced to remember for once that he was a sick man.

At sunrise we came to our ground at Ahmeda, six parasangs [Persian measure of length], and pitched our little tent under a tree: it was the only shelter we could get. At first the heat was not greater than we had felt it in India, but it soon became so intense as to be quite alarming. When the thermometer was above 112°, fever heat, I began to lose my strength fast; at last it became quite intolerable. I wrapped myself up in a blanket and all the warm covering I could get to defend myself from the external air; by which means the moisture was kept a little longer upon the body.

But the thermometer still rising, and the moisture of the body being quite exhausted, I grew restless and thought I should have lost my senses. The thermometer at last stood at 126°.... At last the fierce sun retired, and I crept out more dead than alive. It was then a difficulty how I could

proceed on my journey; for besides the immediate effects of
the heat, I had no opportunity of making up for the last
night's want of sleep, and had eaten nothing. However,
while they were loading the mules, I got an hour's sleep,
and set out, the muleteers leading my horse, and Zechariah,
my servant, an Armenian, doing all in his power to encour-
age me.

So they rode on through the coolness of another night, and
when daybreak again found them on the unshielded plain they
made their preparations.

I got a tattie [shutter] made of the branches of the date-
tree, and a Persian peasant to water it; by this means the
thermometer did not rise above 114°. But what completely
secured me from the heat was a large wet towel, which I
wrapped round my head and body, muffling up the lower
part in clothes.

The next day brought them to the bottom of the mountain
wall among pits of black naphtha "used by the Persians as we
are told it was in (Milton's) hell for lamps, and occasionally
given to their camels."[7]

We arrived at the foot of the mountains, at a place where
we seemed to have discovered one of Nature's ulcers. A
strong suffocating smell of naphtha announced something
more than ordinarily foul in the neighbourhood. We saw a
river:—what flowed in it, it seemed difficult to say, whether
it were water or green oil; it scarcely moved, and the stones
which it laved it left of a greyish colour, as if its foul touch
had given them the leprosy.

Little dreamed the man who loved the soft sea-mists of
Cornwall of the part that the scarred and burning Persian oil-
fields would one day play in political and military history.

Our place of encampment this day was a grove of date-
trees, where the atmosphere, at sunrise, was ten times hotter
than the ambient air. I threw myself down on the burning

---

[7] Scott Waring, *A Tour to Sheeraz*, p. 18.

ground and slept; when the tent came up I awoke, as usual,
in a burning fever.

And now, after three nights in the saddle, and three sleep
less days of fever, they began to climb the mountain ladder t
the Persian plateau.

At nine in the evening we decamped. The ground and
air were so insufferably hot that I could not travel without
a wet towel round my face and neck. This night, for the first
time, we began to ascend the mountains.

There was nothing to mark the road but the rocks being
a little more worn in one place than in another. Sometimes
my horse, which led the way, stopped as if to consider about
the way: for myself I could not guess.

He gave his horse the rein, and rode on drunken with sleep
along paths that hung over dizzy precipices, and up track
where the travelers behind cower with the sense that the mule
must fall back headlong on the hindmost, through desolat
places where the moon plays monkey tricks, sometimes riding
serene and high, and sometimes as the wild path heaves up
ward, seeming to sail level with the traveler's bridle. Through
such "sublime" scenes Martyn dragged himself on, drugged
with overpowering sleep.

My sleepiness and fatigue rendered me insensible to
everything around me. At last we emerged *superas ad auras*,
not on the top of a mountain to go down again, but to a
plain, or upper world.

The first rung of the great ladder was mounted. "We rode
briskly over the plain, breathing a purer air, and soon came in
sight of a fair edifice, built by the king of the country for the
refreshment of pilgrims." Here the thermometer was 110 de
grees, tempered for them, however, by a load of ice bough
from a mountaineer on his way down to the coastal plain.

Next night they climbed the second rung of that great
ladder.

"We ascended another range of mountains and passed

over a plain where the cold was so piercing that with all the clothes we could muster we were shivering." They rode on till eight in the morning through country where mountain was heaped on mountain and stone piled on stone as though in some battle of the elder giants. When Martyn arrived at Kaziroon (Kazerun), "There seemed to be a fire within my head, my skin like a cinder and the pulse violent." Here he lay all day in a summer house in a cypress garden still too feverish for sleep, stretching out a burning hand to dip it in water.

So they made two more great ascents, climbing the rugged hills crowned with the greyish green of the wild almond into a cooler air. On the last night of that climb "the cold was very severe; for fear of falling off from sleep and numbness I walked a good part of the way." And now at last they found a place of rest, never forgotten by any traveler who has made that ride.

> We pitched our tent in the vale of Dustarjan, near a crystal stream, on the banks of which we observed the clover and golden cup: the whole valley was one green field, in which large herds of cattle were browsing. The temperature was about that of spring in England. Here a few hours' sleep recovered me in some degree from the stupidity in which I had been for some days. I awoke with a light heart and said, "He maketh us to lie down in the green pastures and leadeth us beside the still waters."

There were two more nights of travel before Martyn reached his goal, "gasping for life under the double pressure of an inward fire and an outward burning sun."[8]

> Sleepiness my old companion and enemy again overtook me. I was in perpetual danger of falling off my horse, till at last I pushed on to a considerable distance, planted my back against a wall, and slept I know not how long till the good muleteer came up and gently waked me.

On Sunday, June 9, they reached Shiraz the many-gated,

---

[8] Sir Robert Ker Porter, *Travels, I.* p. 687.

set white upon her plain. They halted in a garden outside the walls, and next day rode in through the blind narrow streets to the house of a leading citizen, Jaffir Ali Khan, to whom Martyn had letters bearing the magic signature of Malcolm. The house was thrown open to him.

After the long and tedious ceremony of coffee and pipes, breakfast made its appearance on two large trays: curry, pilaws, various sweets cooled with snow and perfumed with rose-water, were served in great profusion in China plates and basins, a few wooden spoons beautifully carved; but being in a Persian dress, and on the ground, I thought it high time to throw off the European, and so ate with my hands.

The rich and learned Jaffir placed a room at Martyn's disposal, and here he unpacked such books as he had. His host had been once "a great sayer of prayers, and had regularly passed every afternoon for fourteen years in cursing the followers of Omar according to the prescribed form; but perceiving that these zealous maledictions brought no blessings on himself, he left them off and now just prays for form's sake. His wife [a veiled lady whom Martyn never met while living in her husband's house] says her prayers regularly five times a day, and is always up before sunrise for the first prayer." But her husband devoted himself to the pleasures of wealth and literature, excursions to gardens beside living streams, and the company of poets.

Jaffir Ali Khan heard with the interest of a lettered man of his visitor's anxiety for a true and beautiful translation of the gospel, and he introduced a brother-in-law who spoke "the purest dialect of the Persian" and offered his assistance in making a new version. "It was an offer I could not refuse," said Martyn, and he at once prepared for months of virtual solitude, "entrenched in one of Persia's valleys" till the great task should be done.

Chapter 13

A YEAR AMONG THE DOCTORS

Yet with the Friend are we, and the Light of the Eye, and the Path of Expectation.—SHAMSU-D-DIN MUHAMMAD I HAFIZ.

The least of His works it is refreshing to look at. A dried leaf or a straw makes me feel myself in good company. . . . If I live to complete the Persian New Testament, my life after that will be of less importance. But whether life or death be mine, may Christ be magnified in me. If He has work for me to do I cannot die.—MARTYN's *Journal at Shiraz, January* 1, 1812.

HENRY MARTYN, "wearing agreeably to custom a pair of red cloth stockings with green highheeled shoes," went to the palace where a hundred fountains played, and made his bow to the Prince-Governor of Shiraz, in whose city he was now a guest.

On first reaching Shiraz he had found Sir Gore Ouseley, "Ambassador Extraordinary and Minister Plenipotentiary" to the Shah's court, encamped in the plain outside the city walls. When camp was struck and the ambassador and his suite moved on towards Tabriz, Martyn was left alone in that yet medieval Shiraz where the Prince-Governor was an autocratic tyrant ordering the bastinado, where city gates were closed at sunset, where the Vizier sent a train of mules laden with fruit

as a compliment to the stranger, and where men, sipping sherbet cooled with snow, recited the verses of Sadi or of Hafiz
"a poetry which in its endless yet graceful handling of the same
overmastering ideas, has all the fantastic wealth of woven
traceries and colours burnt in glass, of the purple and gold
and crimson shining in the holy place that characterize the art
of the thirteenth century."[1]

Martyn, son of another age and world, knew in Shiraz the
loneliness of a crowd.

> After much deliberation [he wrote to David Brown] I
> have determined to remain here six months. From all that
> I can collect there appears no probability of our ever having
> a good translation made out of Persia. The men of Shiraz
> propose to translate the New Testament with me. Can I
> refuse to stay?
>
> Behold me, therefore, in the Athens of Fars, the haunt
> of the Persian man. Beneath are the ashes of Hafiz and Sadi;
> above, green gardens and running waters, roses and night-
> ingales. How gladly would I give Shiraz for Aldeen!
>
> Now, good Sir, seeing that I am to remain six months
> in captivity, comfort me with a letter now and then.
>
> I am often tempted to get away from this prison, . . . but
> placing myself twenty years on in time, I say why could not
> I stay at Shiraz long enough to get a New Testament done
> there, even if I had been detained there on that account
> three or six years? What work of equal importance can ever
> come from me?

The story of that sojourn has to be pieced together from
Martyn's letters and journal. Letter after letter he sent home
by caravan to the coast or by Tartar courier to Constantinople,
but none yet reached him from Cornwall, and the Indian
packets also were mysteriously delayed.

> Since ten months [he told Lydia] I have heard nothing
> of any one person whom I love. I read your letters inces-

---

[1] *Quarterly Review*, January 1892, on Wilberforce Clarke's translation
of the *Divan* of Hafiz.

santly, and try to find out something new, as I generally do, but I begin to look with pain at the distant date of the last. ...I try to live on from day to day happy in His love and care.

He wrote to Lydia, to David Brown and to Corrie long letters that have to be searched before they yield those little details which give the picture of daily life. For the letters are swallowed up with the one supreme interest of his task. When at length an Indian packet reached him, a Persian friend with unquenchable curiosity about the foreigner was anxious to know "in what way he corresponded." "He made me read Mr. Brown's letter to me," says Martyn, "and mine to Corrie. He took care to let his friends know that we wrote nothing about our own affairs: it was all about translations and the cause of Christ. With this he was delighted."

The *Journal* too, once full of minute and delicate studies in conscience, becomes now a notebook of the progress of translation and of solitary witness to the faith. There are no longer breathings after Brainerd; the man stands alone with Christ. The Martyn that moves among the doctors of Shiraz is clothed with an almost magical calm, with the serenity of a man who has forgotten himself in the service of a Greater.

He set up housekeeping in the room allotted to him by his host, with his talkative Armenian servant to do the foraging.

Victuals are cheap enough ... such a country for fruit I had no conception of. I have a fine horse which I bought for less than a hundred rupees, on which I ride every morning round the walls. My vain servant Zechariah, anxious that his master should appear like an ameer, furnished the horse with a saddle, or rather a pillion which fairly covers his whole back; it has all the colours of the rainbow, but yellow is predominant, and from it hang down four large tassels also yellow. But all my finery does not defend me from the boys. Some cry out "Ho! Russ!" others cry out "Feringhee!" One day a brickbat was flung at me and hit me in the hip. They continued throwing stones at me every day until the

Governor sent an order to all the gates that if anyone insulted me he should be bastinadoed, and the next day came himself in state to pay me a visit.

Most of the day I am about the translation. I am so incessantly occupied with visitors and my work that I have hardly a moment for myself. Even from these Mohammedans I hear remarks that do me good; to-day for instance my assistant observed, "How He loved those twelve persons." "Yes," said I, "and not those twelve only."

Imagine a pale person seated on a Persian carpet, in a room without table or chair, with a pair of formidable mustachios, and habited as a Persian, and you see me. I go on as usual singing hymns at night over my milk and water, for tea I have none though I much want it. I am with you in spirit almost every evening.

The long covered bazaar of Shiraz ("like Exeter Change") was soon seething with rumor about the new foreigner who lodged with the wealthy and respected Jaffir Ali Khan, and who carried letters from that prince of men, the liberal Malcolm Sahib. "This is a man of religion, and his coming here is that he may embrace the true faith and turn Moslem," said some. "Nay," replied the politically minded, "but he will pretend to turn Moslem, and under that pretence he will bring here more and more English, perhaps five thousand men from Hindostan, and at last seize the place." Those who had spoken with Martyn called him a man of God and a doctor of religion. "A beardless boy," said others, "how should he know anything of the faith?" And to settle the question, the learned of Shiraz came one by one to sip coffee and break a lance with the stranger. They never found him inaccessible. His list of visitors, as in all places where he dwelt, was very various.[2]

The prince's secretary who is considered to be the best prose-writer in Shiraz called upon us.

---

[2] For the story of one of these visitors which came to light half a century later, see note on p. 255.

Two young men from the college, full of zeal and logic, came this morning to try me with hard questions.

Before I had taken my breakfast the younger of the youths came, and forced me into a conversation. As soon as he heard the word "Father" in the translation used for "God," he laughed and went away.

Abdulghanee the Jew Mahometan came to prove that he had found Mahomet in the Pentateuch.... He concluded by saying that he must come every day and either make me a Mussulman or become himself a Christian.

Another day it was a Persian general who came out of respect to a friend of Malcolm Sahib, or an Armenian priest who called to see his brother of the west, or the "chief of a tribe which consists of twenty thousand families," or an Indian munshi who recited his own verses while the Persians secretly derided his foreign accent.

The interviews were apt to terminate in deadlock, as host and visitor reached one crucial point.

The Moollah Aga Mahommed Hasan, a very sensible, candid man, asked a good deal about the European philosophy, particularly what we did in metaphysics. He has nothing to find fault with in Christianity, except the Divinity of Christ. It is this doctrine that exposes me to contempt of the learned Mahometans.

Martyn's serenity, his friends soon learned, was never the calm of an unfeeling deadness. They could touch him to the quick by anything that concerned the honor of his Lord.

Mirza Seid Ali told me of a distich [couplet] made by his friend in honour of a victory over the Russians. The sentiment was that Prince Abbas Mirza had killed so many Christians that Christ from the fourth heaven took hold of Mahomet's skirt to entreat him to desist. I was cut to the soul at this blasphemy. Mirza Seid Ali perceived that I was considerably disordered and asked what it was that was so offensive? I told him that "I could not endure existence if Jesus was not glorified; it would be hell to me, if He were to be always thus dishonoured." He was astonished and again asked "Why?" "If any one pluck out your eyes," I replied, "there is no saying *why* you feel pain;—it is feeling. It is because I am one with Christ that I am thus dreadfully wounded."

In spite of the interruptions of garrulous callers, the beloved work went on apace. Sabat's translation, with its fondness for fine words, was found almost useless.

The king has signified that it is his wish that as little Arabic as possible may be employed in the papers presented to him. So that simple Persian is likely to become more and more fashionable. This is a change favourable certainly to our glorious cause. To the poor the Gospel will be preached. We began our work with the Gospel of St. John, and five chapters are put out of hand. It is likely to be the simplest thing imaginable; and I daresay the pedantic Arab will turn up his nose at it; but what the men of Shiraz approve, who can gainsay?

During August Martyn's host, "to relieve the tedium of living always in a walled town," pitched a tent for him in a garden in the suburbs, where he found tranquillity, "living amidst clusters of grapes by a clear stream." Here under an orange tree, with greater freedom from interruption, he sat with Mirza Seid Ali hour after hour at the translation, until the cold at night drove him back to the shelter of the city.

The man who thus spent long hours with Martyn had escaped from the Shiah Islam of orthodox Persia to Sufi mysticism. But in nothing had he gone very deep. He was a man of facile intelligence, who told his friends that it was better to gain information about the faith of the Christians than to loiter away the year in the garden.

From him Martyn tried patiently to understand the Sufi beliefs; but he was met by endless meandering discourses about the unity of all being, from one who was himself but a beginner in the Sufi way. "I came to nothing like a clear understanding of the nature of it," Martyn confessed at the end of the explanations.

The facile shallowness of the man came out in his comments on the New Testament:

Mirza Seid Ali read some verses of St. Paul which he condescended to praise, but in such a way as to be more offensive to me than if he had treated them with contempt. He observed that Paul had not written ill but something like a good reasoner.

There is another circumstance that gained Paul importance in the eyes of Mirza Seid Ali, which is that he speaks of Mark and Luke as his servants.

Can you give me a proof (said he) of Christianity, that I may either believe or not believe—a proof like that of one of the theorems of Euclid?

Yet Mirza Seid Ali had his deeper moments. "You never heard *me* speak lightly of Jesus," he told Martyn; "no, there is something so awfully pure about Him that nothing is to be said." He grew troubled as his intercourse with the saint grew deeper, and said "he did not know what to do to have his mind made up about religion. Of all the religions Christ's was the best, but whether to perfer this to Soofeism he could not tell."

In such disturbance of mind he decided to take Martyn to meet the greatest religious leader and saint of his acquaintance, the Sufi master at whose feet he sat with reverential awe, and to watch the result of the contact. It was a strange and almost silent interview, when Martyn, no stranger himself to the communion of the Christian mystic, was ushered into the courtyard of Mirza Abul Casim, "one of the most renowned Soofis in all Persia."

We found several persons sitting in an open court, in which a few greens and flowers were placed; the master was in a corner. He was a very fresh-looking old man with a silver beard. I was surprised to observe the downcast and sorrowful looks of the assembly, and still more at the silence which reigned.

Martyn sat on the ground among the pupils of the sage, Seid Ali whispering in his ear, "It is the custom here to think much and speak little." After a considerable pause he ventured to ask the teacher, "What were his feelings at the prospect of death: hope, or fear, or neither?"

"Neither," said he, "pleasure and pain are both alike."

I asked, "Whether he had obtained this apathy?"

He said "No."

"Why do you think it attainable?"

He could not tell.

"Why do you think that pleasure and pain are not the same?" said Seid Ali, taking the part of his silent teacher.

"Because," said I, "I have the evidence of my senses for it. And you also act as if there were a difference. Why do you eat but that you fear pain?"

With that brief colloquy they relapsed again into silence, and the sages sat unmoved until Martyn came away, his heart yearning over a young disciple whom he had seen preparing the teacher's pipe with great humility, and who had incurred an orthodox father's wrath and left all to find happiness in mystic contemplation.

From the day of that visit followers of the mystic way, among them the young disciple, began to steal into Martyn's rooms under the sympathetic eye of his host.

"I begin now to have some notion of Soofeism," Martyn wrote. "The first principle is this: notwithstanding the good and evil, pleasure and pain that is in the world, God is not affected by it. He is perfectly happy with it all; if therefore we can become like God we shall also be perfectly happy in every possible condition. This then is salvation."

When they spun interminable theories Martyn was very frank. "There you sit," he told Seid Ali, "and will not take the trouble to ask whether God has said anything or not. No: that

is too easy and direct a way of coming at the truth. I compare
you to spiders, who weave their house of defence out of their
own bowels, or to a set of people who are groping for a light
in broad day."

Yet Sufism as he saw it gave him hope for the spiritual
future of Persia.

> Vast numbers secretly hate and despise the superstition
> imposed on them [he wrote], and as many of them as have
> heard the gospel approve it, but they dare not hazard their
> lives for the name of the Lord Jesus. These Soofis are quite
> the Methodists of the east. From these you will perceive the
> first Persian Church will be formed, judging after the man-
> ner of men.

During the month of Ramadan, when orthodox Moslems
fast by day and feast by night, Martyn was surprised by a
visit from the silent sage himself. He conformed outwardly
to Islam so far as was necessary to avoid shame and punishment; but at heart he was a rebel, and he came now to ask
Martyn for wine, secure that in the Christian's room he would
not be betrayed for breaking the regulations he despised.

"I plied him with questions innumerable," wrote Martyn,
"but the weary old man had no heart for discussion."

> Laying aside his turban, he put on his nightcap and
> soon fell asleep upon the carpet. Whilst he lay there, his dis-
> ciples came, but would not believe when I told them who
> was there, till they came and saw the sage asleep. When he
> awoke, they came in, and seated themselves at the greatest
> possible distance, and were all as still as a church.

So the poor old man awoke from his brief comfort of wine
and sleep to find himself once more a saintly demi-god. "The
real state of this man seems to be despair," wrote Martyn.
"Poor soul, he is sadly bewildered."

When winter came and the translators wrapped sheepskins
round them as they sat at work, Martyn made his Christmas
feast, and bade to it his brethren of the Armenian Church,

ignorant and persecuted, sewing patches on to their new coats for fear they should be taken from them by Moslem neighbors. He also bade the Sufi sage and all his following to celebrate the birth of One whom Wise Men from the East had worshiped. "God will guide whom He will," the poor old man was heard to mutter into his snowy beard; but not another word did he vouchsafe at that strange Christmas feast.

So Martyn reached out towards friendship with these heretics and mystics, for their sakes breaking through the shy, proud reserve of the Britisher, and laying before them all that he had, even his very soul. "I am sometimes led on by the Persians," he said, "to tell them all I know of the very recesses of the sanctuary, and these are the things that interest them."

But long before Christmas time he had awakened hostility amongst the orthodox, and found himself called on to defend the faith before the doctors of Persian Islam. "I am in the midst of enemies," he wrote, "who argue against the truth with uncommon subtlety."

So great was the stir in the city from the presence of the young Frankish teacher that the authorities felt it necessary to assert the true and only faith.

A defense of Islam was prepared, which in the eyes of the learned of Shiraz outweighed all former apologies—"a book which is to silence me for ever," Martyn said. This was the work of Mirza Ibrahim, a majestic and benevolent old man, "Preceptor of all the mullahs," whose manner recalls the traditions of the great medieval doctors, as he meets an opponent with courteous subtlety.

When this work was put into Martyn's hands there fell to him, single-handed and almost without books, the task as knight of Christ of meeting the champion of Persian theology. He replied in a tract, the first of a series, in which he shows an **astonishing mastery of the whole controversy, and in which** he and his opponent throughout preserved high courtesy.[8]

But though Martyn and Mirza Ibrahim might be chivalrous opponents, there were other less courtly antagonists.

As there is nothing at all in this dull place to take the attention of the people, no trade, manufactures or news, every event at all novel is interesting to them. You may conceive therefore what a sensation was produced. Before five people had seen what I wrote, defences of Islam swarmed into being from all the Moulwee maggots of the place, but the more judicious men were ashamed to let me see them.

One of the royal princes was heard to growl that the proper reply to Martyn's writings was the sword. But he remained serene and unmoved among them. "If Christ has work for me to do, I cannot die," he said, and never shirked encounters where he might be called on to confess his faith. Soon all Shiraz was talking of a dinner party at which the great Professor of Canon Law himself had disputed with the stranger.

He invited us to dinner. About eight o'clock at night we went. [October had come and with it the Moslem month of Ramadan, when eating by day is forbidden.] We entered a fine court, where was a pond, and by the side of it a platform eight feet high, covered with carpets. Here sat the Moojtahid in state. The Professor seated Seid Ali on his right hand and me on his left. The swarthy obesity of the little personage led me to suppose that he had paid more attention to cooking than to science. But when he began to speak, I saw reason enough for his being so much admired. The substance of his speech was flimsy enough; but he spoke with uncommon fluency and clearness. He talked for a full hour about the soul. At length after clearing his way for miles around, he said, that philosophers had proved that a single being could produce but a single being; that the first thing God had created was *Wisdom*. . . .

---

[8] The whole controversy was preserved in English, and published by Dr. Lee, the Cambridge Professor of Arabic, after Martyn's death.

And so on—a winding tissue which Martyn, as he sat in silence on the many-colored carpet, had no desire to call in question, being anxious for no useless skirmishes among outworks.

> The Professor at the close of one of his long speeches said to me, "You see how much there is to be said on these subjects; several visits will be necessary; we must come to the point by degrees." Perceiving how much he dreaded a close discussion, I did not mean to hurry him, but let him talk on.

But other listeners were anxious for the clash of arms, and urged Martyn to bring the Professor to grips. He did at length respectfully urge the great lawyer to oblige the company with "something about Islam," and so drew forth a few magisterial statements.

"The Jesus we acknowledge," said he with a contemptuous smile, "is one who bore testimony to Muhammad, not your Jesus whom you call God."

> After this the Koran was mentioned, but as the company began to thin and the great man had not a sufficient audience, he did not seem to think it worth while to notice my objections.

> It was midnight when dinner was brought in: it was a sullen meal. The great man was silent; and I was sleepy.

So quite alone he witnessed to the faith. There is a story, perhaps apocryphal, of Martyn when he went to sit under an awning in the Vizier's courtyard and witness the Moslem Passion Play of the death of Hussein. The drama lasted ten days and was played before an audience that sobbed aloud. The story has it that when a scene was reached in which a Frankish ambassador was made to step forward and implore pardon for the victims, the actor knew no Frankish words to say except a few round English curses picked up from travelers. Martyn, stung to the heart at this, leapt on to the primitive stage, and seizing the actor, taught him to say the Lord's Prayer.

The story may be apocryphal;[4] if so, like many legends it has spiritual truth, being faithful to the daring and the impetuosity of Martyn's solitary witness.

On February 24, the New Testament was finished. Martyn waited for nothing but the scribing of some gorgeous copies for the hands of Persian royalty, before setting out once more on pilgrimage. They could hardly let him go. They took him out to a garden and seated him on a bed of roses, and made him read them the Bible history for hours at a time. "Their love seemed to increase," he said, as the time of his departure drew near. One of them who had seen Martyn's translation of St. Matthew, recited to his friends the story of the Passion of the Lord. "The notes of the nightingales warbling around," said Martyn, "were not so sweet to me as this discourse from the Persian."

Just before he quitted Shiraz, a young man, bred as a doctor of Islam, came begging for an interview. He confessed that he had visited Martyn many times before with the other doctors to heap scorn on the teacher of a despised sect, but at every interview he had found his attitude changing. Martyn's unfailing forbearance to his violence put him to shame, and his calm reasoning laid bare sophistries. At last Muhammad Rahim found himself convinced that the "beardless boy" was right. Then for shame and fear he had kept away from his presence for months. But now he heard that the teacher was going, and he came at last to make confession of his belief. Martyn put into his hands that day a copy of the Book, a Persian New

---

[4] Yet Martyn several times did go to martyr-plays in Shiraz, and we know that he went to the play at the Vizier's in January, 1812. Curiously enough, as E. G. Browne was sitting in a Persian house in 1892, his host, speaking of a similar part allotted to a Frankish ambassador in some recent martyr-plays, said, "How I wish you had been here a little earlier, for then we could have borrowed your hats and clothes for the Firangis, and indeed you might even have taught us some words of your language to put in the mouths of the actors who personated them."—E. G. Browne, *A Year among the Persians*.

Testament that became his lifelong companion. Years afterwards Muhammad Rahim confessed his conversion to a Christian traveler, and showed the book that was his greatest treasure. On one of the blank leaves was written, "There is joy in heaven over one sinner that repenteth.—HENRY MARTYN."

Chapter 14

THE TRAVELER

Suddenly I seem to myself to see holy Martin, the bishop, clad in a white robe, with face like a flame, eyes like stars, and glittering hair; and, while his person was what I had known it to be, yet, what can hardly be expressed, I could not look at him, though I could recognize him. . . . He repeats the name of the cross, familiar in his mouth: next, while I gaze upon him, and cannot take my fill of his face and look, suddenly he is caught aloft, till, after completing the immense spaces of the air, I following with my eyes the swift cloud that carried him, he is received into the open heaven, and can be seen no more. . . . A boy enters with a speaking and sorrowful countenance: "Why so sad and eager to speak?" say I. "Two monks," he answers, "are just come from Tours; they bring the news that Martin is departed."—SULPICIUS SEVERUS, *Life of Martin of Tours* (translated by J. H. Newman).

IN THAT yet medieval Persia, the aspiring poet or man of letters still laid his book before the Shah on his throne of marble spread with cloth of gold. Fateh Ali Shab,[1] ruler of Persia, over-lord of Georgia and Kurdistan, was not only the statesman who received and balanced the claims of embassies from George III, from Napoleon, from the Tzar Alexander and

[1] 1798-1836.

from the Governor General Wellesley. He was, as he sat blaz-
ing with jewels before a prostrate court, the fountain of taste
and the judge of letters for his kingdom. It needed but a
pronouncement of praise in his hollow rolling voice, and the
fortunes of a volume were made.

Henry Martyn, seeing through Persian eyes, determined to
gain for the New Testament the respect yielded to a book
approved at court.

As his translation work drew to a close, he set scribes
preparing two volumes of exquisite penmanship for the Shah
and for his heir, Prince Abbas Mirza, "the wisest of the
princes." The scribes began work in November, 1811. They
brought him the finished volumes in May, 1812, three months
after the translator's work was done. Lingering in Shiraz and
waiting for their manuscript, he "beguiled the tediousness of
the day" by an absorbing study of the Psalms in Hebrew, and
a translation of the Psalter into Persian. It enthralled him so
that he "hardly perceived" the passing of the days. "I have
long had it in contemplation," he wrote to Lydia. "I have often
attempted the 84th Psalm, endeared to me on many accounts,[2]
but have not yet succeeded. The glorious 16th Psalm I hope
I have mastered."

When the scribes brought in their fair copies, Martyn
wrapped up the costly manuscripts uncorrected. He had none
like-minded whom he could put in charge of the precious
volumes, and he was determined to lay the books himself in
the royal hands, correcting them as he traveled. For he knew
that he was a sick man. He must race disease if he desired to
see the Book on its way. A long dispute with a Sufi doctor
would leave him still with a raw pit of pain where his breath
came and went.

He had copies ready for the press. Four were sent by his
direction to India that his friends at Serampore might print

[2] See Chapter VI, p. 96.

his translation.[3] Other copies he carried with him on his wanderings, intending, if he lived, to pass them on to some press in the west, perhaps at his own University of Cambridge. He spent his last hours at Shiraz with his fellow-translator in giving instructions for the care and delivery of the Book in case of his own death.

That done, a little before the closing of the gates at sunset on May 11, 1812, he left Shiraz and joined a caravan outside the walls, starting that night to ride across the great Persian plateau from south to north.

He was riding as servant of the Book to Tabriz where Sir Gore Ouseley lived; for he could only be introduced into the jeweled presence of the Shah by the ambassador who represented his nation.

The air of the uplands was cool enough for day traveling, and the diary is full of notes on the face of the countryside. Here "no cultivation, scarcely any plant except the broom and hawthorn"; then "a vast plain, entirely uninhabited except where the skirts of it were spotted with the black tents of the wandering tribes." On that high plateau it grew cold, even in May: "hoar-frost, and ice on the pools. The highest land between the Persian Gulf and the Caspian Sea." At night they shuddered in open caravan-serais that seemed to let in wind and rain alike. Martyn after a day's ride drew out of its wrappings the precious volume prepared for the Prince, and sat late into the night in some leaky hovel, poring over the correction of his scribe's exquisite Persian lettering.

---

[3] The manuscript arrived safely, but not till 1814. It was published at Calcutta in 1816. Martyn's friend Mirza Seid Ali was actually sent for from Shiraz that he might see it through the press. When he came, he told the Calcutta group that he had with him the translation of the Psalms that had been the solace of Martyn's last months at Shiraz. Martyn no doubt regarded this as an uncompleted task. He had taken no steps to preserve it for the Church. But it formed the nucleus of the beautiful Persian Old Testament published in 1846 in Edinburgh and presented to the Shah in 1848.

After twelve days of riding they came across the poppy
fields to Isfahan, a city of domes and minarets and pigeon
towers, seen from far across the plain. Martyn had for companion in the caravan another Englishman traveling also to
Tabriz to join Sir Gore Ouseley's suite. Consequently they
were lodged as foreigners of mark in one of the palaces of the
Shah. Here they paused a week and there was time for Martyn
to seek out, according to his wont, his fellow Christians of those
parts. He called first on "the Italian missionary, a native of
Aleppo, but educated at Rome. He spoke Latin very sprightly."
Then to Julfa to visit the Armenians, of whose ancient and
desolate Church he was always a lover, and with whom he
spent many hours.

On the first night of June, the caravan left Isfahan, its
plane trees and its fountains, its niggardly merchants and its
dreams of bygone glory. "Soon after midnight we mounted our
horses. It was a mild moonlight night and a nightingale filled
the whole valley with his notes. Our way was along lanes, a
murmuring rivulet accompanied us till it was lost in a lake."

At daylight they rode out of these enchanted scenes on to
the great plain of Kashan where fat melons grow in bare sand,
and far away against the blue stands up a snowy mountain
wall, the northern barrier of the Persian land.

After eight days they came to Teheran, the half-ambitious,
half-squalid city of modern royalty, behind walls of unbaked
clay. They reached those walls two hours before sunrise, and
all the twelve gates were shut.

"I spread my bed upon the high road, and slept till the
gates were open; then entered the city and took up my abode."
Here, at the Persian capital, was the favorite palace of the great
Shah, with a marble bath where his ladies might play, and a
picture gallery for which, when Martyn came, an artist was
painting from memory a likeness of Sir John Malcolm, the
magnificent ambassador whom Persia could not forget.

Here came the first hitch in Martyn's plans. No muleteers could be found at the moment willing to travel to Tabriz, where lay the British ambassador who would introduce him and his book into the royal presence. It meant delay. And Martyn in 1812 could not brook delay. While life was yet in him he must press on with the Book. He held letters of introduction to the Shah's Vizier. Better than lose the time he could not spare, should he not travel alone to the Shah's summer camping ground, a night's journey outside the city, and ask the Prime Minister himself to bring him to the royal presence?

He ventured. He rode out of Teheran alone with his servant, and found the Vizier lying ill on the veranda of the Shah's tent of audience. Only that many colored tent curtain hung between Martyn and his goal. The Vizier had two royal secretaries by his couch.

They took very little notice, not rising when I sat down, as their custom is to all who sit with them; nor offering me a water-pipe. The two secretaries on learning my object in coming, began a conversation with me on religion and metaphysics which lasted two hours. The premier asked how many languages I understood; whether I spoke French; where I was educated; whether I understood astronomy and geography, and then observed to the others that I spoke good Persian. As they were well-educated gentlemanly men, the discussion was temperate.

But Martyn had to betake himself to the caravanserai that night, no nearer to the jeweled figure in the audience tent, fed with words and offered no courteous hospitality. He had not come with the pomp that impresses such diplomats, and the Vizier had no intention of becoming sponsor for a lonely stranger.

Martyn spent the evening on the roof of the inn, sharing the mat of a poor traveling merchant who supposed that the western powers yet paid tribute to Mohammedan masters for permission to live.

Three days later he attended the Vizier's levee bearing the precious Book. All eyes were turned on the solitary Frank. In that court where verbal swordmanship was the art of arts, a discussion was inevitable, but Martyn knew that an angry discussion would ruin his chance of seeing the face of the Shah.

He could not prevent the very clash that he dreaded. "There was a most intemperate and clamorous controversy kept up for an hour or two; eight or ten on one side and myself on the other." He came unfriended; the Vizier encouraged the attack, and the veneer of polish was broken through as they set upon him.

Their vulgarity in interrupting me in the middle of a speech; their utter ignorance of the nature of an argument; their impudent assertions about the law and the gospel, neither of which they had ever seen in their lives, moved my indignation a little.

His indignation, but not his fear. This Martyn seems to have forgotten how to fear. The Vizier who had at first set them by the ears came up at last to the angry group, stilled the hubbub and put to Martyn before them all a crucial question. He challenged the stranger to recite the Moslem creed. "Say God is God and Mohammed is the Prophet of God."

It was an electric moment, the whole court at attention.

I said, "God is God" but added, instead of "Mahomet is the prophet of God," "and Jesus is the Son of God."

They all rose up as if they would have torn me in pieces, snarling out one of the classic fighting cries of the Moslem world, "He is neither begotten nor begets." "What will you say when your tongue is burnt out for this blasphemy?"

He held them in silence.

My book which I had brought expecting to present it to the king lay before Mirza Shufi, the Vizier. As they all rose up after him to go, some to the king and some away, I was afraid they would trample on the book; so I went in among them to take it up, and wrapped it in a towel before them; while they looked at it and me with supreme contempt.

I walked away alone to my tent to pass the rest of the day in heat and dirt.

A message followed him from the Vizier refusing to present him to the Shah and referring him to his own ambassador. "Disappointed of my object in coming to the camp," he says, "I lost no time in leaving it." He found again his English fellow-traveler who had secured muleteers and now set off for Tabriz, traveling for the first nine days along a road where the Shah himself was soon to pass on his way to Sultanieh [Sultaniyeh]. The north wind from the Caspian blew over the mountains, and even at midday in June the air was cool. The fresh tang of the breeze carried Martyn home; he fancied himself trudging the roads near Cambridge with a friend at his side, or following a path by the Cornish shore with one beloved companion. "While passing over the plain, mostly on foot, I had them all in my mind, and bore them all in my heart in prayer."

The shadows of the royal progress lay on all the villages.

All along the road where the king is expected, the people are patiently waiting, as for some dreadful disaster: plague, pestilence or famine are nothing to the misery of being subject to the violence and extortion of this rabble soldiery.

When they had passed the Shah's camping ground at Sultanieh they came into a new world, a country that his been a meeting place of the races of mankind. The speech around them began to change from Persian to Turkish, and the caravanserais were the halting place of men whose mules or camels followed the trade routes of the ancient world from East to West.

We found large bales of cotton brought by merchants from Teheran, intended for Turkey. There were also two Tartar merchants, natives of Astrachan, who had brought iron and tea for sale. They wished to know whether we wanted tea of Cathay.

Here in outlandish parts, the two Englishmen fell sick.

June 25, 1812. After a restless night rose so ill with fever, that I could not go on. My companion, Mr. Canning, was nearly in the same state. We touched nothing all day.

After another night of fever, Martyn was for dragging on, but Mr. Canning was not well enough to start. They had before them a stage of eight or ten hours without a house on the way and they had been unable to eat for two days and were suffering from headache and constant giddiness. No doubt it was wiser to delay, but it added anxiety as to whether their supplies could hold out as far as Tabriz. They were becoming desperately short of money.

Next day the servants were down with fever too, and Martyn's head was "tortured with shocking pains." He put it down to exposure to the sun which had great power even though the wind blew cold.

June 29 was a day of acute pain. "I was almost frantic."

"I endeavoured," he says, his Christianity in 1812 anticipating later teachings, "to keep in mind all that was friendly; a friendly Lord presiding; and nothing exercising me but what would show itself at last friendly.".

The fever passed for that time, leaving him "half dead" but determined to take the road. When they told him at midnight that his horse was ready he "seemed about to sink into a long fainting fit and almost wished it. . . . I set out more dead than alive."

Next day, shivering or burning by turns and almost lightheaded, he reached the outer bulwarks of the mountains that guard Persia on the north, "a most natural boundary it is." The face of the land began to be broken up with very rocky foothills where camels graze on scrubby bushes. His horse threaded his way for him through the boulders, for Martyn in high fever could not make his brain obey him, but traveled bewildered through the past, wandering in "happy scenes in India or England." They lost him once; for riding on ahead he had come to a bridge, and scarce knowing what he did, left his horse and crept under the shadow of the arch, where he sat with two camel-drivers, happy to be still and cool. The caravan passed over the bridge without the sick man's observation, and his fellow-traveler, coming back to search for him, found at first only a grazing horse and feared the worst.

So they passed poor hill villages and came out to the pure clean air, the lovely natural pastures and the churlish shepherds of Azerbaijan. By some miracle Martyn in "fever which nearly deprived me of reason" still sat his horse.

At last, as the dawn of July 7 shone coldly on the Blue Mosque and the Citadel, he reached the gate of Tabriz, and "feebly asked for a man to show me the way to the ambassador's." He had been two months on the road when Sir Gore Ouseley and his lady received him at the point of death.

They did all that they could. The violence of the fever they could not allay for another fortnight, but they "administered bark" and tended him as if he were a son. As he lay there under their kind hands, the sick man knew that he had no more strength to travel, as he had longed, to Damascus, to Baghdad, and into the heart of Arabia to search for ancient versions and perfect the Arabic New Testament. His task seemed dropping from his hands. Sir Gore Ouseley told him that he was too ill to see the Shah or the Prince, and doubtless dreaded another collision between Martyn and the mullahs of the court. But he comforted his guest with the promise that he would give every possible éclat to the Book by presenting it himself. The good ambassador did more. He had extra copies made for high officials of open mind, who might speak well of the Book to the potentate. When at length the New Testament reached the royal hands, the Shah was graciousness itself.

In truth [said the royal letter of thanks to the ambassador] through the learned and unremitted exertions of the Reverend Henry Martyn it has been translated in a style most befitting sacred books, that is in an easy and simple diction.... The whole of the New Testament is completed in a most excellent manner, a source of pleasure to our enlightened and august mind.

If it please the most merciful God we shall command the Select Servants who are admitted to our presence, to read to us the above-mentioned book from the beginning to the end.

Sir Gore Ouseley did yet more. He carried a copy with him to St. Petersburg, and there, at the instigation of a Russian prince, the Bible Society printed the Persian Book, with the British ambassador as volunteer proofreader. Sir Gore Ouseley's Russian edition came into the world in the year of Waterloo, while the sister edition in Calcutta was still struggling through the press.

So Martyn's task passed into other hands, and he lying sick almost to death in a mansion of Tabriz saw nothing more within his strength in the East. The ambassador had handed him a letter; at last, after more than eighteen months, a letter from Lydia. To her and to Cornwall the sick man turned. Would strength be granted him to reach her? Might he not carry home the New Testament, to be printed perhaps in his own Cambridge? If he could only reach Lydia, surely he would be well enough with her to start for more service in the East.

Made an extraordinary effort and, as a Tartar was going off instantly to Constantinople, wrote letters to Mr. Grant for permission to come to England, and to Mr. Simeon and Lydia informing them of it.

We have both those letters written by the hand of a man who tells his correspondent that he has not the strength to search his papers for the last home letters.

"I have applied for leave to come to England on furlough; a measure you will disapprove," so he tells Simeon, his feverish brain remembering the relentless standards of work in the Cambridge parish and the brisk upright figure of the leader who never spared himself. "But you would not were you to see the pitiable condition to which I am reduced." A Henry Martyn's plea against some fancied charge of idleness must have been hard reading to his friend. Then the old passion seizes the sick man, and the pen flies in his feverish hand as he turns to the beloved work and warns Simeon about some publication mooted in Cambridge for Moslem readers. Let it not go to press until it has been approved by men who know the East and know eastern ways of seeing, imagining and reasoning. He tells of the last treatise he had written in Shiraz and, with a rare note of satisfaction in any work of his own, records his hope that "there is not a single Europeanism in the whole of it."

> But I am exhausted; pray for me, beloved brother, and
> believe that I am, as long as life and recollection last, yours
> affectionately,   H. MARTYN.

To Lydia, lest she should dwell on his sickness, he writes of his spiritual solace; "The love of God never appeared more clear, more sweet, more strong." Then, lest she should build on his coming, he adds, "I must faithfully tell you that the probability of my reaching England alive is but small."

The Tartar courier galloped off with the letters and the sick man lay back exhausted. Nothing was left him to do, but to gather strength for the homeward journey.

A month later, "a mere skeleton" after two months of fever, he sat up in a chair and wrote his will "with a strong hand."

> *August* 21-31. Making preparations for my journey to
> Constantinople, a route recommended to me by Sir Gore
> as safer, and one in which he could give me letters of recom-
> mendation to two Turkish governors.

Sir Gore also procured an order for Martyn to use the Government post-horses as far as Erivan. But Martyn had seen the hardships that the levies of royal underlings brought upon the peasants. "These post-horses I was told were nothing else than the beasts the prince's servants levy on every village. I determined not to use them."

Before setting out he wrote a last letter to Lydia, a letter to be read and re-read on her knees where his portrait hung beneath a print of the Crucifixion in a room that looked out across the shimmer of Mount's Bay.

> In three days I intend setting my horse's head towards
> Constantinople, distant above thirteen hundred miles....
> Soon we shall have occasion for pen and ink no more; but
> I trust I shall shortly see thee face to face.
> Belive me to be yours ever, most faithfully and affection-
> ately,   H. MARTYN.

On September 2, 1812, he set out with a little party of guides and servants, while the ambassador and his lady, having done all they could to help him, measured with doubtful eyes the strength of the haggard convalescent against fifteen hundred[4] miles of hardship.

> At sunset we left the western gate of Tabriz behind us.
> The plain towards the west and south-west stretches away
> to an immense distance bounded by mountains so remote
> as to appear from their soft blue to blend with the skies.

He "ambled on" with the keen sense of the convalescent for the beauty and freedom of the outside world, gazing at "the distant hills with gratitude and joy." His way through Azerbaijan and Armenia always tending westward was the "Royal Road" of ancient Persia along which the service of the Great King passed from Susa to the west. It was marked at each twentieth or twenty-fifth mile by a post-station built of mud bricks, such as went to the building of Babylon the great. Here men and beasts fared much alike as to lodging.

In cities where Martyn had letters of introduction he might

---

[4] Dr. George Smith says that the distance from Tabriz to Constantinople is 1500 miles, though Martyn reckoned it 1300.

hire a room from a citizen. "I was led from street to street till at last I was lodged in a wash-house belonging to a great man, a corner of which was cleared out for me."

A room secured, at the end of the day's hard riding there were the perennial discomforts of such travel: mosquitoes and lice, "the smell of the stable so strong that I was quite unwell," and the incessant crowding and chatter of people who could not or would not understand his desire to rest alone. It was always Martyn too who must be the one to wake at midnight, rouse his party and stand urgent over them as they dawdled round the baggage sleepy and loath to start.

The traveling was hard even for a hale man. He crossed the Araxes [Aras]; he left great Ararat upon his left ("so may I, safe in Christ, outride the storm of life and land at last on one of the everlasting hills," he prayed, thinking of Noah); he passed through a rich land of streams where a precious trunk full of books was dropped and soaked, and he had a midnight fire built to dry them. He spent nights in rooms built over or beside the family stable for the sake of the warmth from the beasts in winter, but now in September overpowering in heat and stench; and he rode on, "thinking of a Hebrew letter," and so "perceiving little of the tediousness of the way. . . . All day on the 15th and 16th Psalms and gained some light on the difficulties."

So meditating on his songs of degrees, he came to Erivan, and laid the ambassador's letter before a provincial governor to whom his distant overlord, the Shah, seemed but a shadowy personage.

I was summoned to his presence. He at first took no notice of me, but continued reading his Koran. After a compliment or two, he resumed his devotions. The next ceremony was to exchange a rich shawl dress for a still richer pelisse on pretence of its being cold. The next display was to call for his physician, who after respectfully feeling his pulse stood on one side.

Having sufficiently impressed the thin, sick traveler with
his greatness, he called a secretary to pick up from the floor the
letter of the British ambassador, and to read it in his august
ears. The letter interested him and he grew languidly attentive,
but his hopes were set on some grapes and melons cooling
before him in a marble fountain, and he sent the saint away,
not knowing that he had met a man of God.

On September 12, Martyn left his servants waiting for fresh
horses, and rode alone to visit his brothers the Armenian monks
at Etchmiazin [Echmiadzin], the mother-city of their church.

The wayworn figure rode into "a large court with monks,
cowled and gowned, moving about. On seeing my Armenian
letters they brought me at once to the Patriarch's lodge where
I found two bishops at breakfast." He struck up at once a
friendship with a young monk of his own age named Serope,
"bold, authoritative and very able," and full of reforming plans
for his Church, "but then he is not spiritual." They talked all
day. "When the bell rang for vespers, we went together to the
great Church."

Next day Martyn waited on the Patriarch, who received
him on a throne, surrounded by standing monks. "I told the
Patriarch that I was so happy in being here that I could almost
be willing to be a monk with them."

When the young monk who welcomed Martyn had become
a silvery-bearded bishop he told a European traveler[5] his impressions of that visit. "He described Martyn to me as being
of a very delicate frame, thin, and not quite of the middle
stature, a beardless youth, with a countenance beaming with
so much benignity as to bespeak an errand of Divine love. Of
the affairs of the world he seemed to be so ignorant that Serope
was obliged to manage for him respecting his traveling arrange-
ments and money matters. A Tartar was employed to take him

---

[5] Mr. George Fowler.

to Tokat. He (Serope) was greatly surprised, he said, that Martyn was so eminent a Christian; 'since (said he) all the English I have hitherto met with not only make no profession of religion, but live seemingly in contempt of it.'"

Serope took Martyn in hand, changed most of his traveling kit, and bought him a sword against the Kurdish robbers.

So he left them with new baggage and a new train, "a trusty servant from the monastery" carrying his money.

On September 19 they passed from the Persian province of Erivan to the neighbor province of Kars, and so left the domains of the Shah for those of the Sultan of Turkey.[6]

Troubles began.

> The headman of the village paid me a visit. He was a young Mussulman and took care of all my Mussulman attendants; but he left my Armenians and me where he found us. I was rather uncomfortably lodged, my room being a thoroughfare for horses, cows, buffaloes and sheep. Almost all the village came to look at me.

Each day there were alarms of Kurdish robbers. Martyn's escort met even poor companies of peasants with suspicion and with pieces cocked, and every traveling party was passed with furtive glances and hands lingering on weapons. Each trifling incident of the way revealed that one of the company, the Tartar guide named Hassan, was a man with the nature of that soldiery which could plait a crown of thorns for a scourged prisoner.

> The Tartar began to show his nature by flogging the baggage-horse with his long whip; but one of the poor beasts presently fell with his load.

Or again:

> In this room I should have been very much to my satisfaction had not the Tartar taken part of the same bench. It was evident that the Tartar was the great man here: he

---

[6] Both provinces became part of Russian Transcaucasia after the war of 1828, and several shifts of ownership have since taken place on these frontiers.

took the best place for himself; a dinner of four or five dishes was laid before him. When I asked for eggs they brought me rotten ones.

With a stern vigorous master Hassan might have done good service. With a sick man he showed himself a brute.

September 24. A long and sultry march over many a hill and vale. Two hours from the last stage is a hot spring: the water fills a pool having four porches. The porches instantly reminded me of Bethesda's pool. In them all the party undressed and bathed. The Tartar to enjoy himself more perfectly had his calean [water pipe] to smoke while up to his chin in water.

Kars was left behind, then Erzerum, but fever was winning the race.

September 29. We moved to a village where I was attacked with fever and ague.

October 1. We were out from seven in the morning till eight at night. After sitting a little by the fire I was near fainting from sickness. I learned that the plague was raging at Constantinople and thousands dying every day. The inhabitants of Tocat were flying from their town from the same cause.

October 2. Some hours before day I sent to tell the Tartar I was ready, but Hassan was for once riveted to his bed. However, at eight, having got strong horses, he set off at a great rate. He made us gallop as fast as the horses would go to Chifflik, where we arrived at sunset. I was lodged at my request in the stables of the post-house. As soon as it began to grow a little cold the ague came on, then the fever.

In the night Hassan sent to summon me away, but I was quite unable to move. Finding me still in bed at the dawn he began to storm furiously at my detaining him so long; but I quietly let him spend his ire, ate my breakfast and set out at eight. He seemed determined to make up for the delay, for we flew over hill and dale to Sherean [Sheheran], where we changed horses. From thence we travelled all the rest of the day and all night. It rained. The ague came on.

There was a village at hand but Hassan had no mercy. At one in the morning we found two men under a wain with a good fire; I dried my lower extremities, allayed the fever by drinking a good deal of water and went on. The night was pitchy dark so that I could not see the road under my horse's feet. We arrived at the munzil[7] at break of day. Hassan was in great fear of being arrested here; the governor of the city had vowed to make an example of him for riding to death a horse belonging to a man of this place.

He hurried me away without delay; and galloped furiously towards a village which he said was four hours distant, which was all I could undertake in my weak state; but village after village did he pass till, night coming on, I suspected that he was carrying me on to the munzil; so I got off my horse, and sat upon the ground, and told him "I neither could nor would go any farther." He stormed, but I was immovable, till, a light appearing at a distance, I mounted and made towards it. He brought in the party, but would not exert himself to get a place for me. Sergius told them I wanted a place in which to be alone. This seemed very offensive to them; "And why must he be alone?" they asked, attributing this desire of mine to pride, I suppose. Tempted at last by money they brought me to a stable room, and Hassan and a number of others planted themselves there with me. My fever here increased to a violent degree; the heat in my eyes and forehead was so great that the fire almost made me frantic. I entreated that it might be put out, or that I might be carried out of doors. Neither was attended to; my servant, who, from my sitting in that strange way on the ground, believed me delirious, was deaf to all I said. At last I pushed my head in among the luggage and lodged it on the damp ground, and slept.

October 5. The merciless Hassan hurried me off. The munzil, however, not being distant I reached it without much difficulty. I was pretty well lodged and felt tolerably well till a little after sunset, when the ague came on with a

---

[7] The halting place at the end of each stage of about twenty-five miles.

violence I had never before experienced; I felt as if in a
palsy, my teeth chattering and my whole frame violently
shaken.

Two Persians came to visit him as he lay shivering.

These Persians appear quite brotherly after the Turks.
While they pitied me, Hassan sat in perfect indifference,
ruminating on the further delay this was likely to occasion.
The cold fit after continuing two or three hours was followed by a fever, which lasted the whole night.

October 6. No horses being to be had, I had an unexpected repose. I sat in the orchard, and thought with
sweet comfort and peace of my God; in solitude my Company, my Friend and Comforter. Oh, when shall time give
place to eternity! When shall appear the new heaven and
new earth wherein dwelleth righteousness! There shall in
no wise enter in anything that defileth: none of that wickedness which has made men worse than wild beasts shall be
seen or heard of any more.

There was no later entry in the journal; but he had not
come yet to the end of that impossible ride. Day after day they
dragged him on, waking him out of feverish sleep.

"Up, O ye lovers and away! 'Tis time to leave the world
     for aye;
Hark, loud and clear from heaven the drum of parting calls—
     let none delay;
The cameleer hath risen amain, made ready all the camel
     train,
And quittance now desires to gain: why sleep ye travellers,
     I pray?
Behind us and before there swells the din of parting and of
     bells;
To shoreless space each moment sails a disembodied spirit
     away.
O heart, towards thy heart's love wend, and O friend, fly
     toward the Friend!"[8]

---

[8] Selected Poems from the Divan-i-Shams-i-Tabriz translated by R. A.
Nicholson.

On October 14, 1812, Martyn bade his Armenian servant Sergius make a list of his papers and carry them for him to Constantinople. They had ridden him to death, but there is no story of that deathbed. We know that he came at the last "a young man, wanting still the years of Christ," to Tokat under its weird pile of castellated hill, a city of the copper-merchants, but then grim with plague. We know too that in fever his mind was always moving among friends in India or in England.

So he came to Tokat, and the mule-bells in the narrow streets jingled in dying ears. Or were they sheep-bells? sheep bells on the moors?

They probably laid him down to die amid the babel of an eastern kahn. . . . That everlasting smell of the stable! Why could not the General find a better place for service than the riding school? But then the Lord was born in a stable. A man could worship there . . . . But that raging voice! If only the tormenting flood of words might cease! Was it Sabat or the Tartar? Sons of thunder, both of them. Sons of thunder He called them, yes, and loved them too.

Why that never ending clatter on the cobbles? Little hurrying feet of donkeys. And people too. Surely so many people were never seen in Truro Street before, and all so beautiful. There was Corrie, what a friend he was! and Sally with Cousin Emma, and Sargent and Dr. Cardew (but no matter; the lesson was ready to show up)—and Lydia. Of course she would come at last. How her face was shining like a star. How all the faces shone with the light of God. . . . Was that an Armenian priest standing at prayer? Simeon had surely come at last with the Bread and Wine. How sweet his voice grew, like the music in King's Chapel! "We praise Thee, we bless Thee, we worship Thee, we glorify Thee, we give thanks to Thee for Thy great glory."

"For Thou only art holy; Thou only art the Lord; Thou only, O Christ. . . ."

Some weeks later an Armenian named Sergius, hot from travel, carried a bundle of papers into the house of Mr. Isaac Morier at Constantinople, and said that they came from his master who had died on October 16, 1812, at Tokat, where the Armenian clergy gave him Christian burial.